CAMBRIDGE LIBRARY COLLECTION

Books of enduring scholarly value

History

The books reissued in this series include accounts of historical events and movements by eye-witnesses and contemporaries, as well as landmark studies that assembled significant source materials or developed new historiographical methods. The series includes work in social, political and military history on a wide range of periods and regions, giving modern scholars ready access to influential publications of the past.

Some New Sources for the Life of Blessed Agnes of Bohemia

Walter Seton's 1915 book focuses on one of the key, understudied figures of the early Franciscan movement. Abbess of the Convent of Prague, Blessed Agnes was central to the establishment of the Order of Saint Clare. She presented persuasive arguments to convince the Holy See to permit female Franciscans to live according to their Rule and practise voluntary poverty. Seton's edition, drawn from manuscripts in German libraries, includes the oldest extant Latin version of Agnes's *Life* together with a fifteenth-century German version and German copies of four letters she received from Saint Clare. Praised in the *English Historical Review* in 1916 for its 'admirable thoroughness', this edition sheds new light on Blessed Agnes, whose importance was long overshadowed by her more prominent contemporaries, Saint Clare and Saint Elizabeth of Hungary, her cousin. This reissue makes this valuable primary material accessible again to scholars working on Franciscan history and medieval women's spirituality.

Cambridge University Press has long been a pioneer in the reissuing of out-of-print titles from its own backlist, producing digital reprints of books that are still sought after by scholars and students but could not be reprinted economically using traditional technology. The Cambridge Library Collection extends this activity to a wider range of books which are still of importance to researchers and professionals, either for the source material they contain, or as landmarks in the history of their academic discipline.

Drawing from the world-renowned collections in the Cambridge University Library, and guided by the advice of experts in each subject area, Cambridge University Press is using state-of-the-art scanning machines in its own Printing House to capture the content of each book selected for inclusion. The files are processed to give a consistently clear, crisp image, and the books finished to the high quality standard for which the Press is recognised around the world. The latest print-on-demand technology ensures that the books will remain available indefinitely, and that orders for single or multiple copies can quickly be supplied.

The Cambridge Library Collection will bring back to life books of enduring scholarly value (including out-of-copyright works originally issued by other publishers) across a wide range of disciplines in the humanities and social sciences and in science and technology.

Some New Sources for the Life of Blessed Agnes of Bohemia

Walter W. Seton

CAMBRIDGE
UNIVERSITY PRESS

CAMBRIDGE UNIVERSITY PRESS

Cambridge, New York, Melbourne, Madrid, Cape Town, Singapore,
São Paolo, Delhi, Dubai, Tokyo

Published in the United States of America by Cambridge University Press, New York

www.cambridge.org
Information on this title: www.cambridge.org/9781108017602

© in this compilation Cambridge University Press 2010

This edition first published 1915
This digitally printed version 2010

ISBN 978-1-108-01760-2 Paperback

This book reproduces the text of the original edition. The content and language reflect
the beliefs, practices and terminology of their time, and have not been updated.

Cambridge University Press wishes to make clear that the book, unless originally published
by Cambridge, is not being republished by, in association or collaboration with, or
with the endorsement or approval of, the original publisher or its successors in title.

BRITISH
SOCIETY OF FRANCISCAN STUDIES

VOL. VII

List of Officers of the Society, 1915.

Hon. President :—

PAUL SABATIER.

Committee :—

A. G. LITTLE, *Chairman.*
Professor T. W. ARNOLD.
P. DESCOURS.
Rev. W. H. FRERE.
T. E. HARVEY, M.P.
C. L. KINGSFORD.
Professor W. P. KER.
E. MOON.
Rev. Canon H. RASHDALL.
Rev. H. G. ROSEDALE.
Professor M. E. SADLER.
Miss E. GURNEY SALTER.
WALTER W. SETON.
Professor T. F. TOUT.

Hon. Secretary and Treasurer :—

Mr. PAUL DESCOURS, 65 Deauville Road, Clapham Park,
London, S.W.

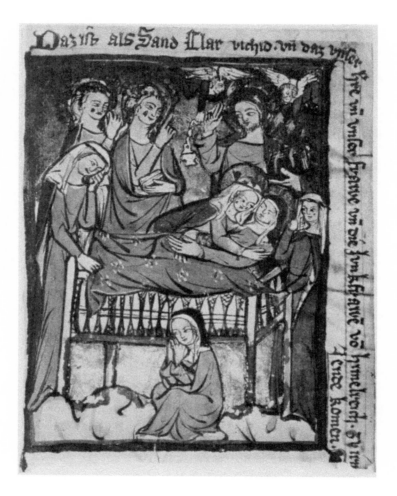

HOW OUR LORD AND OUR LADY CAME TO SAINT CLARE
ON HER DEATHBED.
(From MS. M.281 Royal Library, Dresden.)

SOME NEW SOURCES

FOR THE LIFE OF

BLESSED AGNES OF BOHEMIA

INCLUDING

A FOURTEENTH CENTURY LATIN VERSION

(BAMBERG, MISC. HIST. 146, E. VII, 19)

AND

A FIFTEENTH CENTURY GERMAN VERSION

(BERLIN, GERM. OCT. 484)

BY

WALTER W. SETON

[*Thesis approved for the Degree of Doctor of Literature in the University of London*]

ABERDEEN: THE UNIVERSITY PRESS

1915

CONTENTS.

LIST OF ILLUSTRATIONS.

INTRODUCTION.

I.

BLESSED AGNES OF BOHEMIA.

BLESSED Agnes of Bohemia is a figure but slightly known in Franciscan story. Buried in the folios of the *Acta Sanctorum* of the Bollandists under the date prescribed for her remembrance, 6th March, her life-story has been scarcely remembered, and even to Franciscan students she is known only through the occasional references in the sources and especially by the reflected glory of having had four letters addressed to her by Saint Clare. Never before has her life been presented to English readers. For the last twenty years the loving devotion of followers of Saint Francis has directed the searchlight of literary criticism upon the origins of the Franciscan Order. The great aim has been, and still is, to trace patiently back the paths, often tangled and difficult, which lead to those two great figures, Saint Francis and Saint Clare, which have succeeded in casting a spell over the devotion of the Catholic Church: to learn what really is the "Franciscan spirit" and what factors led to the success of the movement which, beginning in Umbria, spread throughout the world and saved the Church. To many, the magnificence of the triple Church of San Francesco, even though it does contain the bones of the Saint, or the glory of Santa Maria degli Angeli, even though it does enshrine the Portiuncula, fail somewhat in their appeal. They know that it is the rugged simplicity of the windswept Carceri, where the spirit of Francis still dwells and the bare austerity of San Damiano, still pervaded by the holiness of Clare, that made the Order of

VOL. VII.   I

the Brothers Minor a power in the world and in the Church. As we go right back into the thirteenth century, we come to the band of faithful disciples surrounding the person of Saint Francis, names written indelibly in the memories of his chroniclers and his friends. So too there are noble women surrounding the person of Saint Clare, and of these none is worthier to be remembered and reverenced than Blessed Agnes of Bohemia.

Born in 1205 and dying in 1282 after thirty years spent in the world but not of it, and forty-six years spent in religion as a Sister of the Order of Saint Clare, Blessed Agnes was a contemporary of both Saint Francis and Saint Clare. The conversion of Saint Francis had not taken place in the year when she was born: he was still living a life of pleasure. But when at the early age of three she was betrothed to Boheslas, son of the Duke of Silesia, Francis had made the great renunciation; and when at the age of nine years she was betrothed to Henry, the son of the Emperor Frederick II., Clare had already quitted the world and entered her life-long seclusion at San Damiano.

Blessed Agnes came of a stock which was devoted to religion, a stock indeed of which saints were made. One of her ancestors in the royal line of Bohemia, the dynasty known as the Premyslides, was Wenceslas the Holy, known in Christmas story and song as the Good King Wenceslas, who died in 935. It is interesting to see that between the years 1205 and 1227 there lived four royal persons connected with each other by bonds of blood and of marriage, three of whom were destined to be raised to the altars of the Church, and the fourth, Blessed Agnes herself, to be beatified. Saint Elizabeth of Hungary, daughter of Andreas II., King of Hungary, was the first cousin of Blessed Agnes. She was born in 1207 at Pressburg and married at the age of fourteen to Louis IV., Landgrave of Thuringia. Her life was a short one. For in 1227, her husband Louis, who was also canonised, died and she was driven from her palace of the Wartburg by her brother-in-law the Regent, Henry Raspe III., on the pretext that she was wasting the estates by her alms. After suffering the greatest austerities she found refuge at Marburg, where she died on 19th November, 1231, and where she is now buried. She was one of the early members of the Third Order. Reference is made to her in the present life on pp. 64, 78. There can be little doubt that the holiness of the life of Saint Elizabeth was a great stimulus to her kinswoman, Agnes, and was one of the factors which led to her own renunciation. Then too there was Saint Hedwig, likewise a kinswoman of Agnes, for she was the sister of the mother of Andreas II., King of Hungary, uncle of Agnes. She also comes into the story of Agnes ; for as we are told on page 66, when Agnes was three years old, she was sent to the cloister of Trebnitz in Silesia " and was committed to the charge of a nun named Hedwig, who taught the dear child the faith "; and this Hedwig may safely be identified with the Saint of that name. So amid all the political upheavals and disturbances which rent the Holy Roman Empire in the thirteenth century, amid all the quarrels between Pope and Emperor, lived these four saints, Hedwig, Elizabeth, Louis, and Agnes ; and it may be noted that the one of them who was destined to do most for the Church, Blessed Agnes, has never yet been canonised, although popular custom has often described her as " Saint Agnes ".

In order that the life-story of Blessed Agnes may be understood, something must be said as to its historical setting. If there had been nothing else to lend interest to her life, that interest would have been found in her contact with the Emperor Frederick II., who first sought her in marriage for his son, Henry, and then later for himself. The figure of Frederick, with its strange fascination and its inconsistency, threw a glamour over his own generation and has commanded the interest and curiosity of subsequent centuries. Who can tell to what extent Frederick's career might have been altered, if his suit had been successful and if Agnes had become his wife ? How often during the troublous years which followed Blessed Agnes's entry into the Order of Saint Clare must she have thanked God that she had the courage to refuse the hand of the great enemy of the Church, thrice excommunicated, *malleus Romanae ecclesiae*, as Petrarch called him !

Blessed Agnes was the daughter of Premysl Ottocar I., who ascended the throne of Bohemia in 1197. Her mother was Constantia, sister of Andreas II., King of Hungary. At that time Bohemia lay outside the Empire. Ottocar died in 1230, and was succeeded by his son Wenceslas I., brother of Blessed Agnes. It was during his reign, viz. in 1233, that Frederick II., after the death of his second wife Yolanda, sought Agnes in marriage. At the same time she was wooed by Henry III., King of England. Agnes, however, had already made a firm resolve to enter the Order of Saint Clare and succeeded in obtaining the intervention of the Pope, Gregory IX., who, although nominally reconciled to the Emperor Frederick in 1230, probably felt no great regret at the frustration of his suit. In 1253 Wenceslas I. died and was succeeded by his son, Ottocar II., who in 1260 defeated Bela IV., King of Hungary, at the battle of Kressenbrunn and raised the power and influence of Bohemia to its height. Ottocar extended the rule of Bohemia to the shores of the Adriatic and Carinthia ; Istria and even parts of Northern Italy came under his sway. But it was not for long. Rudolph, Count of Hapsburg, was elected King of the Romans in 1273 and claimed part of the territories acquired by Ottocar as vacant fiefs of the Empire. Ultimately Ottocar, deserted by the nobility of Bohemia, was deprived by Rudolph of all lands except Bohemia and Moravia. In 1278 Ottocar made a final attempt to retrieve his failing fortunes by invading the Austrian duchies, but he was overthrown and slain in battle at Durnkrut. Reference will be found to this event in the life of Blessed Agnes, page 110, where it is related how she had a vision showing the coming defeat and the death of her brother's son.

Such was the historical atmosphere in which Blessed Agnes lived her life. Comparatively little did the political movements around and outside her convent walls affect her. The references to historical figures which do occur in the

versions of her life here published are but slight, and yet it
may be observed that practically every historical reference
that does occur can be verified from other sources as in
general accurate.

It is, however, as a Franciscan of the first generation and
as one who took a leading part in keeping alive the spirit and
ideals of the Founder of the Order during the half-century
which followed his death, that Blessed Agnes deserves most
to be remembered. It is indeed a matter for some surprise
that one, who for twenty years was a friend and correspondent
of Saint Clare herself and who was intimately associated with
Saint Clare in the long struggle with the Holy See for the
confirmation of the Rule and the cherished privilege of
Poverty, should be so slightly known to Franciscan students.
The reason has been perhaps the comparative scantiness and
inaccessibility of the materials of her life-story.

If one comes to the reading of the life of Blessed Agnes
after reading the second life of Saint Francis by Thomas of
Celano, or the Legend of Saint Bonaventura, one cannot fail to
notice at once the difference. We are back in the old atmosphere
of the early days of the Order; there is the freshness and naïveté
and austerity of the Portiuncula and of San Damiano. There
is the spirit and the ideals of Francis and Clare. There is the
passionate devotion to the Lady Poverty, which we look for
in vain in the later Franciscans. There is the persistent
refusal to compromise the primitive simplicity of the new
vocation. Throughout the whole life it is impossible to point
to a single incident or statement and say "That is not in
accordance with the Testament of Saint Francis," or "That is
inconsistent with the Testament of Saint Clare". It is not
many Franciscan documents of which this could be said.
When Blessed Agnes resolves to enter the Order of Saint
Clare, she sends for the Brothers Minor to ask what she must
do to give effect to her purpose. "Then the Brothers told her
the Rule of Saint Clare, which was that whosoever would
enter the Order of Saint Clare should, according to the com-
mand of the Holy Gospel, 'sell all that he hath and give to

the poor'." There is the same ring about this as about the conversion of Bernard of Quintavalle. Then again there is the primitive care for the lepers. " For lepers and the sick brothers before the cloister and for other sick folk too she would care specially, with as great devotion and piety as if she were doing so for God Himself." Most significant is her refusal to allow her cloister to hold or to inherit property. " He (the Cardinal-Protector) sent her his letter and besought her most earnestly and counselled her with fatherly sincerity that she and her cloister should hold and inherit property by reason of the widespread want and need of the land. . . . This she withstood with steadfast mind and soul, saying that she would sooner die of want and poverty than be parted from Holy Poverty." We pass to a more detailed consideration of the long struggle for the Privilege of Poverty.

II.

"THE PRIVILEGE OF POVERTY."

One of the most interesting and at the same time one of the most obscure topics in Franciscan studies must naturally be the investigation of the successive stages in the development of the Rules of the Three Orders. This subject, so far as it relates to the First Order and to the Third Order, must lie outside the scope of this study. But perhaps the prime importance of the study of the life of Blessed Agnes of Bohemia 'lies in the contribution which it makes to our knowledge of the intricate negotiations with the Holy See which led up to the final confirmation of the Rule of Saint Clare by Innocent IV. on 9th August, 1253. Much has been written on this subject recently, but it would appear that the contribution made by Blessed Agnes to the ultimate issue has been largely overlooked. An examination of the life of Blessed Agnes and more especially of the numerous papal bulls addressed to her by Gregory IX. and Innocent IV. will give ground for the statement that she must have played no small or unimportant part in the long controversy from which Saint Clare emerged triumphant.

SAINT FRANCIS
(*From MS. M.281 Royal Library, Dresden.*)

In order to state the issues clearly, it will be necessary to recapitulate briefly[1] the events relating to the Rule of Saint Clare, prior to 1234, the date when Blessed Agnes entered the Order.

It was in 1212 that Clare first made her great renunciation and embraced the life of absolute poverty, and in the following year that she was placed by Saint Francis in San Damiano. At that time the newly-formed community of the Poor Ladies had no Rule, but lived as far as possible according to the original Rule of the Friars Minor as approved by Innocent III. In 1215 she obtained from Innocent III. the same "privilege of poverty" which that pontiff had granted to Francis.[2] Reference is made to this oral grant in the Testament of Saint Clare: "*Solicita fui a Domino Papa Innocentio, sub cujus tempore coepimus . . . nostram professionem sanctissimae paupertatis, quam et Patri nostro promisimus, eorum privilegiis facere corroborari*". The essential feature of the "Privilege of Poverty" was that it implied that she and her Sisters were not to be obliged to hold property.

In 1218 Ugolino, Bishop of Ostia, obtained authority from Honorius III. by the bull *Litterae tuae*[3] (7th August, 1218) to receive estates for the purpose of building religious houses for virgins who wished to enter the religious life. As a natural

---

[1] For this recapitulation use has been made largely of Father Cuthbert's admirable Introduction to Mrs. Balfour's *Life and Legend of the Lady Saint Clare*, 1910, and of Père Livarius Oliger's articles, "De Origine Regularum Ordinis S. Clarae," in the *Archivum Franciscanum Historicum*, tom. v., fasc. II. and III., An. 1912.

[2] The question whether it was Innocent III. or Innocent IV. who gave a verbal grant of "poverty" to Saint Clare is a much disputed one. Oliger, after reviewing the evidence, sums up in favour of the view that Innocent III. did make such a grant in 1215; but he bases it mainly upon the reference in the *Legend of Saint Clare*, not on that in her Testament. In this connection the passage in the Berlin MS. [Fol. 192r.] is very puzzling. This MS. clearly attributes the grant to Innocent IV.: but yet it states that the rule was granted "when S. Clare began the order," and also the sentence, "*da schrib ir der babst mit seiner selb hand die erst form vnd mas der regel*," sounds like a reminiscence of a similar passage in the *Legend of Saint Clare* where it is applied to Innocent III. For further discussion of this passage, see p. 25.

[3] Sbaralea, "Bullarium Franciscanum," vol. i., 1.

consequence he himself drew up a Rule, containing provisions for the government of the religious houses coming within his control, and these provisions came to be known as the Hugoline Constitutions. They were not in any sense Franciscan, either in spirit or in form. They were indeed Benedictine, for they definitely placed the houses upon which they were imposed within the Benedictine Order. The constitutions contain the following words :—

"Regulam Beatissimi Benedicti, in qua virtutum perfectio et summa discretio noscitur instituta, quae et a sanctis Patribus a principio devote suscepta est, et ab Ecclesia Romana venerabiliter approbata, vobis concedimus observandam in omnibus, in quibus eidem vivendi formulae vobis a Nobis traditae, cum adhuc essemus in minori officio constituti, contraria \minime comprobatur."

The importance of this was that they were opposed on the most fundamental issue to the Privilege of Poverty, for they deliberately made provision by which property could be held in common and inherited by each house. Ugolino, refusing to recognise the verbal grant made to Saint Clare by Innocent III. and fortified by the bull of Honorius III., *Sacrosancta Romana Ecclesia* [1] (9th December, 1219), which specifically mentions the Poor Ladies of San Damiano, imposed this new Rule upon Saint Clare and her Sisters. This happened while Saint Francis was absent in the East on his missionary tour. Saint Francis returned in 1219, and doubtless by his aid Ugolino was prevailed upon to withdraw his constitutions so far as they affected the most vital question, the Privilege of Poverty, or the freedom from the obligation to hold possessions ; while it would appear that in other respects the practices imposed by the Constitutions of 1219, such as perpetual enclosure, perpetual silence and fasting, were tacitly accepted and remained in force not only at San Damiano, but also in the other houses of Poor Clares which were springing up.

---

[1] Sbaralea, " Bullarium Franciscanum," vol. i., 3.

Ugolino did not however extend his concession to these other houses and they continued to be governed by the Constitutions, without any safeguard of the Privilege of Poverty. In 1228, shortly after the canonisation of Saint Francis, Ugolino, who had by that time been raised to the Pontificate as Gregory IX., in response to the earnest pleadings of Saint Clare granted to her in a letter of 17th September, 1228, the privilege for which she sought. This was, however, entirely a personal privilege restricted to her and to the Sisters of San Damiano.

We come now to the part taken by Blessed Agnes in the long struggle, which had for its object and aim to secure to all the Houses of Poor Clares recognition as part of the Franciscan Order and, in consequence, as participators with the Friars Minor and with the Poor Clares of San Damiano in the Privilege of Poverty.

It can scarcely be doubted that it was at Pentecost, 1234, that Blessed Agnes entered the Convent at Prag, which she had herself founded. The arguments for this date will be discussed in connection with other points of chronology relating to her.[1]

The Convent of Poor Ladies of Prag was then at its foundation in 1234, when Blessed Agnes was installed as Abbess, in precisely the same position as San Damiano had been in 1218, that is to say, it was, formally at all events, under the Hugoline Constitutions, its inmates were regarded by the Holy See as Benedictines, it had not the Privilege of Poverty and so was compelled to receive possessions. How unwelcome this position must have been to Blessed Agnes herself and still more so to Saint Clare can be judged by all that followed and by references in the Life.

On 18th May, 1235, Gregory IX. issued a bull, *Cum relicta seculi vanitate*,[2] to Blessed Agnes and the Poor Ladies of Prag, providing that the revenues of the Hospital of Saint Francis at Prag were to be devoted perpetually to their main-

---

[1] See pages 45-51.
[2] Sbaralea, " Bullarium Franciscanum," vol. i., 156.

tenance; and in July of the same year, the bull *Prudentibus Virginibus*[1] takes the Convent under the special protection of the Holy See.

The year 1238 was one of great importance in the history of the Convent of Prag.

On 18th April, 1238, Gregory IX. makes a great concession[2] to the Abbess and Poor Ladies. By the bull, *Pia credulitate tenentes*,[3] after referring to certain petitions received from them, he accepts their renunciation of the revenues of the Hospital and grants that they should not be compelled to receive possessions. "*Hinc est quod Hospitalis Sancti Francisci Pragensis Diocesis, cum juribus et pertinentiis suis, olim vobis et per vos Monasterio vestro ab Apostolica Sede concessi, vestra libera resignatione recepta, vobis . . . devicti praecibus vestris et lacrymis praesentium auctoritate concedimus, ut invite cogi ad recipiendum de cetero possessiones aliquas non possitis.*"

This was the greatest concession made by Gregory to the Poor Ladies since 1228, when he had granted a similar privilege to Saint Clare and the Sisters of San Damiano. At this point it may be noted that apparently Blessed Agnes resigned the position of Abbess in 1238, at any rate temporarily, a fact which may be deduced from the salutations in subsequent bulls of that year, in which she is addressed merely as *ancilla Christi*.

Blessed Agnes, on receiving this bull granting her request to enjoy the Privilege of Poverty and to be allowed to resign the revenues of the Hospital, must at once have seen the inconsistency of the position taken up by the Pope. The bull, *Angelis gaudium*,[4] of 11th May, 1238, suggests what probably happened. Agnes replied to the bull, *Pia credulitate*, by seeking a further concession. She sends for the papal approbation a Rule based upon that of San Damiano and asks leave to live according to it, instead of according to their present Rule. Gregory replies in this bull, refusing the request of Blessed Agnes and giving certain reasons for his refusal, the chief one being that if he

---

[1] Sbaralea, "Bullarium Franciscanum," vol. i., 171.
[2] See Appendix III., p. 175.   [3] Sbaralea, i., 236.   [4] *Ibid.*, i., 242.

were to agree, it would cause disturbance among other congregations of Poor Ladies, who were living under the Hugoline Constitutions of 1218. The bull was no doubt a great disappointment to Blessed Agnes and her Sisters, who might reasonably have anticipated that their second request, which was merely a corollary to their first, would be granted. No step, however, was taken, as far as can be ascertained, either by Blessed Agnes or by Saint Clare to obtain from Gregory IX. a revision of this decision. They bowed to his ruling.

In 1243, however, Innocent IV. became Pope, after the short and troublous reign of Celestine IV. Before he had been six months on the papal throne, the question had been reopened by Blessed Agnes. She wrote to Innocent, saying how she and her Sisters were troubled in their minds by two phrases in their Rule, viz., " by virtue of obedience" and "the Rule of Saint Benedict," as they feared they were committing mortal sin by observing simultaneously two Rules, the Benedictine and the Franciscan. They petitioned, therefore, for the removal of these disturbing phrases from their Rule. Innocent replied with the bull, *In Divini timore nominis*,[1] of 13th November, 1243, attempting to set their doubts at rest : he repeats precisely the same reasons as his predecessor Gregory IX. had given in *Angelis gaudium*, why the Poor Ladies should continue to live under the Hugoline Constitutions. He then explains away the phrase, "the Rule of Saint Benedict," by saying that it does not mean that they are required to observe the said Rule ! For, he points out, his predecessor Gregory IX. had once stated verbally in the presence of the Bishop of Ostia that this phrase, "the Rule of Saint Benedict," merely pledged the Sisters to the observance of poverty, chastity and obedience.[2] On all these grounds, which

[1] Sbaralea, " Bullarium Franciscanum," vol. i., 315.

[2] This somewhat remarkable assertion of Innocent IV. as to the ruling given by Gregory IX. has recently been examined by Mr. Gilliat-Smith (*St. Clare of Assisi*, pp. 194, 195) and some doubt thrown upon Innocent's remembrance of the incident. But after all it matters little whether Innocent was quoting Gregory rightly or wrongly. The important thing is that Innocent gives to the argument the weight of his own authority.

certainly seem unsubstantial enough, the petition of Blessed Agnes was again refused.

It must be remembered that all this time, Saint Clare and the Poor Ladies at San Damiano were living nominally under the Hugoline Constitutions of 1218, which had never been abrogated except in so far as Gregory's letter in 1228 had placed them in an exceptional position in the matter of holding possessions. The decision of Innocent IV. contained in the bull just discussed, must in all probability have been communicated also to Saint Clare : whether it drew forth from her any remonstrance or not, we do not know. But we do know that in August, 1244, in the bull, *Cum Universitati vestrae*,[1] Innocent IV. sent her exactly the same ruling upon the words, "the Rule of Saint Benedict," which he had sent to Blessed Agnes.

This was followed up in November, 1245, by a reaffirmation of the Hugoline Constitutions in the bull, *Solet annuere*,[2] addressed to all the congregations of Poor Clares. In this bull the Rule to be observed is still that of Saint Benedict. Saint Clare and Blessed Agnes had thus secured from the Holy See the admission that, if they were Benedictines, they were so only in name. Perhaps Innocent IV. was gradually becoming convinced of the inconsistency of his position in this matter and was realising that the Poor Ladies, whether at San Damiano or in the daughter houses, were true Franciscans and should no longer be kept out of their spiritual birthright. Whether that were so or not, it appears clear that Saint Clare and Blessed Agnes did not rest satisfied with their position. This at least may be gathered from the phrase *vestris piis precibus inclinati* in the bull, *Cum omnis vera Religio*,[3] which was issued on 6th August, 1247. In some ways it marks no small progress. The extent of the progress is seen by comparing the Rule as given in this bull with the Rule as laid down in the Hugoline Constitutions and repeated in 1245. There is no further reference to the words which had caused

[1] Sbaralea, "Bullarium Franciscanum," vol. i., 350.
[2] *Ibid.*, i., 394.   [3] *Ibid.*, i., 476.

so much doubt and distress, "the Rule of Saint Benedict".[1]
On the contrary they are enjoined to live "according to the
Rule of Saint Francis so far as it relates to three things,

[1] This question of the references to the Benedictine Rule in the earlier
versions of the Rule of Saint Clare is discussed in greater detail in the present
writer's Introduction to the *Rewle of Sustris Menouresses enclosid*, recently
edited for the Early English Text Society and the Philological Society. The
following passages from that Introduction are relevant by way of illustration :—

"Ever since the middle of the eighteenth century the question has been
debated whether S. Clare at her profession adopted the Benedictine Rule, and
whether and if so in what sense the Clarisses in the early history of the Order
were Benedictines. . . .

"The day following her profession S. Clare was committed by S. Francis
to the Convent of S. Paulo near Bastia, which followed the Benedictine Rule,
whence shortly afterwards she was transferred to another Benedictine House,
S. Angeli de Panso on the slopes of Mount Subasio. It was not long, however,
before she was brought to San Damiano, and there formed the community of
Poor Ladies, living, as far as can be ascertained, in accordance with the 'formula
vitae' given to her by S. Francis.

.   .   .   .

"These facts Père Oliger [in his articles, "De Orig. Regul. Ordin. S.
Clarae," *Archivum Franciscanum Historicum*, 1912, pp. 181-4, 203-5, 446-7]
explains by referring to the XIIIth Canon of the Lateran Council, which had
been held in 1215 and which required that no new 'religion' should be founded
in the Church, but that those who felt led to a religious vocation should attach
themselves to one of the already existing Orders, e.g. the Benedictine or the
Augustinian. As an illustration he asserts that S. Dominic '*formaliter* Regulam
S. Augustini accepit '. He infers that the references to the Benedictine Rule in
the Hugoline Constitutions and in the later Bulls of the Holy See addressed to
S. Clare must not be understood to imply that the Poor Ladies were regarded as
following the Benedictine Rule otherwise than 'formaliter,' that is as a kind of
ecclesiastical fiction. . . .

"This repeated protest on the part of the Poor Ladies themselves and the
tone of the responses from the Holy See make it difficult to accept Père Oliger's
view that the observance of the Benedictine Rule by the Clarisses was a mere
formality, and that it must not be understood as having constituted a real obligation ; they make it hard to suppose that it is in any sense comparable with
S. Dominic's relation to the Augustinian Rule. One illustration which Père
Oliger himself gives seems to prove rather more than he intends it to show.
He quotes the case of the Clarisses of Barcelona who, in 1514, refused to be
reformed, and contended that they were not Clarisses, but in reality Benedictines, giving as evidence for this the Bulls of Innocent IV., in which they were
bidden to live after the Rule of the Holy Father Benedict; and ultimately they
went over to the Benedictine Order. This may certainly show the confusion
which arose in later years as to the Rules which governed individual Houses of
Poor Clares, some of which had no desire to accept the settlement of 1253; but
it also proves that the Benedictine character of the Hugoline Constitutions was

obedience, surrender of private property, and chastity ".[1]
Further it is provided that Sisters once professed could only
leave their convent to go to another by direction of the
Minister-General of the Order of Friars Minor or of the Pro-
vincial, thus conceding the claim of Saint Clare that the
Minister-General should be the spiritual Superior of the
Clarisses. Further a special formula for the profession of
Sisters is given, in which the vow is made "to God and to
Blessed Mary ever-virgin, *to Blessed Francis* and all the
Saints". Again it is provided that the Sisters should sing
the offices "according to the use of the Order of the Friars
Minor". The care of all the congregations of Poor Ladies
is definitely handed over to the Minister-General and the Pro-
vincials of the Order of the Friars Minor. The election of the
Abbess is to rest with the congregation, but the confirmation of the election with the Minister-General. So far all this
is exactly what had been the heart's desire of the Saints.
But what of the Privilege of Poverty? It was precisely at
this point, the most vital of all, that the Pope held back.
They were still to be allowed to receive and hold bequests and
possessions; and in order to remove any technical objection
thereto, the possessions were to be held for them by a Pro-
curator. After all, the battle for the full Franciscan liberty
was not yet won!

Nor were the ideals of Saint Clare and Blessed Agnes
shared by all the communities of Poor Ladies, which owed
allegiance to Saint Francis. For in 1252 Innocent IV. issued
a bull, *Nostro decet provenire*,[2] to the Bishop of Ostia, after-

something real as well as formal, if the Sisters at Barcelona were able thus
successfully to appeal to the Hugoline Constitutions to show that they were
Benedictines and not Franciscans. Special emphasis has been laid here on this
matter as it is one of the few doubtful conclusions among those reached by Père
Oliger in his otherwise most valuable treatise, which one must challenge."

[1] It is difficult to see much ground for the view maintained by some writers,
e.g., Lempp and Eubel, that in the passage quoted above the name " Francis "
has been substituted by a verbal slip for " Benedict ". If it were an isolated
case, that might be believed : but the change is systematic and deliberate. See
further Gilliat-Smith, *St. Clare of Assisi*, pp. 247-248.

[2] Sbaralea, i., 601.

wards Alexander IV., instructing him that the Poor Ladies of
S. Angeli Esculan were not to be compelled to exchange
the Hugoline Constitutions for the Rule as revised by the
bull of 6th August, 1247.

There is little to record between 1247 and 1253, the year
of Saint Clare's triumph and death. In September, 1252,
however, Raynaldo, Bishop of Ostia and Protector of the
Order, hearing of the serious illness of Saint Clare, hastened
to her bedside and was implored by her to secure from the
Holy See the ratification of the Rule as given by Saint
Francis and in particular the Privilege of Poverty. Almost
a year later the Rule was finally approved in the bull, *Solet
annuere*,[1] of 9th August, 1253, which reached Saint Clare in
time to cheer her last days on earth.

In December, 1254, Innocent IV. died and was succeeded
by Alexander IV., formerly Bishop of Ostia. Neither the
Latin lives of Blessed Agnes, published by the Bollandists,
nor the versions here published, make clear what happened in
the Convent at Prag, after Saint Clare had obtained for San
Damiano the Privilege of Poverty: but it would appear that
Blessed Agnes received from Saint Clare the Rule as approved
in 1253, and that she "besought the Pope Alexander that he
also should confirm to her likewise and to her cloister the same
rule of perpetual poverty, to the end that neither she nor the
cloister should ever receive any property or inheritance. This
the Holy Father the Pope granted according to her desire."
Sbaralea's *Register of Franciscan Bulls* does not, however,
contain any documentary evidence of this application to
Alexander IV. and of his granting of the desired confirmation.[2]
Indeed no further bulls appear relating in particular to the
Poor Ladies of Prag: nor were they necessary, for the perse-
verance of the two Saints had been rewarded by their success

---

[1] Sbaralea, i., 671.

[2] There is however a Bull extant showing such a confirmation granted by
Alexander IV. on 23rd October, 1259, specially to the Clarisses of Panso (*ibid.*,
ii., 367): and there may have existed a similar Bull granted to the Clarisses of
Prag.

in wringing from the Holy See the one Privilege which they sued, the Privilege of possessing nought.

III.

MANUSCRIPT SOURCES OF THE LEGEND OF BLESSED AGNES.

For the purposes of this study of the sources of the Legend of Blessed Agnes seven Manuscripts have been used, containing either the Legend itself or the Letters from Saint Clare to Blessed Agnes or both. It is highly probable that other manuscripts exist containing similar material, but those which will now be described are the only ones which the present writer has found.

Three manuscripts are contained in the Royal Library of Bamberg, viz., Misc. hist. 146 E. VII. 19, Misc. hist. 146 E. VII. 54 and Misc. hist. 146 E. VII. 56. A detailed description of these manuscripts has been published by Leitschuh in his *Katalog der Handschriften der Kön. Bibliothek zu Bamberg*,[1] but it will be well to give some account of them here with special reference to their contents as relating to Blessed Agnes.

   I. Misc. hist. 146 E. VII. 19, XIV. century, is a quarto volume containing 224 leaves of vellum, measuring 185 mm. × 130 mm. It contains *inter alia :—*

      (i.) Fol. 1v.-138v. A German version of the Legend of Saint Clare and other matter relating to Saint Clare.

      (ii.) Fol. 139r.-157v. A German version of the four Letters from Saint Clare to Blessed Agnes. Rubr. *Dise brief sant die selig sand Clar der edeln kvniginn der heiligen jvnkfrawen Agnesen, des aller edelsten kvnges tohter von Pehaim.* Incip. *Der ersamen vnd aller heiligsten jvnkfrawen Agnesen.* Explic. *an disen gegenwertigen briefen.*

      (iii.) Fol. 157v.-158v. A German version of the Benediction of Saint Clare. Incip. *In dem namen*

---

[1] Vol. i., part II., pp. 241 and foll. ; Bamberg, 1897.

des vaters . . . Explic. *daz dv alle zeit seist in im. Amen.*

(iv.) Fol. 158v.-217r. The Legend of Blessed Agnes in Latin. Rubr. *Incipit prologus in uitam inclite uirginis sororis Agnetis.* Incip. *Crebris sacrarum uirginum* . . . Explic. *laudabilis & gloriosus in secula seculorum. Amen.*

The Latin text here published is the text contained in this MS. Fortunately it is possible to determine the date and provenance of this MS. fairly closely. On the last folio are found the following lines rubricated :—

> Swer an disem bvch werd lesen
> Der schol des gemant wesen
> Daz er gedenk durch got swester
> Katherin hofmenin dez ist ir not
> Die daz bvch geschriben hat
> Daz ir got helf avz aller not
> Vnd geb ir ze lon
> Die himelischen kron. Amen.

Now it is known that Katherin Hofmenin was Abbess of the Clarisses in Nürnberg from 1380-1382 and again from 1389-1393 ; and she is believed to have entered that convent in 1336, coming from Gründel See.[1] She appears to have died in 1393. According to these dates she would probably have been sixty years old when she became Abbess, and it may safely be conjectured from her description of herself in this colophon as ' sister,' as well as on other general grounds, that she wrote the MS. before she became Abbess, i.e., before 1380.

We may accordingly assume that this MS. was written in Nürnberg some time before 1380. At

---

[1] Ussermann, *Episcopatus Bambergensis*, 1802, p. 443 : "Catharinae Hofmannin a. 1380 que post biennium Agneti rursus cessit per septennium, qua denuo a. 1389 munus dimittente, Catharina iterato id usque ad a. 1393 tenuit. Hacc jam a. 1336 ex Grundlacensi coenobio huc advenisse legitur."

the dissolution of the Nürnberg convent about
1600 it passed into the possession of the Convent
of Banz, near Langheim in the diocese of Bamberg.
In 1802 the libraries of the convents in the diocese of Bamberg were merged in the Royal Library
of Bamberg, and among the MSS. so acquired was
Misc. hist. E. VII. 19.[1]   It will be referred to as B1.

II. Misc. hist. 151 E. VII. 56, early XV. century, is a quarto
volume containing 210 leaves of vellum, measuring
177 mm. × 128 mm.   It contains:—

(i.) Fol. 3v.-162v.   A German version of S. Bonaventura's Legend of Saint Francis.

(ii.) Fol. 162v.-210v.   A German version of the
Legend of Blessed Agnes of Prag, being a translation of the Latin version contained in B1.
Rubr. *Hye hebt sich an die vorred des lebens
der edlen heiligen iungfrawen swester Agnesen des
ordens der heiligen iungfrawen sand Claren von
Prag zu Peheim.*   Incip. *Der strengen heiligen
iungfrawen.*   Explic. *vnd lebt dar nach mang iar
in ewigkeit, amen.*   The MS. breaks off after the
first miracle.   It will be referred to as B2.

III. Misc. hist. 147 E. VII. 54, late XIV. or early XV.
century, is a small quarto volume containing 264 leaves
of vellum, measuring 150 mm. × 104 mm.   It contains
inter alia:—

(i.) Fol. 1r.-160r.   A German version of the Legend
of Saint Clare and other matter relating to Saint
Clare.

(ii.) Fol. 160r.-181v.   A German version of the
four Letters from Saint Clare to Blessed Agnes.

(iii.) Fol. 181r.-183r.   A German version of the
Benediction of Saint Clare.

The whole of this material is practically identical
with that contained in B1.

---

[1] For this information as to the history of the MS., the author is indebted to
Herrn Oberbibliothekar Fischer of the Bamberg Library.

It is again possible to settle the date and provenance of this MS. ; for at the end of the Benediction (fol. 183r.) the scribe adds in red ink the words, *Vnd ich auch M. wisentaverin.* This identifies her as Margaret von Wisenthau, who succeeded Katherin Hofmenin as Abbess of the Convent of the Clarisses in Nürnberg from 1393 to 1395, and again from 1401 to 1403, when she died.[1] It is probable that she wrote the MS. before she became Abbess in 1393. The history of the MS. is the same as that of B1.[2] It will be referred to as B3.

The fourth Manuscript is Cod. germ. mon. No. 539 in the Hofbibliothek, Munich. It is a folio volume containing 304 leaves of vellum, measuring 313mm. × 209mm. It is described on the label of the binding as " Legende der Heiligen circ init. XV.," and on the inside of the cover as " ein passional von fremden heilligen ". It is written in two columns, with headings and capital letters rubricated. The Manuscript, as its title implies, contains the lives of a number of saints, and on page 3 of the Index is the following entry :—

Von sant Angnesen der hohgeporen furstin vnd edeln junkfrawen des kungstohter von Prog vnd jezunt ein mitgesellin vnser heylligen vnd wurdigen Muter sant Claren in den hymelischen frewden.

The Legend of Blessed Agnes occupies folios 232r.-261v. Rubr. *Hie hebt sich an.* Incip. *Der strengen heilligen junkfrawen* . . . Explic. *loblich vnd erlich von ewen zu ewen. Amen.* This Manuscript will be referred to as M.

The fifth Manuscript is Cod. 132 Helmstadiensis in the Herzogl. Bibliothek, Wolfenbüttel, XV. century. It is a folio volume containing 287 leaves of thick paper, measuring 316 mm. × 205 mm. It contains *inter alia :—*

---

[1] Ussermann, l.c. : " Margaretha a Wisenthau duobus annis praefuit. Agnes Gansmannia . . . sex annis clavum moderabatur, quem a. 1401 Margaretha rursus duobus annis tenuit."

[2] See p. 18.

(i.) Fol. 153r.-205r. A German version of the Legend of Saint Clare and of Saint Clare's sister, Saint Agnes.

(ii.) Fol. 205r.-213v. A German version of the four Letters from Saint Clare to Blessed Agnes. Rubr. *Dezenn brieff sant die selige sant Clara.* Incip. *Der ersamen vnde allerheiligsten juncfrawin.* Explic. *an dezen gegenwertigen brieffen.*

(iii.) Fol. 213v.-214r. A German version of the Benediction of Saint Clare. Incip. *In dem namen des vatir* . . . Explic. *das du alle zeit seist mit ym. amen.*

(iv.) Fol. 257v.-287r. A German version of the Legend of Blessed Agnes. Rubr. *Hye hebit sich an.* Incip. *Der gestrengen heiligen incfrawen* . . . Explic. *sprach sie alle zeit Deo gracias.*

This Manuscript will be referred to as W.

The sixth Manuscript is M.281 in the Königl. Bibliothek, Dresden, XV. century. It is a quarto volume containing 247 leaves of vellum, measuring 160 mm. × 110 mm. It is in German throughout and is beautifully illuminated with miniatures representing scenes in the life of Saint Clare.[1] It contains *inter alia* :—

(i.) Fol. 1r.-150v. The Legend of Saint Clare and of Saint Clare's sister, Saint Agnes.

(ii.) Fol. 150v.-175r. The four Letters from Saint Clare to Blessed Agnes. Rubr. *Dise brief sant die selig Sand Clar.* Incip. *Der ersamen vnd aller heiligsten jvnkfrawen.* Explic. *an disen gegenwertigen briefen.*

(iii.) Fol. 175r.-176v. The Benediction of Saint Clare. Incip. *In dem namen des vaters* . . . Explic. *daz dv alle zeit seist in im. Amen.*

This Manuscript will be referred to as D.

The seventh Manuscript is Germ. Oct. 484 in the Königl. Bibliothek, Berlin, XV. century. It is a quarto volume containing 332 leaves of paper, measuring 213 mm. × 151 mm. The Manuscript was formerly No. 1153, in the collection of

---

[1] The Miniatures from this MS. are reproduced as illustrations of this volume by permission of the authorities of the Royal Library of Dresden.

Sir Thomas Phillipps. It consists principally of the lives of Saints and of miscellaneous theological material.

(i.) The Legend of Blessed Agnes occupies folios 177r.-214v. Rubr. *Von sant agnes der kunigin von behem.* Incip. *Hie vahet an daz leben vnd lesen.* . . . Explic. *heiligsten vnd loblichsten junckfrawen sant Angnes von Brag. Amen.*

(ii.) Fol. 215r.-222v. contain the four letters from Saint Clare to Blessed Agnes. Rubr. *Hie nach volgend etlich santprief.* Incip. *Der ersamen vnd aller heiligsten junckfrawen agnessen* . . . Explic. *als vil ich mag an dissen gegenwirtigen prieffen.*

(iii.) Fol. 222v.-223r. contain the Benediction. Incip. *In dem namen des vaters* . . . Explic. *daz du alle zit syest in im. Amen.*

The German text of the Legend here published is the one contained in this Manuscript: it will be referred to as Ber.

It would be beyond the purpose of this work to enter into a detailed examination of the dialect of the Berlin MS., but it may be mentioned that it appears to be written in the dialect generally known as "Oberdeutsch," with some distinct evidences of Swabian provenance.

The enumeration of the Manuscript sources for the life of Blessed Agnes would be incomplete without reference to two other subsidiary manuscripts, to which recourse may profitably be had in considering later on the chronology of Blessed Agnes.

One is a magnificent folio Breviary, written in 1356 and belonging to the Convent of the "Ordo Cruciferorum" of Prag, which Order Blessed Agnes herself brought to her native city. The Breviary was courteously placed at the disposal of the present writer by General und Grossmeister Franz Marat. It contains two important references to Blessed Agnes which are discussed on page 48, and its authority is high as being the earliest MS., at present known, containing such a reference.

The other is Manuscript I.C. 24. in the Universitäts-Bibliothek, Prag, which contains *inter alia* a recension of the Bohemian chronicle generally known as the Pulkavova chronicle, having been written by Pulkava († 1380). This manuscript likewise gives an important reference to Blessed Agnes which is discussed on page 49.

It thus appears that five manuscripts contain versions of the Legend of Blessed Agnes, viz. B1., B2., Ber., M. and W.; and that five contain the Letters from Saint Clare to Blessed Agnes and the Benediction of Saint Clare, viz. B1., B3., Ber., W. and D. Even a cursory reading of the MSS. makes it clear that the versions of the Legend are so closely alike as to indicate a common source, and that B3., Ber., M. and W. are all translations either of the Latin B1., or of a closely allied text. It is possible, however, to go further and to define, provisionally at any rate, their relation to one another.

The existence of the Latin text B1. itself suggests an original Latin source for the Legend. The Bollandist editors of the *Acta Sanctorum* state[1] that two legends of Blessed Agnes were written before 1328 at the instance of Elizabeth, Queen of Bohemia, in support of the petition for her canonisation, one in Latin and the other in Czech. This statement is so important that it is desirable to quote it in full :—

10. *Ut jam dicta supplicatio felicem exitum sortiretur, videntur mandante Elisabetha Regina undequaque conquisita illustriora Acta et miracula, atque ex iis duplex vita B. Agnetis confecta, cuius altera sermone Latino, altera Bohemico fuit exarata : prior datur ex vetusto codice Ecclesiae Pragensis eruta, cuius aliquod apographum extat in collegio Clementino Societatis Jesu apud P. Joannem Tannerum : et hanc statueramus solam dare, omissa Vita posteriore, quam ex duobus etiam vetustis codicibus descriptam Latinitate donavit vir eruditus e Societate etiam Jesu Georgius Crugerus. Verum dum utramque inter se contulimus, deprehendimus illustres rerum circumstantias cum variis miraculis addi, et quia hactenus etiam inedita est, judica-*

---

[1] *AA. SS., Mart.,* I., p. 503.

vimus ipsam quoque praelo dignam esse, et priori addi debere. Codicum horum MSS., quibus Crugerus usus est, alter appellatur Crumloviensis, alter Veleslavius : imo unius auctor creditur B. Agneti coaevus extitisse, et de eo accipienda esse ista verba infra num 18. *relata : " Haec habui e veteri manuscripto coaevi auctoris, quae de insolita virgunculae regiae ante sacrum parthenonem virtute paucis annotarem ". Ceterum ut ex dictis patet, ut explicarentur obscura, huic inde interposuit pauca jam memoratus Crugerus.*

Assuming the existence of a Latin original, the question immediately suggests itself: Is B1. the Latin original? A detailed comparison of B1. with the German versions shows that this cannot be the case.

The five versions appear to fall into two groups derived from a Latin original, which may for convenience be described as [Latin] X and [Latin] Y.[1] It can be shown that in the X group should be placed B1. and Ber. ; in the Y group B2., M. and W.

The first point to establish is that B1. and Ber. have a common Latin source (X) which differs from the common Latin source (Y) of B2., M. and W.

The following are examples of additions common to B2., M. and W. (which accordingly must have existed in Y) but which are not found in either B1. or Ber. (and which thus must have been absent from X).

[2] Fol. 164v., l. 17. *In pane & vino ieiunauit :* M., W., and B2. add " *vnd prachs irm leib ab das sy nit in korung viel* ".

Fol. 165r., l. 22. *Percipere potuisset :* M., W., and B2. add " *vnd dennoch nit wol wann sy von den menschen nit gelobt wolt werden* ".

Fol. 166r., l. 21. *Sed deus magnus :* M., W., and B2. add " *vnser herr Jhesus Cristus* ".

Fol. 170v., l. 27. *de Terdento :* M., W., and B2. add " *in welschen landen* ".

---

[1] An alternative hypothesis of the inter-relation of the MSS. will be found in Appendix IV., p. 176.

[2] In these examples the references are to the folios of B1., the German quotations are from M.

Fol. 173r., l. 1, *peripsima propter Cristum :* M., W., and
B2. add "*daz die swester ir zell vnd wonung rein vnd
sauber funden vnd daz sy in reinikeit wurd vor dem
anplik gotes vnsers herrn gefunden vnd in rehter dymutikeit*".

On the other hand examples can be given of
additions common to B1. and Ber. which M., W., and
B2. agree in omitting.

Fol. 167r., l. 13, *ad capellam domus regie [uel] ad ecclesiam
kathedralem :* Ber., "*in ir capel, die sy in ir kuniglichen phaltzen het oder zu den rechten tům*". M., W.,
and B2. omit reference to the cathedral.

Fol. 17or., l. 17. *Cruciferos cum rubea cruce & stella :* Ber.,
"*Crützherren vnd tragent rötte crütz vnd einen sternen*".
M., W., and B2. omit reference to "*& stella*".

Fol. 197r., l. 9, *clauus qui cum uiolencia impulsus fuerat :*
Ber., "*der . . . nagel . . . da mit auch der sarch aller
krefftigest verschlagen was*". M., W., and B2. omit.

These examples of omissions and additions might be
multiplied and a large number of further instances will be seen
in the notes to the Latin text : but even more conclusive than
these turns of expression are points of difference in the narrative, slight though they may be in intrinsic importance :—

Fol. 166r., l. 12, *cuidam ex nunciis imperatoris :* Ber.,
"*einer von des keissers botten*" ; whereas M., W., and
B2. state "*einem aus den poten des kungs*," attributing
the dream to the King of England's envoy, instead of
to the Emperor's envoy.

Fol. 17ov., l. 31, *septem uirgines :* Ber., "*siben junckfrawen*" ; whereas M., W., and B2. say "*sechs*".

Fol. 176r., l. 3. B1. and Ber. tell how Blessed Agnes herself
fell ill, and how the fishes were miraculously provided
for her refreshment. But M., W., and B2. apply the
story to King Ottocarus, "*und der selb kunk Octagarus
in solche armut fiel*," etc.

Fol. 190r., l. 25, *quam unum cum peccato :* M., W., and B2., "*denn vil mit beswerung der sund*". Probably Latin Y had "*multa*" instead of "*unum*".

Now assuming that B1. and Ber. belong to a group having a common source X, what is the relation between them ; and can Ber. be regarded as being actually derived from B1. ?

In any case Ber. is a very free translation of its Latin original, and in this respect it differs markedly from the members of the Y group, which are very literal and even slavish translations. Ber. contains some passages of considerable length, to which nothing corresponding will be found in B1. As both these texts are here published, it is unnecessary to point out many of these additions, but two or three of the more substantial ones may be noted.

> Fol. 192v., l. 17. At the end of Chapter IV. Ber. adds a paragraph in praise of obedience : "*Wann da mit werden sy den martarrer gelichet . . . vnszers lieben herren Jhesu Cristi*". This addition is interesting as containing the Latin quotation in the German text, "*propter te mortificamur tota die*," which the translator carefully renders into German. This passage is one which may well be a quotation from a sermon, added by the writer of Ber.
>
> Fol. 193r., l. 32 (Ber.), shows a similar quotation, "*als auch vnser lieber her sprichet in dem ewangelio ' selig sind die armen, wann daz himelrich ist irer '*".
>
> Fol. 193v., l. 28. Ber. adds another allusion, "*als auch der heilig sant Laurencius von dem schatz der im geben ward, den gab er durch gottes willen vnd gabs den dürfftigen vnd den armen*".
>
> Fol. 192r., l. 32. "*Wann da sant Clar den orden anfeng, da bat sy den selben babst, daz er ir die regel rechter armůt wolt bestetigen vnd beiden vns zu trost vnd vnsren orden zu eren vnd zu bestetigung. Da schrib ir der babst mit seiner selb hand die erst form vnd mas der regel.*" This is the most important addition found in Ber. as

compared with B1. It bears a remarkable verbal similarity to a passage in the Legend of Saint Clare, and it
may perhaps be suggested that the translator had
access to that Legend.

The possibility must not be overlooked that the
translator of Ber. may have made additions which
were entirely original or were derived from another
source, but while making allowance for this possibility
it appears probable that Ber. was working from a Latin
source which contained much that is absent from B1.
Between the Latin source of the X Group and the
Berlin version there must be hypothecated another
Latin version X1., which contained the source of these
additions which differentiate Ber. from B1.

The inter-relationship of the members of the Y group must
now be considered.

While there is a close similarity between the three members
of the Y group, M., W., and B2., so close indeed that they
may properly be described as one version, yet there are a large
number of minor differences among them. Standing between
Latin [Y] and the three German texts must be assumed a
hypothetical common German source which will be described
as [Y1]. Notwithstanding these close resemblances between
the three texts, there are also minor points of difference, in
the majority of which M. and W. agree together as against
B2. These variations are set out in the notes to the Latin
text here published. A close examination of M. and W.
affords a good deal of ground for the hypothesis that W. has
actually been copied from M. Here are some examples :—

M. (Fol. 235r.), " *das ir gemahel der vorgenant herzog von
polonii* ‖ *vnd nun*," etc. The word " *starb* " is added
‖ *starb*

below in a later hand. W. (Fol. 260r.) copies this :
" *das ir gemahel der vorgenant herzog von polony vnde
nun*," etc., leaving out the verb " *starb* " altogether.
But B2. has " *starb* " quite correctly.

B1. (Fol. 205v., l. 12) gives "*capillos sancte Agnetis quos habet celerius apportate*". Both M. and W. translate this : "*bringt mir des wassers von sant agnessen,*" perhaps thinking of water in which some relic of Blessed Agnes had been placed.

B1. (Fol. 210v., l. 17). "*Et multi alii a diuersis egritudinibus liberati.*" Both M. and W. after translating this add the word "*Nota*".

B1. (Fol. 168v., l. 8), "*ac se contulit excusandum sororisque propositum detegendum*". B2. gives "*nam ers zu im zu beschuldigen sein swester*"; but M. and W., "*do nam er zu im die poten des keisers zu beschuldigen sein mumen,*" inserting the words "die poten des keissers" which have somehow crept in and which destroy the sense. It is remarkable, however, that M., W., and B2. all give "*be*schuldigen" where the sense requires "*ent*schuldigen ": the fact that this mistake occurs in all three proves a common German source for all three, and also suggests that the Latin source used by Y1. read "accusandum " instead of "excusandum ".

These examples, and others which might be given, certainly strongly support the view that W. is a slavish copy of M. ; but there are other variants between M. and W. which are difficult to account for thus. On the whole it seems safe to assert that W. is a descendant from M., but probably not a direct copy from it.

The results thus obtained from an examination of the five MSS. containing the Legend of Blessed Agnes can to some extent be supplemented and even confirmed by a similar treatment of the five MSS. containing the four Letters from Saint Clare to Blessed Agnes and the Benediction. The material under consideration is, however, much smaller in extent: and the variants, while numerous, are slighter and consequently the inferences to be derived are more problematic.

It has already been mentioned (pp. 16-22) that the five MSS. in question are B1., Ber., W. (which have already been considered) and B3. and D. For the purposes of this study the text of the Letters and the Benediction contained in B1., being the oldest version at present known, has been taken as the standard and is published here. The more important variants are given in the foot-notes : slight verbal differences are not recorded and differences of dialectic form are disregarded.

It may first be noted that the Dresden text, D., is practically identically the same as B1. No important variant between these two can be found : even the dialect is the same. Further there are several striking similarities which suggest that D. may have been copied from B1., or from a copy of B1. Here are some examples :—

> The rubricated heading of the second letter in both B1. and D. is "*Daz ist der ander brief*" ; while B3. gives "*der ander brief*," and W. has no heading at all.
>
> The heading of the fourth letter in B1. is "*Daz ist d' virde brief*". D. has precisely the same, even copying the contraction "*d'*" (which contraction, though generally so common, does not happen to occur elsewhere in either MS.).
>
> B1. (Fol. 139v., l. 2) reads "*aller erwe[r]gsten lebens*," the "*r*" being added in red ink. D. copies it exactly, including even the red ink, while B3. and W. give "*erwirdigsten*".

It is difficult to account for these and other similar details, except on the hypothesis that D. is derived in some way from B1. It is safe to assign D. to the X group.

On the other hand two MSS., viz. B3. and W., agree in scores of small variants from the B1. text. As will be seen from the foot-notes, some of these variants are additions common to both, others are omissions common to both, others are different ways of expressing the same sense. There are a fair number of indications which suggest that W., the later text, is in some way derived from B3.

> Thus in Letter I. (see B1. Fol. 142v., l. 24), where B1. has "*denne die ere*" : B3. read originally "*denne ere*" and

di has been added by a later hand in the margin. W. reads "*denne ere*" without any addition of *di*.

In Letter II. B1. (Fol. 145v., l. 2) reads "*vnd, als die ander Rachel, alle zeit ansehest,*" etc. : B3. is identical, except that "*alle zeit*" is added by a later hand in the margin. W. is identical, except that it has no "*alle zeit*".

Still the W. text shows a good deal of independence. There are a number of cases in which W. has a different reading, when B1. and B3. agree. But there is so general an agreement between B3. and W., that B3. may be held to belong to the Y group, which we have hypothecated in the consideration of the text of the Legend.

It remains to refer to Ber. In considering the text of the Legend in Ber. it was seen (p. 25) that that text is to a large extent independent of the others : that it has a number of substantial additions not found in any of the other versions. So too with the Ber. text of the Letters. It shows many variants, not of a very important character ; but apparently only one variant in which Ber. agrees with B3. and W.

The result of this investigation of the inter-relation of the seven MSS., which contain either the Legend or the Letters, or both, can be represented in diagrammatic form [1] as follows :—

A. MANUSCRIPTS CONTAINING THE LEGEND.

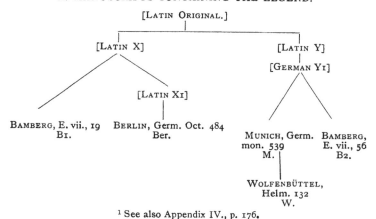

[LATIN ORIGINAL.]

[LATIN X]   [LATIN Y]

[GERMAN Y1]

[LATIN X1]

BAMBERG, E. vii., 19   BERLIN, Germ. Oct. 484   MUNICH, Germ.   BAMBERG,
B1.   Ber.   mon. 539   E. vii., 56
M.   B2.

WOLFENBÜTTEL,
Helm. 132
W.

[1] See also Appendix IV., p. 176.

B. MANUSCRIPTS CONTAINING THE LETTERS.

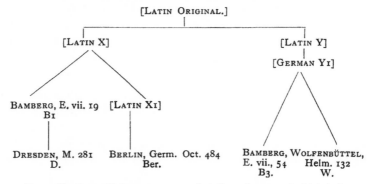

Note.—Versions which are not extant, but the existence of which is hypothetical, are placed in brackets.

IV.

PRINTED SOURCES OF THE LEGEND OF BLESSED AGNES.

Reference has already been made to the printed sources for the Life of Blessed Agnes. It is unnecessary to enumerate all the references to her life which are to be found in many different chroniclers and historians. The main source of information hitherto available is to be found in the two Latin lives and other related material published in the *Acta Sanctorum*, under the date 6th March, the second of which lives is the longer and more detailed. The account given by the Bollandist editors of the source of the two versions published by them is quoted on pages 22, 23. From this it appears that the first Life is a copy taken from a very ancient MS. in Prag which was one of the two versions, viz. the Latin one, prepared some time before 1328 in support of the application for the canonisation of Blessed Agnes initiated by Elizabeth, Queen of Bohemia. The second Life purports to be a compilation made by the Jesuit, Georgius Crugerus, from two ancient MSS., one known as "Crumloviensis," the other as "Veleslavius"; one of the two MSS., but the Bollandists omit to define which, "is believed to be the work of a contemporary of Blessed Agnes".

If the two Bollandist Lives are compared, first the one with the other and then with the manuscript versions already described, it immediately becomes apparent that with all their differences the various versions, manuscript and printed, are substantially the same : the narrative follows the same course in them all : the same main incidents occur and generally in the same order. They all have a common source, a Latin one. The Bollandists do not appear to have supposed that the Latin document prepared for the canonisation application, which according to them was the one source of the first Life, was also one of the two sources upon which Crugerus drew for his compilation which forms the second Life, but that is one obvious explanation of the close similarity between the two Bollandist lives. Another explanation is that both Tannerus, the copyist of the first Bollandist life, and Crugerus, the compiler of the second life, were using a common Latin source, differing from both the Latin lives.

If the two Bollandist Lives are compared in detail with the MSS. versions, it is by no means easy to place them in position, but some provisional conclusions can be reached.

It will be found that there is a much closer connection between B1. and the first Bollandist Life (Boll. I.) than between B1. and the second Bollandist Life (Boll. II.). Similarities not only in the matter of incidents recorded, but also in actual wording, can be traced. Some of the more striking may be given :—

Incidents recorded :—

B1. Fol. 163v., l. 23. *" Cum per annum integrum proficiens eisdem commansisset."* Boll I. agrees : *" iter per anni orbem formavit"*. But Boll. II. makes no reference to the " one year ".

B1. Fol. 165r., l. 30. *" Vnde & annunciacionem dominicam inter ceteras festiuitates quoad uixit ardentissima deuocione colebat."* Boll. I., *" quam ob caussam festum ejusdem, quo salutarem Angeli voce nuntium accepit, praecipua veneratione . . . re colebat"*. Boll. II. is silent as to her special reverence for the Annunciation.

B1. Fol. 176r.-177v. The stories about the miraculous provision of the fishes and of the loaves are not given in detail in either of the Bollandist Lives. But Boll. I. has a reference to them :—

" *Quam tamen brevi et panibus mundissimis et fundulis . . . ad limina ejus depositis, atque per ostiariam repertis, Cristus mitigavit*".

Boll. II. has no reference to these incidents at all.

Matters of Wording :—

Fol. 164v. l. 18.

B1.	*Boll. I.*	*Boll. II.*
Quum pueri prefati ducis lacticiniis utebantur.	*Cum filii, filiaeque ducis Austriae lactariis vescebantur.*	*Austriae duces, liberi principes, lacticiniis vescerentur.*

Fol. 170r. l. 13.

B1.	*Boll. I.*
Ad imitacionem beate Elyzabeth consobrine sue, hospitale . . . in pede pontis ciuitatis Pragensis ad honorem sanctissimi confessoris Francisci construxit, quod redditibus & possessionibus amplis ditauit.	*Nosocomium ad imitationem S. Elisabethae cognatae suae, perpetuis redditibus fruens, sub nomine D. Francisci prope Pontem constituit.*

Fol. 180v. l. 4.

B1.	*Boll. I.*	*Boll. II.*
Benigna et Petrusca.	*Benigna et Prisca.*	*Benigna et Wratislava.*

If the whole section containing the miracles (B1. Fol. 200r.-215v.) is compared with Boll. I., § 16-21, and with Boll. II., § 64-84, it will be seen that :—

(i.) Boll. I. follows precisely the same order as B1., but omits five of the miracles ; whereas Boll. II. follows an order which is largely different and omits the same five miracles as Boll. I. and omits an additional one.

(ii.) B1. gives the proper names in almost every case more fully than either Boll. I. or II., e.g. *Donika filia*

Domazlai Desquotz, Psribko famulus Cunssonis de Hermanitz ; and in some cases gives the name where Boll. II. has no name at all.

(iii.) Boll. II. contains much verbiage, but not a single fact or incident which is not in Bı.

Speaking generally of the whole of Bı. as compared with the two Bollandist lives, Bı. is a good deal fuller and more detailed than Boll. I. and less detailed than Boll. II. The probable explanation is that the Bamberg text represents substantially the original Latin narrative prepared in support of the canonisation application : that Boll. I. is merely a curtailed or abridged version of Bı. ; that Boll. II. is a compilation in which one factor is either Bı. or its abridged form Boll. I., while the other factor is the Czech narrative prepared for the canonisation application. But it is dangerous to dogmatise as to the composition of Boll. II., as the Czech narrative is not at present known. Further it can scarcely be profitably or successfully discussed whether the Bollandist versions should be classified with the X group or with the Y group. The criteria for differentiating these two groups are so comparatively slight that they cannot well be traced in the Bollandist versions.

V.

AUTHORSHIP OF THE LEGEND.

There is little in the Bollandist Lives in the way of internal evidence to indicate the authorship or source of the original Latin legend. But the prologue to the Legend as contained in Bı., B2., M., and W., does give some fairly definite information which must of course be taken with caution and reserve. From the prologue it would appear that it was composed by a Friar Minor at the request of the Clarisses of Prag : as there is no clue to his identity, we may refer to him as *Anonymus Pragensis* (by analogy of *Anonymus Perusinus*). Clearly he is a man who is writing of a town which he knows personally and of people known to him. His descriptions of the exact position of the House of the Crucigeri and of the House of the Clarisses are those of an eye-witness.   His claim to have derived his materials partly from his own observation (*aliqua quidem uisa*) and partly from others who were themselves participators (*alia uero ab hiis quibus acciderant narrata*), though not free from a certain conventionality, is yet substantiated by the general style of his narrative and specially by the ample details of proper names and place names which are found in BI., the earliest form of the Legend at present known.   Many of these names can be identified as local names from contemporary chronicles.[1]   If then the original Latin version was, as has been suggested, one of the versions prepared in support of the application for canonisation of 1328, it would follow that it came into existence at some time between 1281/82, the year of Blessed Agnes's death, and 1328, the year when that application was begun.   Even at the latest possible date, circ. 1328, there would still be persons in Prag whose memories would go back to events in 1281/82.   It is more probable, however, that the Legend came into existence a good deal earlier than 1328; for the cult which justified or prompted the application for canonisation must have grown up at a date nearer that of the death of Blessed Agnes.

This theory as to the origin of the Legend is supported by a passage in the BI. text.   In the miracle recorded in BI., Fol. 203r., Elizabeth, Queen of Bohemia, promises at a time of dangerous sickness that, if she is cured through the merits of Blessed Agnes, she will strive with all her might to secure her canonisation (*si per merita eius gloriosa tam grauem languorem euaderet, pro canonizacione ipsius totis uiribus & omnibus quibus posset conatibus uellet fideliter laborare*).   What more likely than that such a hint should be included, if the narrative were written in support of an anticipated canonisation? and what more unlikely than that it should be included if the narrative were composed after the application for canonisation had proved abortive?

[1] See Note XIX., p. 173, Note XXIV., p. 174, and particularly Note XXVI., p. 174.

VI.

NICHOLAS GLASSBERGER'S USE OF THE LEGEND.

A special interest attaches to the B1. text through the fact that it can be shown to be one of the sources used by Nicholas Glassberger, the fifteenth century Franciscan chronicler. Moreover new light is thrown on a point hitherto obscure, viz. Glassberger's allusions to a "maior chronica".

Nicholas Glassberger entered the Franciscan Order in 1472. He was the author of the Chronicles which are preserved in one MS. only and which have been published in the *Analecta Franciscana*, Tom. II. Glassberger is also known to have copied with his own hand a MS. of the "Chronicles of the XXIV. Generals," a work of uncertain authorship which was composed about 1360: this copy, known as the "Hall Codex," was completed by him in 1491.

The Quaracchi editors of the "Chronicle of Nicholas Glassberger" in their introduction state:—

"*Pluries auctor meminit cuiusdam maioris Chronicae* (pp. 15, 58, 83, 84), *quae non alia videtur esse ab ea, quam alias vocat 'antiquam Ordinis Chronicam'* (XXIV. Gen.)., *ubi revera inveniuntur quae narrat. Solummodo* (p. 83) *verba: 'quam in maiori chronica* posui' *scrupulum animo iniicere possent. Tamen paucis verbis exceptis, eadem iterum inveniuntur ibidem.*"

The reference on page 15 (*Anal. Franc.*, Tom. II.) is to Fr. Agnellus Pisanus and his companions and how they were ill-treated by certain Black Monks, and certainly a fuller version of that incident is found in the "Chronicles of the XXIV. Generals" (*Anal. Franc.*, Tom. III., pp. 24-26).

The reference on pages 83 and 84 is to Bertholdus de Ratisbona and contains the word "*posui*" which has troubled the Quaracchi editors. Still as the fuller narrative is contained in the XXIV. Generals (*Anal. Franc.*, Tom. III., pp. 238, 239), the editors have remained satisfied with their theory that the "*maior chronica*" is identical with the "Chronicle of the XXIV. Generals".

The reference on page 58 is, however, to the story of Blessed Agnes, contained in pages 56-58. The Editors refer to an account of Blessed Agnes which is contained in the "Hall" Codex of the XXIV. Generals (*Anal. Franc.*, III., pp. 183, 184). Evidently they have had some misgiving as to their theory about the "*maior chronica*," for in their footnote to the reference on page 15 they say :—

"*Chronica maiora citata usque nunc nondum inventa sunt*".

It will be found that Glassberger's account of Blessed Agnes (*Anal. Franc.*, II., pp. 56-58) is a word-for-word copy of a part of the text B1. The relevant passages are set out in parallel columns :—

B1. Text [Fol. 170v.].	*Anal. Franc.*, II., pp. 57-58.
Venientes autem quinque sorores ordinis sancte Clare de Terdento, que ad peticionem ipsius de fauore sedis apostolice sibi fuerant destinate, cum magna spiritus exultacione ab ipsa recepte, memoratum cenobium honorifice introducte sunt. Et in proxima festiuitate sancti Martini septem uirgines de regno Bohemie generis ualde clari, sponso uirginum castitatis nexibus uinciri cupientes, habitu & conuictu adiuncte sunt sororibus antedictis. Considerans tandem uirgo prudens quod in naufraga uita presenti continue fluctibus nostre mortalitatis iactamur, nec superna contemplari ualemus propter tumultum mundanarum causarum, amore celestium arden-	*Eodem anno venerunt de Tridentino Pragam quinque sorores Ordinis sanctae Clarae, per dominum Papam Gregorium nonum dictae dominae Agneti petenti destinatae, quas ipsa cum magna spiritus exultatione susceptas in memoratum coenobium sancti Salvatoris introduxit. Et in proxima festivitate sancti Martini septem virgines clari generis et sanguinis de regno Bohemiae, sponso virginum castitatis nexibus vinciri cupientes, habitu et convictu coniunctae sunt sororibus antedictis. Agnes autem tamquam virgo prudens cogitans et considerans, quod in naufraga vita praesenti continue fluctibus nostrae mortalitatis iactamur, nec superna*

cius inflammata, in Penthecoste proximo sequenti, presentibus septem epyscopis et domino rege, fratre suo ac regina cum multis principibus & baronibus, nec non innumera utriusque sexus diuersarum nacionum multitudine, spreto regni fastigio et omni gloria mundana contempta, cum septem nobilissimis regni sui uirginibus, ut columba innocua de diluuio nequam seculi ad archam sacre religionis conuolauit. Cumque in monasterio, crinibus tonsis, uestes regias deposuisset, fletibus et luctui, ut Hester altera, apta indumenta suscepit—quatenus Clare matris sue pauperi se habitu conformaret & gestu. Sic sic elongauit fugiens a periculosis mundi procellis [et] salutis sue anchoram supra petram que Cristus est fiducialiter collocauit. Ad hanc religionis solitudinem pennis affeccionis transmigrauit, ut in ea puritatis & pacis interne soliditatem seruando, suauitatem eterne dulcedinis palato mentis pregustaret. In hoc antro paupertatis amore pauperis crucifixi et dulcissime matris eius usque ad mortem se recludens, quasi mirra electa suauem diffudit fragranciam sanctitatis.

contemplari valemus propter tumultum mundanarum causarum, amore coelestium ardentius inflammata, in Pentecoste proxime sequenti, videlicet

Anno Domini 1236, *praesentibus septem Episcopis et domino Wenceslao rege, fratre suo, ac Cunigunde regina, filia quondam Philippi, regis Romanorum, cum multis principibus, baronibus, nec non innumera utriusque sexus diversarum nationum multitudine, spreto regni fastigio et omni mundana gloria contempta, cum septem aliis nobilissimis regni sui virginibus ut columba innocua de diluvio nequam saeculari ad arcam sacrae Religionis convolavit. Cumque in monasterio, crinibus tonsis, vestes regias deposuisset, fletibus et luctui, ut Esther altera, apta indumenta suscepit, quatenus Clarae, matri suae pauperi, se habitu conformaret et gestu. Sic se elongavit fugiens a procellosis mundi fluctibus, et salutis et spei suae ancoram supra petram, quae Christus est, fiducialiter collocavit. In antro ergo paupertatis amore pauperis Crucifixi et dulcissime Matris eius usque ad mortem se recludens, per annos 55 quasi myrrha electa suavem diffudit fragantiam sanctitatis. Ad hanc misit Christi virgo sancta Clara plures epistolas consolatorias et instructivas. Eius virginis vita et modestia ac sanctitatis et miraculorum gesta singulari Legenda in maiori chronica exprimuntur.*

Again Glassberger under the date 1281 gives an account of the death and burial of Blessed Agnes (p. 95). This is also copied from B1. The passage is as follows :—

B1. Text [Fol. 197v.].   *Anal. Franc.*, II., p. 95.

Quibus propter occupaciones diuersas, secretiori dei consilio aliud ordinante, uenire recusantibus—paulo enim ante mortem suam inclita uirgo predixerat quod nec epyscopus nec aliquis alterius religionis prelatus quam frater minor, et talis frater qui prius numquam uisus est in terra Bohemie, corpus eius sepelire deberet—adueniens uenerabilis pater, frater Bonagracia generalis minister quartadecima die a transitu eius, in sequenti die, uidelicet in dominica de passione, preciosum illud pignus cum multis qui tunc aderant fratribus deuote ac honorifice in capella sacratissime uirginis Marie, in qua tempore debilitatis audiebat missarum sollempnia, sicut ipsa petiuerat, sepeliuit. Vbi miri

Eodem anno visitando Provinciam Alamanniae pervenit frater Bonagratia, Minister Generalis, in Pragam Provinciae Bohemiae, ubi sexto nonas Martii soror Agnes, Ottokari, primi regis Bohemiae filia Ordinis sanctae Clarae, feliciter in Domino obdormierat et quarta decima a transitu eius in sequenti die, videlicet in Dominica de Passione, pretiosum illud pignus cum multis qui tunc aderant fratribus devote ac honorifice in capella sacratissimae Virginis Mariae, in qua tempore debilitatis audierat Missarum solemnia, sicut ipsa petiverat, sepelivit, ubi miri odoris fragrantia sorores causa orationis intrantes diebus pluribus respergebat. Haec paulo ante mortem suam inclyta

odoris fragrancia sorores causa oracionis intrantes diebus pluribus respergebat.

virgo praedixerat, quod nec Episcopus nec aliquis alterius Religionis Praelatus quam Frater Minor, et talis frater, qui prius nunquam visus est in terra Bohemiae, corpus eius sepelire deberet ; quod factum est per hunc Ministrum Generalem. Vide Legendam eiusdem virginis.

We may even without undue presumption go so far as to suggest that in B1. we have the actual MS. from which Glassberger was copying. On page 57 the Quaracchi editors emend the text : " *Sic se elongavit fugiens a procellosis mundi fluctibus et salutis,*" etc. : they explain in the note that the MS. of Glassberger reads "*sic sic*" for "*sic se*"; and that they have to add "*et*" after "*fluctibus*". Now it will be noticed that B1. likewise reads " *sic sic*" and likewise is without the "*et*" after "*fluctibus*". It is most unlikely that Glassberger was copying from another MS. which contained these same peculiarities.

Following upon the end of the Legend of Blessed Agnes in B1. is a short passage apparently unconnected, the object of which is not at all clear. It will be found that Glassberger has used this passage in two places : it appears in his own Chronicle (*Anal. Franc.*, II., p. 57), and also in his copy of the " XXIV. Generals " in the section which he has added, as already stated (*Anal. Franc.*, III., p. 184). The passage in the original and in the two copies by Glassberger are set out in columns below :—

B1. Text. Fol. 217r.	*Anal. Franc.*, II., p. 56.	*Anal. Franc.*, III., p. 184.
Cristo deuota uirgo domina Agnes, soror Vencezlai quarti regis Bohemie, suscepit ordi-	*Hoc tempore Christo devota virgo, domina Agnes, filia regis Ottokari et soror Wenceslai*	*Haec ante conversionem suam ad imitationem, sicut ipse sanctus Pater Fran-*

nem sancti Francisci: ad cuius imitacionem sicut pater sanctus Franciscus sub typo trium ordinum, tres ecclesias erexit, ita ipsa tres sollempnes ecclesias construxit in Praga. Primam uidelicet in honore saluatoris omnium, in qua se cum sororibus suis recollegit. Secundam in honore sancte dei genitricis Marie et beati Francisci pro fratribus minoribus iuxta se diuina sibi & sororibus ordinis Sancte Clare ministrantibus. Terciam in hospitali suo eciam in honore sancti Francisci pro ordine cruciferorum tunc de nouo per fratres minores de mandato ipsius domine Agnetis creato, uidelicet cruciferis stelliferis quibus ipsum hospitale copiosissime de propriis bonis regalibus dotatum conmisit, ut ipsi debilibus & infirmis & omnibus miseris personis ibi receptis, tam in temporalibus quam in spiritualibus, fideliter

quarti, regis Bohemiae, audiens de sancta Clara et de beato Francisco, iam noviter in coelis glorificato, qui sub typo trium Ordinum tres ecclesias erexit, ad eius exemplum tres solemnes ecclesias Pragae construi propriis sumptibus fecit: Primam in pede pontis Pragensis in hospitali suo, quod amplis redditibus et possessionibus dotatum pro infirmis, velut consobrina sua Elisabetha construxerat, aedificavit in honorem sancti Francisci, in quam collocavit Cruciferos cum rubea stella et cruce, qui de novo per Fratres Minores ad preces dictae virginis Agnetis instituti fuerant, ut infirmis ministrarent et de necessariis sollicite providerent; secundam in honorem Salvatoris omnium erexit, qua, pretiosis reliquiis Sanctorum, vasis et ornamentis ad cultum divinum pertinentibus decorata, se postmodum cum sororibus inclusit;

ciscus sub typo trium ordinum tres ecclesias erexit, ita ipsa tres solemnes ecclesias construxit in Praga: primam videlicet in honorem Salvatoris omnium, in qua se cum suis sororibus recollegit; secundam in honorem beatae Virginis Mariae et beati Francisci pro fratribus Minoribus iuxta se divina sibi ministrantibus; tertiam in hospitali suo etiam in honorem sancti Francisci pro Ordine Cruciferorum tunc de novo per fratres Minores de mandato ipsius sanctae dominae Agnetis creato, videlicet Cruciferis stelliferis; quibus ipsum hospitale copiosissime de propriis bonis regalibus dotatum commisit, ut ipsi debilibus et infirmis et omnibus miseris personis ibi receptis tam in temporalibus quam in spiritualibus fideliter ministrarent.

necessaria   ministra-   tertiam   in   honorem
rent.   sanctae Dei Genitricis
Mariae et sancti Fran-
cisci iuxta suum monas-
terium   pro   Fratribus
Minoribus, ei et eius so-
roribus divina celebra-
turis, fabricari iussit.

From these extracts one fact emerges which seems indisputable, that Nicholas Glassberger had access to the document B1. or to some closely similar version. It may be argued that Glassberger composed his own Chronicle at a later date than 1491, which is the date when, according to his own statement, he completed the " Hall " Codex of the " XXIV. Generals " ; that by that later date he had discovered the text B1. in Nürnberg (where he was confessor of the Clarisses), and that this is why the passages quoted from B1. by him in his own Chronicle are not found in the Chronicle of the " XXIV. Generals ". That argument is however upset by the fact that the quotation in the Hall Codex of the "XXIV. Generals " given above is clearly dependent upon the isolated passage at the end of B1., that is to say, Glassberger must have been acquainted with B1. in 1491 when he finished the Hall Codex.

The line of investigation with respect to Glassberger, his " maior Cronica " and his use of the Bamberg MS. containing the B1. Text was completed up to this point, when, arising from it, a fresh line of investigation opened up, which adds the strongest possible confirmation and carries what has already been said beyond the region of conjecture.

One of the Collection of Manuscripts known as the " J. P. Ceroni's Handschriften-Sammlung " which was acquired by the city of Brünn in Austria in the early part of the nineteenth century, and which was described in detail by Dr. Beda Dudik[1]

[1] J. P. Ceroni's *Handschriften-Sammlung*, Brünn, 1850. In this description of the MS. it has been necessary to rely entirely on Dr. Dudik's account of it, as the present war makes it impossible to examine the MS. itself or obtain

supplies the clue. Its number in the Ceroni collection is 292, and it is stated to be a quarto MS. of the fifteenth century containing 352 leaves. It is a chronicle of Bohemia, its title being given on folio 13 :—

"Incipit maior cronica boemorum moderna".

Fortunately the preliminary material gives the name of the author as follows :—

Ex Bohemorum Regum Spectabili ac Illustri prosapia oriundo sibique plurimum Serenissimo principi Domino Johanni Marchioni Mantuano frater Nicolaus natus de Bohemia, educatus in Moravia ordinis minorum de observancia minimus promptam ad sua beneplacita voluntatem. Dum, Serenissime princeps, causa deuocionis pridem Conventum nostrum in vrbe imperiali Nurenberg visitastis, interrogatus ego minimus a dominacione vestra de Kunsza, seu Kunsack quod consistit in provincia bohemie. Sed quia propter perfidiam hussitarum Situs Civitatum Bohemie et similiter Castrorum et opidorum nomina sunt immutata et etiam aliqua in Regno Bohemie loca et civitates desolate et presertim monasteria olim a Regibus fundata funditus etiam euersa : Ideo statui modernum situm Breviter in hanc cartam redigere.

Here, then, is a fifteenth-century chronicle of Bohemia describing itself as "*maior cronica*," written by a Friar of the Strict Observance named Nicholas, living in the Franciscan convent of Nürnberg in the fifteenth century. The question at once suggests itself: Is the friar Nicholas Glassberger and is the Chronicle the missing "*maior cronica*" to which he himself alludes in his extant work?

Dudik has carefully analysed the MS. and has come to the conclusion that it is a compilation of several older documents. The groundwork is the Bohemian chronicle of Pulkava, which exists in either three or four separate recensions, both Latin

accurate information about it. The author intends to investigate the MS. further when opportunity offers.

and Czech, which were composed at any rate before 1380 when Pulkava[1] died.

The author has also used other chronicles of lesser importance and several lives of the Saints, including in particular a Legend of Blessed Agnes and one of Saint Clare. Under the year 1236, embedded in the extracts from the Pulkavova Chronicle, comes the following passage relating to Blessed Agnes :—

Eodem anno Christo devota virgo, domina Agnes, soror Wenceslai regis, considerans quod in naufraga vita praesenti continue fluctibus nostre mortalitatis iactamur nec superna contemplari valemus propter tumultum mundanarum causarum, amore celestium ardencius inflammata in Penthecoste presentibus septem episcopis et domino rege, fratre suo, ac regina cum multis principibus et baronibus necnon innumera utriusque sexus diuersarum nacionum multitudine, spreto regni fastigio, et omni gloria mundana contempta, cum septem nobilissimis regni sui virginibus ut columba innocua de diluvio nequam seculi ad arrham sacre religionis sancte Clare in monasterium, in honore Salvatoris mundi et sancti Francisci, quod propriis sumptibus pro sororibus fieri procuravit, ipsa conuolavit et usque ad finem vite sancte constitucionis proposito perseueravit, prout in legenda eiusdem virginis clarius patet.

It will be seen that this passage is substantially identical with the passage quoted on pages 36, 37 from Nicholas Glassberger's Chronicle and the B1. text. Again under the year 1238 the "*maior cronica*" states :—

Anno Domini M°CCXXXVIII°. per sanctissimum patrem Gregorium papam IX. confirmatus est ordo fratrum

---

[1] Pulkava (Přibík) was from 1373-78 rector of the school of St. Giles at Prag. He was a friend of Charles IV., who gave him his autobiography to translate into Bohemian and ordered him to write a new Bohemian Chronicle. The Chronicle runs from Babel to A.D. 1330: it was originally intended to go to A.D. 1350. The most modern edition of the Pulkavova Chronicle is that of the late Prof. Josef Emler in *Fontes Rerum Bohemicarum*, vol. v. (Ac. Prag. Nadáni Palackeho).

Cruciferorum cum stella rubea a sancte Agnetis mandato de novo per fratres Minores creatus, videlicet Cruciferis et Stelliferis, quibus beata Agnes adhuc in secolo existens hospitale in pede pontis Pragensis in honore sancti Francisci edificavit et copiosissime de propriis bonis regalibus dotavit et ipsum hospitale admisit, ut ipsi debilibus et infirmis et omnibus miseris personis ibi receptis tam in temporalibus quam in spiritualibus fideliter necessaria ministrarent.

This passage may be compared with those quoted on pages 39-41 from Glassberger's Chronicle, from the Hall Codex of the Chronicle of the "XXIV. Generals," and from B1.

Again under the year 1281 the "*maior cronica*" refers thus to the death of Blessed Agnes :—

Anno Domini MCCLXXXI., vi°. nonas Marcii beata Agnes, filia quondam Otakari primi regis Boemie tercii, apud sanctum Franciscum in monasterio virginum in Domino feliciter obdormivit et angelicis fulta presidiis ad eterna gaudia letanter intravit, que fuit in religione XLVI. annos.

This passage is a very close copy of a passage contained in Folio 194v. of the B1. text.

It can, however, scarcely be doubted that in the Ceroni MS. we have to do with a hitherto unknown work of Nicholas Glassberger. For Glassberger was certainly from Moravia : he describes himself as "*Nicolaus de Moravia*".[1] He was a redoubtable opponent of the Hussites,[2] referred to in the passage quoted above. The reference to John, Marquis of Mantua, gives the right chronological setting ; for John Francis Gonzaga, fourth Marquis of Mantua (born 10th August, 1466, died 29th March, 1519), succeeded his father in 1484 : Glassberger makes a reference to his predecessor who was Marquis in 1415, when the Chapter was held at Mantua.[3]

---

[1] *Anal. Franc.*, II., p. ix.   [2] *Ibid.*, p. 467.

[3] "*Oretur pro bono statu magnifici viri domini Johannis Francisci domini Mantuani et pro felicitate . . . totius eius prolis*" (*Ibid.*, p. 272).

VII.

THE CHRONOLOGY OF BLESSED AGNES.[1]

The new manuscript sources for the Life of Blessed Agnes, which have already been described, contain fortunately some chronological details which make it possible to settle some disputed points concerning dates in her career.

As to the date of her birth, no question arises. There is unanimity in assigning January, 1205, as the date of her birth.

The two events, the dates of which are in dispute, are :—

(1) her entry into the Convent, which she herself founded at Prag ;

(2) the day of the week, the day of the month and the year of her death. For reasons which will appear later, it will be found convenient to treat the second point first.

The feast of Blessed Agnes is observed in Prag, as well as in some other places, and by the Franciscan Order on 2nd March. On the other hand her feast is observed elsewhere on 6th March, and the Bollandists have given her life in the *Acta Sanctorum*[2] under that same date. Further it is disputed whether she died in 1281 or 1282 or even 1283.

Let us first set out the statements of the authorities as at present known.

The Compendium of Georgius Bartholdus Pontanus[3] asserts that she died on 6th March.

The Bollandist Editors in their Introduction to her Life in *Acta Sanctorum*[4] state that she lived until 1282 and died on 6th March, being the twenty-fourth day of Lent and being a Friday.

The first Life published by the Bollandists states[5] :—

"*Anno Servatoris mundi millesimo ducentesimo octogesimo primo, sexta Martii die, cum sex et quadraginta annos in coenobio . . . decurrisset,*" Blessed Agnes died.

---

[1] A large portion of this section is reprinted from the author's article which appeared in the *Archivum Franciscanum Historicum*, fasc. II., 1914.

[2] Mart. I., 502-32 (ed. III., 501-30).   [3] L.c. 509.

[4] § II., n. 7, p. 503.   [5] C. III., n. 15 ; p. 512.

The second Life in *Acta Sanctorum*, which is a compilation made by Georgius Crugerus, S.J., gives the following information: § IX. "*In coenobio . . . ab anno MCCXXXV. usque ad annum MCCLXXXI. vitam religiosam per annos omnino XLVI. . . , traduxit Agnes.*"[1] § XIII. "*Annus MCCLXXXI. vertebatur, et recte magna parte ab acta hyeme ver primum se aperiebat.*"[2]—The same Life states that she fell ill: *dimidia porro jam Quadragesima et ultra*, to which a footnote is added by the Editors: *scilicet die 24 Quadragesimae, si dies obitus signetur;* and further[3] that she lay unburied: *a die VI. Martii in diem usque decimum.*

With respect to the year, Wadding gives it as 1283.[4] Nicholas Glassberger assigns her death to the year 1281.[5] There are, however, three lines of investigation independent from one another, which seem to establish the day of the month on which Blessed Agnes died as being 2nd March, not 6th March.

I. The fourteenth-century Bamberg MS., B1., gives a very clear and precise statement as to the date :—

It states[6] that Blessed Agnes fell seriously ill on the Sunday in the third week of Lent: *Die uero dominica tercie quadragesimalis ebdomadis adueniente, senciens instare suum felicem transitum.* It describes how she exhorted the sisters throughout the night (i.e. Sunday), how on the following day she was filled with great joy: *die altera secunda videlicet feria quadam cepit hylaritate perfundi*, and how on that same day (i.e. Monday) soon after Nones she died :

---

[1] L.c. n. 30 (p. 520).   [2] N. 58 (p. 527).   [3] N. 59.

[4] *Annales Min.* ad an. 1283, n. 2 (V², 122); he quotes Gg. Barthold. Pontanus, *Bohemia pia* [Francofurti, 1608], l. IV.

[5] "*Sexto nonas martii*" (= 2) : *Analecta Francisc.* II. (1887), 95. Arturus, a Monasterio, O.F.M., *Martyrologium Franciscanum*, II. edit., Paris, 1653 (I. edit., *ibid.* 1638), 100, 101, speaks of her *sub die 6 martii;* Fort. Hueber, O.F.M., *Menologium . . . Sanctorum . . . ex triplice Ordine . . . S. Francisci*, Munich, 1698, col. 650, fixes her death as occurring on 6th March, "*sed . . . eius encomium die 22 februarii reposuimus ob dicendorum copiam* "; cf. col. 586-8; Vigilius Greiderer, O.F.M., *Germania Franciscana*, I., Oeniponte, 1777, l. IV.: Provincia Bohemiae ; 698-703, follows the Bollandists'(701).

[6] Fol. 192r.

*Circa horam qua saluator humani generis . . . tradidit
spiritum, hec deo gratissima famula in manus patris celestis
animam suam commendans, anno gracie millesimo ducentessimo
octogesimo primo, sexto nonas marcii* [i.e. 2nd March] *in domino
feliciter obdormiuit.*   Our MS. further records how the body lay
two weeks unburied (*duabus septimanis stans inhumatum*); and
how she was buried by Bonagracia, "*quarta decima die a transitu eius in sequenti die, uidelicet in dominica de passione*".

It will be seen that this version contains an abundance of
precise and circumstantial evidence, which is absent from the
Bollandist versions.

The German Bamberg version (B2.), the Munich text
(M) and the Wolfenbüttel text (W) all give precisely the
same chronological details as those given in B1. : in other
words, they agree in stating Monday, 2nd March, as the day
of her death.   So also the Berlin text, while giving an account
in somewhat different language, agrees in all substantial
details.

Before passing on to the two other independent sources it
will be well to examine this evidence.   As regards the year it
soon becomes clear that the year must be 1282.   If the year
1282 is assumed, all works out consistently.   In 1282 Ash
Wednesday fell on 12th February; the Sunday in the third
week of Lent would be 1st March : if Blessed Agnes died on
the following day, it would be Monday, 2nd March : Passion
Sunday fell on 15th March, i.e. just fourteen days from the
day of her death.—If however the year 1281 is taken, not one
of these dates will fit in, as in that year Ash Wednesday fell
as late as 5th March.   The explanation as to the year is a
simple one.   The MSS. which give 1281 are calculating the
year according to the system by which the New Year begins
on 25th March.[1]   Those authorities which state 1282 are
using the system of reckoning in which the year begins on
1st January.

---

[1] In many parts of Europe in the XIII. century the ecclesiastical year
began on 25th March ; while the civil year began either at Christmas or on 1st
January.   It would appear that this was the case in Bohemia.

But how have the Bollandists and others got at the date Friday, 6th March? Probably thus: instead of *sexto nonas Marcii* they [1] have read *sexto Marcii*, omitting the word *nonas*. Having thus reached the wrong day of the month (the 6th), they have calculated the day of the week and have found that in 1282 6th March fell on a Friday. But this produces a mistake in the facts. The second Bollandist life states that Blessed Agnes lay unburied from 6th March to 10th March, i.e. four days only, which is inconsistent with the evidence that she lay unburied fourteen days.

To sum up the evidence so far: The Bamberg version with its related texts shows that Blessed Agnes died on Monday, 2nd March, 1282.

II. The next line of evidence in order of date is derived from the Breviary of the Ordo Cruciferorum of Prag referred to on page 21.

This Breviary has, fortunately, been exactly dated by the scribe, himself a former Grossmeister, as having been completed in 1356. A rubricated statement on the first folio refers to Blessed Agnes and says of her death: "*anno incarnationis eiusdem MCCLXXXI°. VI°. nonas [= 2] martii celum petivit regnatura cum Christo*". And in the Kalendar of the Breviary under the date 2nd March we find: "*Obiit beata agnes fundatrix ordinis fratrum cruciferorum cum stella*". The Grossmeister of the Order states that his Order has always observed the feast of their foundress on 2nd March.

III. The third line of evidence is as follows: Reference has already been made to the Bohemian chronicle known generally as the *Pulkavova chronicle*, having been written by Pulkava. The exact date of its composition is uncertain and several recensions of it exist, but at any rate Pulkava died in 1380, so that the chronicle is not later than the last quarter of the fourteenth century.

References to events in the life of Blessed Agnes occur in

---

[1] The fault does not necessarily lie with the learned Bollandists themselves, but rather with the sources of which they made use: but in any case they have assumed responsibility for the mistake.

some recensions and are omitted in others. One of the best MSS. however is that numbered *I. C. 24* in the University Library of Prag. On Folio 85, in a list of members of the Bohemian Royal House, occurs the following: "*Anno domini M°CCLXXI. VI°. nonas Marcii obiit illustris virgo agnes filia prziemysl . . . Item . . . cenobium [construxit] . . . in quo sub regulari habitu annis XLVI. degens, obdormivit feliciter in domino*".

As regards the date of the death of Blessed Agnes, we thus find three independent sources combining to establish 2nd March, 1281/82, and all of them sources which come within one hundred years of her death, while one (*Bamb. E. VII.* 19) is all but contemporary.

From considering the date of the death of Blessed Agnes, we pass to the consideration of the date of her entry into the convent at Prag. Here again the exact date and the year are both in dispute.

The second Bollandist life in the *Acta Sanctorum* gives the date as 25th March, being the feast of the Annunciation of Our Lady.[1] As to the year the second life is not self-consistent: for it states, § II., 5[2]: *Eius vocalem e coelo explicationem eventus ipse postmodum sub annum Domini MCCXXXIV firmavit, cum Agnes . . . purpuram . . . abiecit;* whereas in § VIII., 27[3] the year is given as MCCXXXV.

The *Letopisy Ceske* (A.D. 1196-1278) contained in *Fontes Rerum Bohemicarum,*[4] states under the year 1233: *Agnes . . . assumpsit habitum pauperum dominarum.* The *Kronika Neplachova* in the same,[5] gives precisely the same statement. The *Kronika Marignola* in the same,[6] refers to the canonisation of S. Elizabeth in 1232 and adds: *anno sequenti* [i.e. 1233] *sancta Agnes . . . intravit claustrum.*

But the Pulkavova Chronicle, to which reference has

---

[1] § VIII., n. 27 (p. 519).   [2] P. 514.   [3] P. 519.
[4] Prag, 1874, vol. II., p. 284.   [5] Vol. III., p. 472.
[6] The author is Friar Ioh. de Marignollis, O.F.M. of Florence; *ibid.,* III., 603.

already been made, speaking of the year 1236 says: *Eodem anno . . . domina Agnes Penthecoste in monasterium . . . convolavit.*

The same year, viz. 1236, is given by Albertus Stadensis, in his Chronicle[1] and also by Nicholas Glassberger:[2] *Eodem anno in die Pentecostes . . . domina Agnes . . . se reddit Ordini pauperum Dominarum.* Unfortunately neither the Latin text in Bamberg *E. VII. 19* nor any of the German translations give the year of her entry, while all agree in saying that it took place at Pentecost.

On the other hand it is very difficult to understand how the year can be 1236, as a Bull of Gregory IX., dated 30th August, 1234, addressed to Blessed Agnes " *Sincerum animi tui fervorem*,"[3] takes the monastery and hospital at Prag into the protection of the Holy See; and another of the following day, 31st August, 1234, " *Sincerum animi carissimae*,"[4] addressed to Brother John, Minister of Saxony, and Brother Thomas, Custos in Bohemia, bids them appoint Blessed Agnes to the office of Abbess of the Poor Ladies of Prag.

These dates seem to be conclusive as a *terminus ad quem*, and while it must be admitted that the evidence is somewhat contradictory, the most probable date would be Pentecost, 1234.

There is one line of evidence which must not be altogether overlooked, but upon which too much reliance must not be placed. Practically all the authorities agree in stating that Blessed Agnes lived forty-six years in religion, whatever other dates they give. This would point to a clear tradition arising probably at the time of her death, that she had then completed forty-six years in religion. But if the date of her death is taken as a fixed point, viz. March, 1281/82, then by deducting forty-six years, we reach not 1234, but 1235. This calculation

---

[1] Quoted in *AA. SS.*, Mart. I., 502, § I., n. 4 (ed. III., 501).

[2] *An. Fr.*, II., 56 f.

[3] Sbaralea, *Bullar. Franc.*, I., 134; Potthast, *Reg.*, n. 9519.

[4] Sbaralea, I., 134; Potthast, n. 9523.

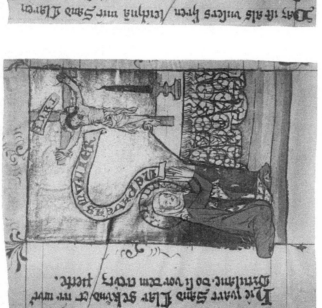

HORTULANA, MOTHER OF SAINT CLARE PRAYING BEFORE
THE CRUCIFIX.

(From MS. M.281 Royal Library, Dresden.)

HOW THE BODY OF OUR LORD APPEARED TO SAINT CLARE
FROM OUT OF THE CHALICE.

(From MS. M.281 Royal Library, Dresden.)

however can scarcely hold its ground against the more direct evidence already quoted.

The final result of this inquiry is then the establishment of the following dates :—

> Pentecost, 1234 (11th June), Blessed Agnes enters the Convent of the Poor Clares at Prag.
>
> 31st August, 1234, Blessed Agnes is nominated as Abbess by Pope Gregory IX.
>
> 2nd March, 1281/82, Blessed Agnes dies.
>
> 15th March, 1281/82, Blessed Agnes is buried.

VIII.

THE LETTERS FROM SAINT CLARE TO BLESSED AGNES.

The four Letters from Saint Clare to Blessed Agnes have long been known to students of Franciscan literature.[1] Hitherto only the first Letter has been known in a MS. version. The first Letter is contained in Nicholas Glassberger's copy of the "Chronicles of the XXIV. Generals," the Hall Codex finished by him in 1491. Father Paschal Robinson, O.F.M., discussing the writings of Saint Clare in an article in the *Archivum Franciscanum Historicum*[2] so recently as 1910, writes thus of these letters :—

> "We are without any clue to the origin of the copies of these Letters that have come down to us. It would not be surprising, however, in view of what we know of the Clares' praiseworthy custom of transcribing all their documents, if some industrious disciple of the Blessed Agnes had copied them before the Poor Ladies had left Prague and thus preserved them to posterity. The elder Locatelli in his biography of Saint Clare speaks of Saint

---

[1] According to Sbaralea (Suppl. ad Script. O.M., 1806) the letters of Saint Clare were first published at Alcalá in 1508 under the auspices of Cardinal Ximenes, but Paschal Robinson shows that Sbaralea is mistaken and that the letters were first published by the Bollandists in the *Acta Sanctorum* in 1668 ; it is in this form that they have generally been known.

[2] *Ibid.*, iii., 434-40.

Clare's letters to Blessed Agnes as existing in some MSS.
at Prague—a reference which is just vague enough to be
practically worthless.   In vain I have tried to trace up
any such MSS.   However at least one of these Letters
is found in a late fifteenth-century codex at Ala [1] in the
Tyrol."

Although no MSS. of the Letters have yet come to light
in Prag itself, yet Father Paschal Robinson's suggestion is
strongly supported by the discovery of the five MS. versions
(B1., Ber., W., B3., and D.), the relation of which to one
another and to the versions of the Legend has already been
discussed.   It is regrettable that no one of these MSS. gives
us the text in Latin and that consequently the earliest known
version of the text, viz. that contained in the fourteenth
century MS., B1., is itself a translation.

There appears little reason to doubt the authenticity of the
Letters.   They have been accepted as the genuine work of
Saint Clare by the Bollandists and by Franciscan critics
generally, although Père Van Ortroy now denies their authenticity altogether.   They constitute the larger part of the
writings of Saint Clare which are accepted as genuine.   The
fact that the Letters are contained in B1. carries their pedigree
back nearly 300 years beyond the earliest date to which (with
the exception of the first one in the Hall Codex) they have
hitherto been traced, viz. from 1668 to 1380.

It is not easy to determine with any degree of certainty
the date or occasion of their composition.   There are however
some features in the MS. versions which differ from the
printed versions and which aid in fixing the date.

The first Letter may be assigned to the period preceding
the entry of Blessed Agnes into the Convent at Prag.   The
most likely date for that event is, as already shown, Pentecost,
1234.   In the opening address this Letter differs from the
three others in not referring to Blessed Agnes as a sister of
the Order.   Moreover it is noticeable that in all the MS.
versions she is addressed in the first Letter in the plural

[1] Correct " Ala " into " Hall," near Innsbruck.

(ewres *aller heiligsten wandels: als* ewerr *vnd seiner wirdikait gezvmen*); while in the three other Letters she is addressed in the singular (*daz er* dich *als vil gezieret hat . . . vnd* dich *erlevhtet*). This is quite consistent with the theory that the first Letter was written to her, when she was still in the world at her brother's court: while the others were written to her after she had taken the veil.

The date of the second Letter may also be fixed provisionally from internal evidence. The fact that it refers to her as being now in religion gives a *terminus a quo,* viz. Pentecost, 1234. Saint Clare in this letter advises Agnes to "follow the counsel of our honoured father, Brother Elias the General".[1] It is known that Elias of Cortona was deposed from the Generalate at the Chapter held at Pentecost, 1239: and so this date forms a *terminus ad quem* for the composition of the letter. The frequent references in this letter to her renunciation of the glory of the world and especially her refusal of the Emperor suggest that the letter was written not long after Agnes' entry into the Convent, i.e. nearer 1234 than 1239.

The date of the third Letter cannot be satisfactorily determined. The passage on p. 160, in which Saint Clare gives some guidance to Blessed Agnes in the matter of fasting, has been interpreted by some in such a way as to indicate a date. Père Lemmens regards the passage as relating to the Rule generally known as the Hugoline Constitutions. But as Père Livarius Oliger, quoting also Wauer, points out, the words of this passage do not agree with the text of the Hugoline Constitutions and those Constitutions required even severer fasting. Moreover the Hugoline Constitutions were probably

---

[1] Some critics, as Father Robinson points out, have found in the expression here applied to Elias in the Latin text, viz., "*ministri generalis totius ordinis,*" an indication of a late source for the Letters. If the words "*totius ordinis*" are an authentic part of the original version, it would be dangerous to found an attack upon the authenticity of the Letters on this. But it is deserving of notice that in B1. and in all the four other MSS. there is nothing whatever to correspond to the words "*totius ordinis*". It seems unwise to use the words as a weapon either of assault or defence.

never observed in San Damiano, while Saint Clare was Abbess. Père Oliger holds that these directions as to fasting refer rather to the original *formula vitae* granted to Saint Clare by Saint Francis.   If it be so, then it appears likely that the Letter was at any rate written before May, 1238, for in that month Gregory IX. in his Bull, "*Angelis gaudium*," refused to grant permission to Blessed Agnes to follow the practices of San Damiano and required her to conform to the Hugoline Constitutions.   On the other hand, the letter is almost certainly nearer to 1234, the beginning of Agnes' life in the Convent; for it is scarcely likely that she would have allowed four years to elapse before obtaining the advice of the foundress of the order in the matter of fasting.

In the case of the fourth Letter, the MS. versions agree in containing one definite indication of date, which is absent from the Latin text of the Bollandists.   The tone of the last sentences of the letter has caused some critics to believe that the letter was one of the last written by Saint Clare before her death.   " Fare thee well, dearest daughter," she writes, " with thy daughters unto the throne of glory of Almighty God." But this possibility is strengthened by the previous sentence :—

" *Die selben, mein töhter vnd ze aller vorderst die aller weisest jvnkfrawe Agnes, mein swester, enpfelhent sich dir vnd deinen tohtern.*"

"The same, my daughters and chiefest of all the most prudent virgin Agnes my sister, commend themselves to thee and to thy sisters."

In this sentence the "Agnes" mentioned is nominative and is mentioned as one of the persons who sends greetings to Blessed Agnes.   In the Bollandist version the "Agnes" is vocative and is one of the persons greeted by Saint Clare.

" *Filiabus tuis me et filias meas, dignissima . . . nostra Soror Agnes, diligenter commenda in Domino. Vale, o dilectissima cum filiabus tuis usque ad thronum gloriae magni Dei, etc.*"

The explanation is, that in the MS. versions the Agnes in question is not Agnes of Bohemia, but Agnes, the sister of Saint Clare. This Agnes was Abbess at Monticelli for about thirty years. When Saint Clare was dying she was summoned back to San Damiano : she was with her when she died and she herself died three months after Saint Clare. This reference to her as being with Saint Clare proves that the letter was written within a very short period before Saint Clare's death, viz. 11th August, 1253.[1]

IX.

THE BENEDICTION OF SAINT CLARE.

Following immediately after the fourth Letter in all the MS. versions comes the document which is known as the Benediction of Saint Clare, being like the Letters in German. Our knowledge of the Benediction of Saint Clare has hitherto been based on printed sources only. In the *Seraphicae Legislationis Textus Originales*[2] the editors print a version of the Benediction which, as they state, is reproduced from the earliest version then known, viz. the one contained in the "Chronicles of Mark of Lisbon," published in an Italian version at Venice in 1582.[3] Following Mark of Lisbon's text, they give also a French translation of the Benediction, which shows certain variants as compared with the version of Mark. The Quaracchi editors do not specifically state that no earlier or MS. version of the Benediction is known, but this may perhaps be implied from the fact that Mark of Lisbon's text is the one used. The MS. versions contain the variants which are peculiar to the French text.

Mark of Lisbon's text corresponds with that of B1., as printed on pages 164, 165, down to line 8, where it ends : *a piu di quel ch'io posso. Amen* (B1. *mer den ich mag*). The French text contains the additional lines, but without anything to correspond with the following in B1. :—

---

[1] It is of course quite possible that S. Clare may have sent her sister Agnes's greetings to Agnes of Bohemia, without her sister being present with her : but the explanation given above seems on the whole the most likely.

[2] *Quaracchi*, 1897, p. 281.   [3] T. 1, l. 8, c. 34, p. 240.

1. *vnd nach meinem tode.*

2. *vnd mit den'ain gaistlich vater und muter ir gaist-*
   leich sun vnd töhter gesegent hat.

On the other hand the Capuchin translation of 1659 contains, as the Quaracchi editors point out, certain additions to the French text and these additions are precisely the same in contents as those just mentioned as being found in B1. It has been suggested that these modifications are due to the Reform of the Order associated with Saint Colet. But Saint Colet was not born until 1381, and did not enter religion until 1406, and B1. was written at the latest before 1393 and probably earlier. Accordingly this theory of Coletan influence falls to the ground, and it may be assumed that in the text of B1. we have the most primitive version at present known of the Benediction and that Mark of Lisbon's text represents a later and less accurate form. Thus the Bamberg MS. also carries the pedigree of the Benediction of Saint Clare back about two centuries, viz. from 1582 to 1380.

Some light is thrown on the whole question by Father David de Kok's recent article, "De Origine Ordinis Saint Claræ in Flandria".[1] He gives another Latin version of the Benediction, viz. that contained in the MS. of P. Sebastian Bouvier, but it may be doubted whether P. Bouvier had access to sources as early as B1. It will be noticed that P. Bouvier's version contains words corresponding to "vnd nach meinem tode" but' nothing to correspond to "vnd mit den . . . gesegenne wirt". From P. Bouvier's MS. it appears that the Benediction was sent by Saint Clare shortly before her death to Ermentrude, the foundress of the Clarisses in Flanders. He writes:—

> "*Paulo ante suam mortem B. Clara benedictionem hanc*
> *Ermentrudi misit.*"

Whether the Benediction, as found in B1. and the other German versions, was originally an appendix to the fourth Letter to Blessed Agnes or whether it was sent to her at

---

[1] *Archiv. Franc. Hist.*, vii., fasc. II., 243-46.

some later date is an obscure point : but the comparison with the Bouvier text would suggest that the Benediction was a kind of " Circular " document sent by Saint Clare to several houses, and among others to those presided over by Blessed Agnes and by Ermentrude. This agrees with the statement of Thomas of Celano in the Legend of Saint Clare that she shortly before her death sent "*omnibus Dominabus Monasteriorum pauperum, tam presentibus quam futuris, largam benedictionis gratiam*".

There are several persons and bodies to whom thanks are due for help given in this study of the Legend of Blessed Agnes. The authorities of the Royal Libraries of Bamberg and of Dresden, of the Ducal Library of Wolfenbüttel, of the Court Library of Munich, and of the University Library of Prag have sent over precious MSS. from their collections for use in London and have allowed the author to keep them for unusually long periods.[1] Professor Robert Priebsch has given continual help and encouragement and has frequently suggested fresh lines of investigation. Mr. A. G. Little has given valuable advice on the Franciscan aspects of the study. Professor W. E. Collinson and Mr. H. N. Fryer have helped to elucidate some problems in the German text and Mr. L. Solomon some in the Latin text. Father Michael Bihl, O. F. M., of Quaracchi has made some most useful suggestions. The author received much help and courtesy during his investigations in Prag from Dr. Vácslav Rezníček of the Museum of the State of Bohemia, from General und Grossmeister Franz Marat, and from Canon Dr. Podlaha of the Cathedral Library. To all of these he tenders his most sincere and grateful thanks.

[1] Two of the MSS. are still (June, 1915) in the author's safe-keeping for obvious reasons !

TEXTS.

[In editing the Latin and German texts the following principles have been followed :—

Contractions universally recognised are not indicated in the text.

Italics are reserved in order to indicate that the editor is departing from the MS. Where a letter is changed, that letter is put in italics and the MS. reading given in a footnote: where a word or letter is supplied it is placed in italics between square brackets.

In order to render the texts more easily legible, the capitalisation of the MSS. has not been followed : all proper names are spelt with capitals, whether the MS. does so or not: and capitals not required for proper names or for the beginning of sentences are not kept.

In the German text, the "mutation" is represented in various ways, sometimes by an "e" over the vowel, sometimes by one sign and sometimes by a slightly different one. It is represented in the printed text uniformly by ¨ over the vowel. In some cases the MS. gives ¨ over "w" or over "y," but in these cases it has not been preserved.]

INCIPIT PROLOGUS IN UITAM INCLITE UIRGINIS SORORIS [Fol. 158 v.]
AGNETIS, ORDINIS SANCTE CLARE DE PRAGA BOHEMIE.

CREBRIS[1] sacrarum uirginum sororum ordinis sancte Clare de
Praga precibus sum pulsatus | ut illustrissime uirginis, sororis [Fol. 159 r.]
Agnetis, filie incliti domini regis Bohemie conscriberem uitam
& actus, ne ipsius eximia sanctitas dampnoso reticeretur silencio ; cuius eterna memoria merito cum laudibus debet esse, 5
pro eo quod ipsam inscrutabilis dei sapiencia uelud lucernam
in candelabro militantis ecclesie posuit, et igne sue gracie
clementer accendit, quo feruide arsit in se per uite meritum,
aliisque clare luxit salutiferum per exemplum. Cui quidem
peticioni racionabili atque pie bonam habui uoluntatem par- 10
endi ob spem retribucionis sempiterne. Sed consideracione
sollerti ad hoc insufficientem me senciens & indignum, cala-
mum asscribendi continui, pauens im|perito sermone fuscare [Fol. 159 v.]
quod claris & magnis laudum preconiis fuerat depromendum.
Tandem reuerendi patris mei ministri super hoc obedienciali 15
precepto constrictus, negocium supra uires meas assumpsi,
malens sub sarcina tanti laboris humiliter parendo deficere
quam uoluntati precipientis pertinaciter contra ire, cum in-
obediencia quasi peccatum ariolandi[2] uel scelus ydolatrie
censeatur. Sed quia non sumus sufficientes cogitare aliquid 20
ex nobis, sed sufficiencia nostra ex deo est, qui miseria sua
grata operatur in nobis & uelle & perficere pro bona uoluntate, ideo adiutorii mei totam fiduciam ponens in ipso,

---

[1] M. and W.: "Der strengen heilligen Iunkfrawen vnd swester *agnesen dez
kungs tohter von pehem* des ordens . . . pin ich mit pet genotet". The words
in italics are redundant. B2. is correct : "Der strengen heiligen iunkfrauen vnd
swester des ordens der heiligen iunkfrauen sand Claren von Prag".

[2] M., W. and B2. : "Wann ein vngehorsamer mensch wirt geschetzet pey der
sund wider die kristenheit vnd got ".

[Fol. 160 r.] de hac eximia uirgine alia scribere non intendo quam | ea
que habere potui ab hiis personis, que uirtutum eius mag-
nalia conuersando cum ipsa suis oculis conspexerunt, quarum
assercioni ob uite ipsarum meritum non facile quis potest re-
5 fragari ; et mira que per ipsius merita tam in uita quam post
felicem eius transitum dominus dignanter effecit, aliqua quidem
uisa, alia uero ab hiis quibus acciderant narrata & sub fideli
asseueracione recepta ad meam noticiam peruenerunt.   In processu uero huius hystorie non semper secundum ordinem tem-
10 poris res gestas descripsi propter confusionem uitandam, sed
quecumque alicui materie competebant siue eodem siue diuersis
patrata forent temporibus, pro simplicitatis mee modulo sic
[Fol. 160 v.] compendiositer et conuenienciter | potui coaptaui, ut breuitate
gaudentes materiam fastidiendi non habeant.   Et ut affectus
15 fidelium ad imitacionem huius praeclare uirginis ardencius
inflammetur, totius uite ipsius decursus tredecim continetur
capitulis infra scriptis.   In primo enim de ortu ipsius & conuersacione in etate primeua.   In secundo de sanctitate uite
quam habuit post mortem parentum apud germanum[1] suum
20 degendo.   In tercio qualiter ordinem sanctissime uirginis Clare
intrauit.   In quarto de magna eius humilitate & obediencia.
In quinto de sancta & uera paupertate ipsius.   In sexto de
graui maceracione carnis.   In septimo de studio oracionis &
mira deuocione ipsius circa sacramentum altaris.   In octauo
[Fol. 161 r.] de feruentissimo amore | crucis Cristi.   Nono de multa caritate
26 ipsius erga sorores & afflictos.   Decimo de reuelacionibus di-
uiniter sibi factis.   Vndecimo de transitu eius et de hiis que
in eo facta sunt.   Duodecimo de sacri corporis eius sepultura.
Postremo de miraculis uirtute diuina patratis.

[1] M. and W. : " pey irm oheym ".   B2. omits.

Von sant Agnes der kunigin von Behem die in sant Claren orden kam, ir leben.

Hie vahet an daz leben vnd lesen der kunigen Angnes von
Behem, die in sant Claren orden lebet sechs vnd viertzig jar
in volkumner seligkeit vnd übung aller tugend; vnd ist als ir
leben hie geschriben vnd begriñen in trizehen sch[t]ucken
oder capitel mit gar kurtzen worten durch daz, das die es 5
lesen oder hörent lesen vrsach werd genumen alles vrtrutz,
vnd doch alle andechtige hertzen erman an zeheben zu loben
den ewigen got vnd sein wunder zu erkenen, der so gar wunderlich gewirckt hat mit einer so gar hochen fürsten. Das
erst[1] capitel ist von ir kintheit, wie sie gelept hat. Daz ander, 10
wie[2] heiligklich sy da lept nach irs vater vnd muter tod, do
sy by irem bruder was, der kunig nach irem vater was. Das
tryt, wie sie in sant Claren orden kam. Daz vierd, | von ir [Fol. 178 r.]
grossen demuttigkeit vnd von ir gehorsam. Das funfft, von
ir waren vnd willigen armût. Das sechst, von der strenge 15
vnd grosse kestigung, die sy ir selbs an det. Das subent, von
irem gebet vnd von ir andacht, vnd von der andacht die
sy zu vnsers herren fronlichnam het. Das acht, von der
inbrinstigen inhitzigen mynn,[3] die sy zu den schwestren het
vnd zu allen denen, die in beschwerd vnd arbeit warent lybs 20
oder hertzen. Daz zehent, von der offnung heimlicher ding
die ir von got geoffenbart ward. Das eilft, von irem end[4] vnd
wie sy begraben ward. Daz zwelft, von den zeichen die nach
irem tod geschachen.

---

[1] See note I., p. 169.   [2] MS. " sy " crossed out.

[3] The text is here obviously defective. It can be conjecturally amended by
comparison with B2., M., and W. by adding here [*die sy zu den martter vnsers
herren Jhesu Cristi het. Das neunt von der lieb vnd mynn.*] It is probably the
recurrence of the word " mynn " which has caused the error and been the source
of the confusion.

[4] The text may here again be conjecturally amended by inserting [*Das zwelft*]
after or instead of vnd, and altering zwelft in next clause to [*trizehent*].

INCIPIT UITA ILLUSTRISSIME UIRGINIS SORORIS AGNETIS
ORDINIS SANCTE CLARE DE PRAGA: & PRIMO DE
ORTU IPSIUS ET CONUERSACIONE IN ETATE PRIMEUA.

Candor lucis eterne et speculum sine macula dei maiestatis,
et ymago bonitatis patris eterni, dominus Jhesus Cristus, cuius
miseraciones super omnia opera eius, mundi termino iam
[Fol. 161 v.] uergente, miserie sue liberis recordatus, de excelso habi|-
5 taculo suo dignatiue prospexit super filios hominum sedentes
in tenebris & umbra mortis. Et ut in seculis superuenient-
bus habundantes diuicias gracie ac bonitatis sue ostenderet, de
massa humani generis, quasi de tenebris lucem fecit splendes-
cere mirande sanctitatis, cum Agne[te]m felicissimam hora ista
10 nouissima tamquam luciferum in tempore suo produxit, et
uelud uesperum super filios terre consurgere fecit: ut eius
conuersacione preclara splendore ueri syderis populus gencium
qui ambulabat in tenebris, pedes affeccionum suarum dirigeret
in uiam pacis.

15 Ex inclita namque prosapia, ut pote regie stirpis progenita,
[Fol. 162 r.] quia pater eius Premisserius dictus Otakarus, illus|tris rex
Bohemie; mater uero Constancia, soror domini Andree, regis
Vngarie, patris sancte Elyzabet: et tota progenies utroque
parente regalis, originem nobilem morum elegancia mirifice
20 uenustauit. Cuius mater, cum adhuc eam gestaret in utero,
uidit sompnium euidens presagium fiendorum. Videbatur enim
sibi quod intraret cameram in qua uestes sue regie preciose &
multe seruabantur. Quas conspiciens uidit inter eas tunicam
& pallium coloris grisei, ac cordam qua sorores ordinis sancte
25 Clare cinguntur. Cumque ualde miraretur quisnam uestem
tam rudem & simplicem inter uestimenta eius preciosa po-
suisset, audiuit uocem dicentem sibi "Noli mirari, quia proles
[Fol. 162 v.] quam | portas tali ueste utetur, et erit lumen tocius Bohemie!"
Futurorum quoque prescius deus, qui prius uult ostendere
30 uentura quam fiant, ortam in mundum Agnetem paruulam
miro quodam instinctu pretendere fecit signis corporeis future
ymaginem sanctitatis. Nam iacens in cunis sepe a nutrice sua
inueniebatur, habens manus & pedes in modum crucis can-

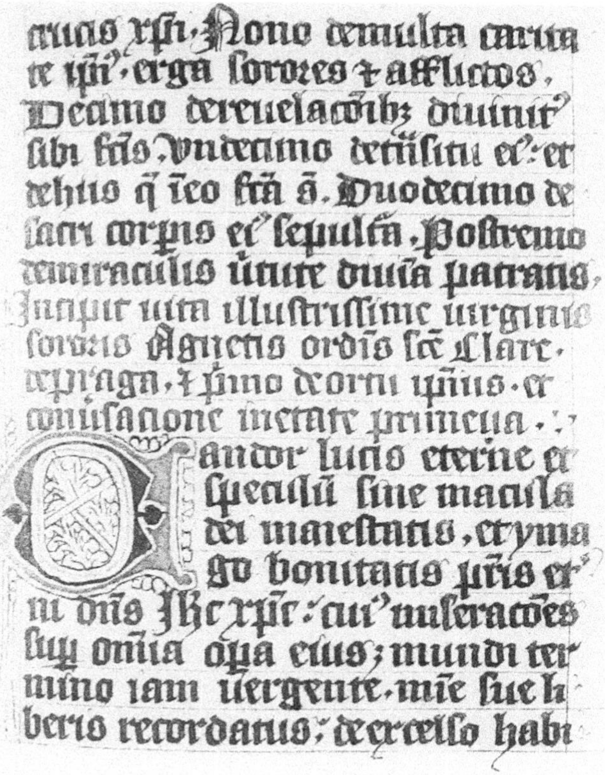

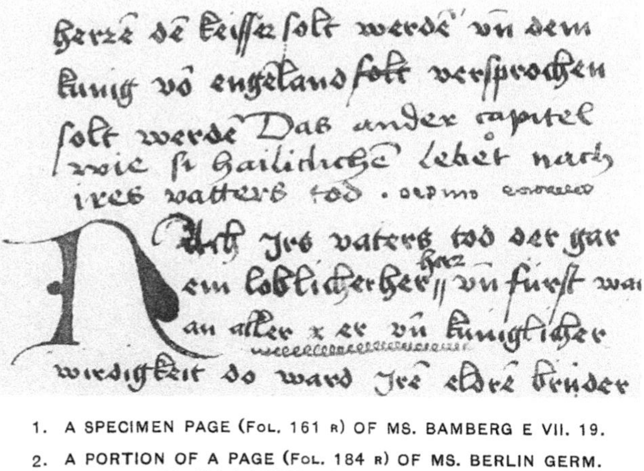

1. A SPECIMEN PAGE (FOL. 161 R) OF MS. BAMBERG E VII. 19.

2. A PORTION OF A PAGE (FOL. 184 R) OF MS. BERLIN GERM. OCT. 484 SHOWING THE THREE HANDS.

DAS ERST CAPITEL VON IRER KINTHAIT.

Unser herr Jhesus Cristus, der da ist ein schin vnd ein glantz des ewigen liechts vnd ein spigel aun masen vnd ein bild der güt[1] des ewigen vatters, des güt[2] vnd erbermd übertrifft alle seine werck, der | wöll von seiner gotlicher güt[3] [Fol. 178 v.] vnd erbermd der cristenheit zu hilf kumen mit seiner hilf vnd 5 stür, die ietzunt zu vall vnd zu verbend ser was geneigt, vnd den die do sassent in der feinsternus vnd dem schatten des tods, den wolt er ein nuw liecht geben wunderlicher heiligkeit vnd lobliches bild an der aller heiligsten vnd loblichsten künigin Angnessen, die also ein edel lucern vnd also ein 10 liechter morgenstern vnd also ein clarer abentstern an dem jungsten zit der welt hat volbracht vnd[4] gegeben, mit dem sy bereittet den weg des liechtes vnd des fryds, mit dem sy machent[5] wider keren zu got vnd zu dem ewigen leben.

Sy was von gar edlem vnd künglichem geschlecht bürtig. 15 Ir vater was genant Ottokarus,[6] vnd was künging zu Behem gar gewaltig vnd rich, mainhafftig vnd bekant ver vnd nach über al. Ir mutter hiesz Constancia vnd was des küngs Andreas[7] von Vnger, | der sant Elszbehten vater was, des [Fol. 179 r.] selben schwester was ir mutter, vnd waz von vater vnd muter 20 jetweter syten von künglichen stamen eren vnd wirdigkeit geborn. Do sy ir muter trug, do sach sy in irem schlaff ein gesicht [das][8] gar mercklich was vnd ein sagung kinftiger ding ; sy sach das ir kamer vol edler[9] vnd gar kostperen kleider was ; vnder den künglichen vnd kospperen kleidern da sach sy 25 ein gewant, daz was graw von grawer farb tůch gemachet, vnd by dem grawen gewant was ein seil, also die schwestren von sant Claren orden tragen. Da wundret sy ser wem dis ruch

---

[1] MS. " gyt " crossed out.   [2] *Ibid.*
[3] MS. " gvt " crossed out.
[4] Some object is required here to make sense, e.g. " ein beispiel ".
[5] MS. " machent " ; either a slip for singular " machet " or an unusual dialectic form.
[6] MS. " Karolus " crossed out and " Ottokarus " substituted.
[7] " Andreas " added in MS. in different hand.
[8] MS. " die ".
[9] MS. adds " cleider " deleted.

cellatos, ad designandum quod is qui pro nobis crucis amara
sustinuit intra mentis ipsius ubera, tamquam mirre fasciculus
erat continue moraturus & quod uirginitatem florigeram eidem
perpetue seruare deberet.

5 Cum autem ad tercium etatis annum peruenisset, paren-
[Fol. 163 r.] tibus suis eam generose ut | decuit maritare uolentibus, despon-
sata est cuidam duci Polo*n*ie,[1] illucque cum nutrice sua &
honesto comitatu deducta in monasterio quod *T*reb*n*ier[2]
dicitur honorifice recepta est, vbi primum ex ore filie sancte
10 Hegwidis[3] morum & fidei rudimenta docili corde suscepit, ibi
denique manens, quamuis infantula nichil puerile gessit in
opere: quin pocius dominabus monasterii ad persoluendas
horas canonicas chorum intrantibus, ipsa coram ymaginibus
Cristi & uirginis gloriose oracionem dominicam & salutacio-
15 nem angelicam flexis genibus frequencius iterando Cristo &
uirgini matri eius offerebat deuote, socias suas ad simile crebris
sermonibus exhortabat.

[Fol. 163 v.] Factum est autem, | diuina prouidencia pro ea aliquid
melius disponente, ut mortuo sponso suo duce predicto iam
20 sexennis patri redderetur; et ab eodem in claustro Doxan[4] in
regno Bohemie pro ampliori morum informacione et capes-
cenda litterarum noticia monialibus ibidem domino famulanti-
bus studiosius commendaretur. Et cum per annum integrum
proficiens eisdem commansisset, doctor internus spiritus sanctus
25 qui mora non indiget ad docendum, tanta cor eius unccione
miserie sue perunxit & docuit,[5] ut quod aliis leccio cottidiana
tribuere solet, illi spiritus sanctus suggerebat. Etatem itaque
moribus transiens, aliarum puellarum insolencias uitabat &
[Fol. 164 r.] ludos: solus eam sancte oracionis locus, scilicet | ecclesia
30 delectabat.

Octauo igitur etatis sue anno nobilis Cristi discipula de
monasterio ad paternos lares reducitur; ibique propter morum
ipsius grauitatem quam in omnibus actibus perferebat, non

---

[1] MS. "Polomie".   [2] MS. "creb = mer".
[3] See note II., p. 169.   [4] *Ibid.*, III., p. 170.
[5] M., W. and B2.: "daz sy den andern frawen all tag ein leczen las Das der
heillig geist als durch sein gut in. yr wurkt".

vnd vngeschaffen gewant angehört; do sprach ein stim zu ir:
" fraw, dich sol[1] dis gewandes nit enwundren, wenn des kind
daz du treyst by dir in deinem lyb, daz sol das gewant tragen
vnd sol | ein liecht vnd ein geziert werden alles des lands von [Fol. 179 v.]
Behem.   Vnser her Jhesus Cristus, dem alle kinfftige ding 5
gegenwirtig sint, wirt an dissem kind zeigen sein kunfftige
heiligkeit vnd sein übung." Da es geboren ward vnd in der
wiegen lag, wenn denn sein ammen über es kam, so fand sy
es allzit lygen, daz es sein hendlin crutz wisz über sein
hertzlin geleit het, zu einem zeichen daz ir die marter vnd 10
der tod vnsers herren stethlichen in irem hertzen wonnet, als
ein miren bischelin, daz es auch an ir darnach erfült ward;
vnd da sy ir reinikeit vnd magtum vnsrem herren ophern
vnd sy sich im gemechlen [ward] mit stetter truw vnd gantzer
mynn.   15
   Da sy tryer jar alt ward, do ward sy gemechelt dem hert-
zigen von Polonie vnd wart im auch gesant mit [irer][2] ammen,
die des | kindes pflag; vnd sant mit ir gar grosse vnd herliche [Fol. 180 r.]
geselschafft vnd ward einer closter frawen bevolhen die heisz
Hedewig,[3] die lert daz lieb kind den gelaben vnd waz dar zu 20
gehört.   Vnd wie sy dann doch gar ein kleines[4] vnd junges
kind was, so tet sy nit kindlicher werck weder mit spil noch
mit andren dingen, als die andren kind, sunder aller ir flisz lag
an gebet; vnd so die andren frawen zu kor gengen, so geng
es all zit mit in zu kor, vnd bettet denn, vnd veinet gar vil vor 25
vnser lieben frawen bilt vnd vor vnsers herren marter bilt, vnd
lasz die wil Aue Maria, vnd opfert ir gebet vnser lieben frawen
gar andechtiglichen, vnd manet ir | gespilen gar flissigklichen, [Fol. 180 v.]
vnd sprach zu inen daz sy auch also deten vnd got dem
herren dieneten.   Do sy nun jetz sechs jerig was, als es got 30
wölt, do starb der hertzog dem sy gemehelt ward, wann got
het sy zu einem bessren erwölt vnd höheren geachtet vnd
geordent.   Do ward sy irem vatter dem künig wider gesant,
der befalch sy in ein ander closter daz[5] sy da solt lernen die

---

[1] MS. " niten " deleted.
[2] MS. " seiner," by mistake for feminine.   [3] See note II., p. 66.
[4] MS. " kind was " deleted.   [5] MS. " was " deleted.

solum a parentibus, uerum eciam ab omnibus sibi conuiuenti-
bus karissimo uenerabatur affectu.   Tempore tandem aliquo
interiecto, ab imperatoris Friderici filio perinter nuncios post-
ulatur in coniugem et a parentibus dicto iuueni mediantibus
5 prefatis nunciis desponsatur.   In qua desponsacione quoddam
contingit non tacendum.   Nam nomen uirginis celebre quod
pene omnibus erat notum, in ipsa desponsacione nullus astan-
[Fol. 164 v.]   cium ualuit recordari, ut hoc clareret indicio quod non | homini
mortali sed agno sine macula, in cuius libro nomen eius
10 memoriter scriptum erat Agnes federe perpetuo esset copu-
landa.   Denique ratificatis sponsalibus iuxta desponsacionem
imperatoris, cum regalis magnificiencie apparatu per patrem
in Austriam mittitur processu temporis per ducem Austrie
imperatoris filio in consortem tradendam.[1]   Manens autem in
15 curia ducis prefati nulli uoluptati carnis animum dedit, sed
per totum aduentum, cum omnes de familia ducis secundum
morem patrie carnibus uescerentur, ipsa sola in pane & uino
ieiunauit.[2]   At in quadragesima communi quum pueri prefati
[Fol. 165 r.]   ducis lacticiniis utebantur, ipsa tum pane et | uino contenta.
20 Nolens tamen ab hominibus uideri ieiunans, totam quadragesi-
mam sic cautissime ieiunando transegit quod preter nutricem
suam & quasdam ipsius secretarias uix[3] aliquis alius hoc percipere potuisset.[4]   Sic ipsa Jhesu Cristi mortificacionem an-
helans circumferre in corpore suo, carnem teneram macerabat,
25 concupiscencias eius loro parsimonie constringendo, ne uiuens
in deliciis coram deo mortua censeretur.   Elemosinis denique
& oracionibus insistendo, intemerate matri Cristi quam sibi
patronam elegit, se suamque pudiciciam commendabat, pre-
cando deuote ut digna fore posset imitatrix ac socia eius
[Fol. 165 v.]   uirginee puritatis.   Vnde & an|nunciacionem dominicam inter
31 ceteras festiuitates quoad uixit ardentissima deuocione colebat,

---

[1] M. and W. : " Do sўch nun etwas vil zeit verlof, do wart sy von dem
herzogen von osterreich des keisers sun vereinigt zu einem erben fur die vermehlung wann sy was got vermehelt ".   B2. stops at " erben ".

[2] M., W. and B2. add : " vnd prachs irm leib ab das sy nit in korung viel ".
[3] MS. " nix ".

[4] M., W. and B2. add : " vnd dennoch nit wol wann sy von den menschen
nit gelobt wolt werden ".

bücher vnd alle kunst. Da sy da ein jar zu schůl was gewessen, do nam sy der heilig geist der lerr selb gegen ir an vnd
erlücht sy mit seiner gnad also, daz sy me von gnaden kumt
denn ander ir gespilen von kunst oder von lernen, vnd daz sy
an kunst vnd sytten vnd an aller loblicher wandlung vnd[1] 5
wysheit[2] mer zu nam denn daz sy es an den jaren oder von
natur mecht haben erzugt. Alle kintliche verlassen spil ver-
meid sy mit grossem flisz, vnd aller ir trost vnd kurtzwil lag an
gebet, vnd daz sy dick vnd vil in der kirchen | möcht sein. Vnd [Fol. 181 r.]
do sy acht jar alt was, die edel jungerin vnd nachvolgerin 10
vnsres lieben herren, da nam sy ir vatter wider vsz dem closter
zu im, vnd was gar tugenhafftiges lebe[n]s vnd loblicher sytten
vnd mynnklicher wanlung gegen allen lutten, daz sy gemynt
ward nit allein von iren frunden, sunder auch von allen den
die sy erkantten oder von ir horten sagen; vnd erschal die mer 15
ir tugent vnd irs guten leben ver vnd nach über all, daz sy all
lüt mit lob in irem mund trugen. Do vernam des keissers
Friderichs sun als vil von der junckfrawen vnd von iren lob
vnd iren tugent, daz er grosse begirt gewan das sy im zu
einem gemahel mecht werden vnd sant beide der keisser vnd 20
sein sun gar | herlich vnd loblich botten an iren vatter, das [Fol. 181 v.]
man im disse lobliche junckfrawen solt zu der ee geben. Daz
lisz der vatter der kunig zu gan vnd gelopt sy des keissers
sun zu einem gemahel zegeben. Do geschach es in der gemahelschaft ein wunde[r]lich ding; do man der junckfrawen 25
namen solt nemen, als es gewunlich ist, do en was neimen
vnder in allen der der junckfrawen namen genenen kind
oder mocht, der doch vil nach allen menschen kunt was.
Da mit wolt got zu erkenen geben, daz sy keinem tödlichen menschen zu gemehelt solt werden, sunder dem 30
himelschlichen kunig. Do disse gemahelschaft zwischen ir
vnd des keissers sun bestettiget ward, do sant sy ir vatter,
der kunig, dem hertzogen von Polonien[3] mit kuniglicher wir-
digkeit vnd bereitschaft | vnd herlicher geselschaft, als es seinen [Fol. 182 r.]
kuniglichen eren vnd des keissers wirdigkeit vnd herschaft 35

[1] MS. "wyscheit".   [2] Ibid.
[3] " Polonien " is a scribal error, as the Latin text gives " Austrie ". It is
probably a reminiscence from p. 67, l. 17.

pia meditacione reuoluens quomodo intacta puella rore sancti
spiritus fecundata humani generis conceperit ac germinauerit
saluatorem, saluo priuilegio uirginali, sola digna nomine
uirginis & matris.

5   Igitur mirabili uirtute dei qui reprobat consilia principum,
factum est ut procelato et dissimulato prefato connubio,[1]—
dum iam quartum decimum annum attigisset, ad terram na-
tiuitatis sue iterum reducitur. Et ecce non multo post
tempore imperatoris [2] & regis Anglorum [3] nuncii ad parentes
10 uirginis uenientes certatim petebant, ut eorum domino in
[Fol. 166 r.] coniugem tra|deretur. Ipsisque ibidem moram trahentibus,
cuidam ex nunciis imperatoris [4] militi utique clare fame digna
relacione uisio monstrata est. Videbat namque in sompnis
coronam mire magnitudinis super caput uirginis descendere:
15 quam illa deponens, capiti suo superposuit incomparabiliter
meliorem. Euigilans autem mane & uisa mente pertractans ac
aliis referens, ut animalis homo expers intelligencie spiritalis,
interpretabatur legacionem suam finem cupitum sortituram :
quod uidelicet Agnes, Anglorum rege despecto, eum qui
20 maioris dignitatis est scilicet imperatorem acciperet in mari-
[Fol. 166 v.] tum. Sed deus magnus [5] reuelans in celo | misteria, hoc
sompnio uoluit indicare quod Agnes sponsa Cristi mox
futura, pro dyademate regni corruptibilis inmarcessibili corona
glorie ad ipso esset perhenniter coronanda.

---

[1] M. and W. : " geschah das sy nun in ir vermehlung die do offenbar was
die sy got getan het. Do was sy xiiij jar alt." B2. : " geschach das sie nun in
irer uermehlung die offenbar was viertzehen iar alt warde ". Probably Y was
corrupt at this point.

[2] M.: " nit lang noch dez keisers syn. Do komen die poten des kungs von
engellant zu irm vater, etc." W. : " nicht lang dornoch qwomen die poten
vnd des konigis von engelant ".

B2. : " Vnd nit lang nach dem zeit des keisers vnd do chomen die poten des
kunges von engelland ".

[3] See note V., p. 170.

[4] M., W. and B2. : " einem aus den poten des kungs ".

[5] M., W. and B2. add : " vnser herr Jhesus Cristus ".

zimlich was, das er die gemahelsaft solt verrichten, wann wie
der keisser, vnd nach der masz vnd wissz als im der kunig
seinen willen dar an zu erkenen[1] gab. Do was sy in des
vorgenanten herzogen hoff also daz sy sich enzoch von aller
lyplicher wollust vnd woltlicher fröd vnd trost; vnd do alle 5
die die in des herzogen hoff waren in dem advent fleisch[2]
assen nach ir gewunheit, do vastet sy allen advent also daz sy
nit anders ass denn wein vnd brot, vnd in der gemeinen
fasten, da daz gesind alles ass milch vnd kesz nach irer
gewonheit, | do über vastet sy alle die fasten vsz, vnd wolt dar [Fol. 182 v.]
zu nit anders essen denn wein vnd brot, vnd det doch daz 11
also heimlich, daz das neimen weist noch bevand denn ir[3] amm
vnd etlich irer junckfrawen, die ir gar heimlich waren. Also
kestiget sy iren zartten jungen lyb in ir kindheit durch vnsren
lieben herren Jhesu Cristi irs gemahels willen, daz sy da mit 15
doch ettwaz seiner mynn vnd seines lydes widergelten vnd
gedancken möcht. Sy gab auch gar vil almůssen durch got;
an gebet vnd andacht übet sy sych gewonlichen, vnd erwölt ir
vnser lieben frawen gottes muter zu einer sundren muter vnd
patrone, vnd eret sy vnd deint ir mit grossem flisz vnd andacht,— 20
vnd befalch ir ir küszheit vnd iren magtum, daz sy ir solt ein [Fol. 183 r.]
beschirmerin vnd behütterin ir megtlicher küszheit vnd reinikeit, daz sy möcht werden ein ware nachvolgerin irer reinikeit,
die allein wirdig ward daz sy wer muter vnd magt. Vnd
darum eret sy daz hochzit vnser lieben frawen in der vasten, 25
die Anunciacio, vntz an iren tod für alle die hochzit die imer
in dem jar waren, wann daz selb hochzit ein anfang was
vnser seligkeit vnd aller hochzit. Nun geschach es von
vnsers herren ordnung, der den rat vnd den willen der fürsten
dick wider tribt vnd verwirft, daz die brolaff zwischen ir vnd 30
des keissers sun | verzogen ward vntz daz sy tryzeen jar alt [Fol. 183 v.]
ward;[4] vnd do sy in daz vierzeent jar geng, do ward sy wider
in ir land gefurt, daz sy ir frund solt sehen. Vnd do sy do by
iren frunden was, vnlang darnach da kam ir botschaft daz ir
gemahel des keissers sun tod wer. Darnach über etwen vil 35

De sancta uita quam habuit post mortem parentum
apud germanum suum degendo.

Cum autem pater eius clare memorie rex Ottakarus ex
hac uita migrasset, mansit apud germanum[1] suum, regni
successorem dominum inclitum Venzezlaum, et crescens per
etatem corporis, crescebat amplius per affectum deuocionis, de
5 uirtute proficiens in uirtutem. Consurgens enim diluculo
mutabat habitum & que secretorum eius erant conscie com-
[Fol. 167 r.] itabantur ; dedicaciones ecclesiarum que multe sunt | in
Praga deuotissime perlustrabat, et inclusas circa easdem uisitans, illarum se oracionibus instancius commendabat. Sepe
10 uero cum sese [*calefaceret*][2] rediens post laborem, propter
asperitatem algoris uisi sunt pedes eius sanguine rubricati ;
eo quod per artam uiam contendens intrare ad uitam, cus-
todiebat uias duras. Die[3] tandem clarius lucescente, ad

---

[1] M., W. and B2. : "irem fetern".
[2] MS. "talem faceret". The German versions justify reading "calefaceret".
[3] M., W. and B2. : "eins tags".

zyt vnd auch nach irs vatters tod do komen potten zu iren [1]
fründen, daz man sy dem keisser solt zu einem gemahel geben ;
vnder des kömen auch des kunigs von Engenland [2] botten dar
vnd würben mit allem flisz das irem herren von Engenland
wurd. Da sy also wider strit vmm sy wurbent, do was gar 5
ein manhafftiger vnd achtberer her do, einer von des keissers
botten, dem ward ein mercklich ding gezeigt. Er sach in
seinem slaff, daz sich ein | cron von dem himel herab leisz über [Fol. 184 r.]
ir hopt, die was michel vnd grosz vnd gar schön vnd wunig-
klich. Do nam sy die cron von irem hopt vnd leit sy von ir 10
vnd satzt [3] ir selber da ein vil bessere vnd ein herliche cron vff,
die waz schöner denn die erst was ; da mit wolt got zu erkenen
geben, daz er sy geachtet vnd fürsehen het zu höher er vnd
wirdigkeit denn alle küngrich sind. Daz verstunt er aber nit
vnd wand es bezeichnet, daz sy seinem herren dem keisser 15
solt werden vnd dem kunig von Engenland versprochen
solt werden.

DAS ANDER CAPITEL WIE SI HAILICH[LI]CHEN LEBET NACH
IRES VATTERS TOD.

Nach irs vaters tod der gar ein loblicher her vnd fürst was
an aller er vnd kuniglicher wirdigkeit, do ward irem eldren
brüder | daz rich nach seinem vatter. Do bleib sy by im vnd [Fol. 184 v.]
nam zu am lyb, also nam sy auch zu von tag zu tag an der 21
andacht vnd an götlicher lieb vnd an heiliger vnd tugent-
licher öbung. Sy stunt vil frü vff vor tag vnd wandlet ir
gewant vnd geing vss mit iren junckfrawen zu allen den
kirchen vnd gotzhüssren da denn kirchwichen was, vnd sůcht 25
den aplas da mit grosser begird vnd andacht, vnd geng auch
zu allen clostren die da warent gar vil dar vmm gesessen, vnd
bevalch sich andechtlich vnd demietiglichen in ir gebet ; vnd
so sy dem wider hüm kam vnd sy wermen solt, so waren ire
zarte fusz zerschrunden vnd zerprochen beide von arbeiten 30
vnd von gan die bössen vnd scharpfen weg | vnd auch von frost, [Fol. 185 r.]
daz sy ir vil dick pludent. Vnd so es recht kalt ward, so
geng sy zu kirchen in ir capel,[4] die sy in ir kuniglichen phaltzen

---

[1] MS. "vatter" deleted.   [2] See note V., p. 170.
[3] MS. "schatz" deleted.   [4] See note VI., p. 170.

capellam domus regie [*uel*] ad ecclesiam kathedralem [1] procedens, nobilium commitatiua stipata non uanis affatibus
hominum sed diuinis eloquiis erat intenta ; et ecclesiam uel
capellam ingrediens, missas plures quas poterat deuotissime
5 audiendo persistebat & nunc psalmos penitenciales cum aliis
[Fol. 167 v.] oracionibus, nunc uigilias | pro defunctis, debita domino cum
intencione persoluens, indefessum ab oracione spiritum non
relaxabat. Cernens autem quia preterit figura huius mundi,
moleste iam ferebat terrenam fugacem gloriam ; & secularis
10 ornatus decorem proposse deuitans, sub uestibus auro textis
ut regiam prolem decebat, ciliciolum clam portabat. Cubi-
culum suum apparatu magnifico decoratum deuitans, iuxta
lectum delicatum super stramentum durum & humile decu-
babat. Talia fuerunt in domo fraterna eius conuersacionis
15 insignia, talis affectus celestium & contemptus terrenorum.
Sed quia tam luminosa lucerna subter modio [2] latere non potuit,
[Fol. 168 r.] uirtutum ac nominis eius fama ad instar olei | per adiacentes
prouincias circumquaque diffusa, eciam usque ad imperatorem
peruenit. Qui sicut prius ad patrem, ita secundo ad fratrem
20 uirginis nuncios destinauit, multis promissionibus interpositis,
postulans ut sororem suam eius coniugio non negaret. Quo
uotis annuente petentis, uirgo Cristi cogitans que sunt domini,
ut corpore & spiritu sancta existens, cum lylia continencium
uirginum [3] celestem agnum sequi ualeret, nulli se mortalium
25 cuiuscunque status uel prominencie nupturam proponit. Et
ut in suo proposito, quod deo inspirante conceperat, securius
permaneret, manum mittens ad forcia, nobili Cristi uicario,
domino pape Gregorio nono per honestos nuncios & discretos
[Fol. 168 v.] suum | ocultum intentum patefecit. Qui felix antistes tam
30 generose uirginis deuocioni congaudens, per eosdem nuncios

---

[1] M., W. and B2. omit reference to the cathedral altogether; but it is found
in Ber. See note VI., p. 170.

[2] M., W. and B2. : "vnter dem klein steinlein". Y must have had some other
word than "modio".

[3] The common German source of M., W. and B2. must have misunderstood
sense and failed to recognise the quotation from Rev. XIV. 4 : for M., W., B2.
read : "vnd daz zepter der lilgen mit der schar aller heilligen iunkfrawen moht
noch tragen vnd als ein dymutigs lemlein moht noch folgen".

het oder zu den rechten tům mit grosser vnd herlicher gesel-
saft vnd wolt [*nymmer*]¹ vnnutz wort oder red haben mit den
sy geng, noch von in hören, sunder all zit redt sy von got
vnd von nutzb[*e*]ren besserlichen dingen, vnd blieb denn in
der kirchen, vnd hört alle die messen die ir werden mochten 5
mit grosser andacht. Sy ward auch ansehend vnd mercken
die vnstetigkeit vnd die falsheit disser welt, wie gar vnsted
vnd falsz ist die er vnd fröd disser ² welt; vnd ward ir gar
widerzem daz ir alle weltliche gezeirt vnd fröd ein pein vnd
marter was. | Vnder dem gulden vnd kostperen gewand trug [Fol. 185 v.]
sy heimlichen an irem zarten lyb ein hert herin hemd, vnd ir 11
küniglich bett, daz ir mit aller gezeirt vnd wirdigkeit wol
bereit waz, liesz sy es ston vnd wolt nit daran ligen, vnd heisz
ir ein deimiettig vnd gar ein hert bett machen neben irem
küniglichen vnd wol bereiten bett, vnd lag denn vff dem herten 15
bett.   Also lebt sy by irem bruder, da sy dannocht in der
welt waz, in küniglicher er vnd wirdigkeit ; vnd also ein starck
vnd ein clar liecht seinen scin nit verbergen mag, es liechtent
als vmm sich, daz eyder mag geseichen, also durch brach vnd
durch geng der lymunt irer loblicher sytten vnd wandlung 20
vnd ires ³ durch alle die land ver vnd nach.   Vnd vernam auch
der | keisser Fryderrich als vil lobs vnd seligkeit von der junck- [Fol. 186 r.]
frawen, das er ir grosslichen [*begert*] ⁴ zu der ee, vnd als er botten
vmb sy het gesant an iren vatter, also sant er aber botten an iren
brüder vnd warb mit allem flisz vmm sy.   Do sy daz vernam, 25
do nam sy ein manlich hertz an sy vnd sprach ⁵ daz sy keinen
tödlichen gemahel nymmer wolt nemen ; sy het sich gemehelt
vnd entheyssen dem himelschlichen künig in stetter trew vnd
mynn vnd lieb, an dem wölt sy stet belyben vntz an iren tod ; vnd
sant da bryff an babst Gregorium mit gar erberen botten, vnd 30
det im iren willen vnd fürsatz kunt, daz sy den keisser vnd all
man verschmehen wolt vnd got in ewiger küscheit vnd reinig-
keit | wölt deinen vntz an ir end, vnd bat in ernstlich daz er sy [Fol. 186 v.]

---

¹ MS. "myner ".   ² MS. " fröd " repeated, deleted.
³ A substantive is apparently omitted here, probably "namens ".
⁴ MS. reads " gebert ".
⁵ MS. here reads "in vnd all tödlich keisser vnd fürsten," thus breaking
the sense.

ipsam graciosis litteris in domino confortauit, propositum
eius sanctum commendans pariter & confirmans, adoptatamque
in filiam multis spiritalibus donis inuisit, cunctis diebus suis
eam prosequens pii patris affectu. At Cristi famula, de hiis
5 qui a summo pontifice receperat in responsis multa spiritus
consolacione repleta, statim propositum suum germano suo
domino regi Venzeslao intrepide propalauit. Quo rex audito
non sine magna turbacione ac se contulit ¹ excusandum sororisque propositum detegendum imperatori nuncios destinauit.
[Fol. 169 r.] Ad quorum lega|cionem imperator fertur taliter respondisse,
11 " Si a quocumque homine nobis hec iniuria illata fuisset, tante
despeccionis obprobrium uindicare nullatenus cessaremus.
Sed quia nobis maiorem dominum perelegit, hoc despectui
nostro nequaquam asscribimus, cum instinctu diuino istud
15 factum esse credamus ". Vnde intencionem bonam uirginis
magnis extollens laudum preconiis, preciosa ei munera &
reliquias multas transmisit, hortans per litteras & inducens ut
quod salubriter cepit feliciter consumaret.

Qualiter ordinem sancte clare intrauit.

Uolens igitur felix uirgo quod mente tractauerat cupito
[Fol. 169 v.] effectui man|cipare, uocauit fratres minores ² quos intuitu dei
21 pre ceteris religiosis ampliori prosequebatur affectu, petens ab
eis informari de qualitate regule ordinis sancte Clare, que

---

¹ M. and W. : "do nam er zu im die poten des keisers zu beschuldigen sein
mumen vnd sant dem keiser behendiklich potschaft ". But B2. : " nam ers zu im
zu beschuldigen sein swester ". It is curious that all three versions read " beschuldigen," where the sense demands " entschuldigen ". See further comment
on this on p. 27.

² See note VII., p. 171.

nem in sein schirm, das weder ir bruder noch nemen hindren möcht iren guten fursatz.

Do daz der babst Gregorius vernam, der ein liebhaber waz oder ein mynner aller heiligkeit vnd seligkeit vnd aller ding da gottes lob vnd er vnd der sel heil vnd seligkeit anligen mag, da der vernam daz so ein hohe edle fürstin die grösten er vnd wirdigkeit der welt het versprochen, do ward er gar frö vnd lobt got vnsren herren Jhesum Cristum inerlichen darum vnd schreib ir gar einen lieblichen tröstlichen bryff, an dem er sy tröst vnd sterckt sy, daz sy stet belib an irem heiligen gutten fürsatz, vnd nam sy im selbs do zu einer sundren tochter vnd | zu einem kind, vnd alles daz daz sy an in [Fol. 187 r.] begert, daz wolt er sy geweren.

Do ir brüder sach daz er kein volgen an ir fand vnd das sy den keisser vnd all mann mit festen gemůt vnd fürsatz versprochen het, da *s*enet[1] er sich dar vff, wie er sich gegen den keisser enschuldigen möcht. Vnd do daz der keisser vernam, da sprach er "Het mir disse schmacheit oder vner jeman anders erbotten, ich liesz es nymer vngerochen; syt aber disse junckfraw ir den obersten herren erwölt hat vnd sich dem gemehelt hat, so wil ich sie[2] yemer dester lieber vnd dester werder han," vnd lobt sy grosslichen gegen den fürsten vnd allen lütten, vnd sant ir gar kosper vnd edel gab,[3] vnd kleinetter[4] vnd vil heiltums des grösten | heiltumsz [Fol. 187 v.] des man haben mag, vnd mant sy[5] an seinen briffen daz sy starck vnd stet belyb an irem heiligen vnd loblichen fürsatz.

Das drit capitel wie si in sant Claren orden kam.

Do begert disse selige lobliche junckfraw, das sy iren willen vnd ir langen begirt möcht mit den wercken erfillen, vnd sant nach den myndren brudren,[6] die sy mynt für all ander geistlich lüt, vnd bat die daz sy ir rietten, wie sy in sant

[1] MS. "sendet" deleted: "senet" added in margin.

[2] MS. "sich" altered to "sie".

[3] MS. "des man haben mag" deleted.

[4] MS. "klainëinetter".

[5] MS. adds "daz sy" deleted.

[6] See note VII., p. 171.

adhuc uiuens pro tunc circa ciuitatem Assisii apud sanctum
Damianum inclusa cum sacris uirginibus morabatur, & quasi
thus ardens in igne ac redolens in diebus estatis suarum odore
uirtutum mundi climata respergebat. Edocta uero a fratribus
5 quod regula memorata intrare uolentibus ordinem supradictum secundum tenorem sacri ewangelii suadet omnia sua
uendere et ea pauperibus erogare, Cristoque pauperi in pau-
[Fol. 170 r.] pertate & humilitate famulari, celesti mun|ditate perfusa "hoc
est" ait "quod cupio, hoc est quod totis precordiis concu-
10 pisco". Mox ergo aurum & argentum, iocalia quoque preciosa
ac ornamenta diuersa iussit distrahi & pauperibus dispergi,
cupiens facultates suas per eorum manus in celestes thesauros
deportari. Denique ad imitacionem beate Elyzabeth con-
sobrine sue, hospitale sollempne pro infirmis in pede pontis
15 ciuitatis Pragensis ad honorem sanctissimi confessoris Francisci construxit, quod reddditibus & possessionibus amplis
ditauit, Cruciferos cum rubea cruce & stella[1] ibidem collocans,
qui predictorum infirmorum curam gererent, et prout uni-
[Fol. 170 v.] cuique opus esset, de necessariis omnibus sollicite | prouiderent.
20 Monasterium quoque fratrum minorum in honore prefati
confessoris gloriosi intra urbem pragensem propriis sumptibus
fieri procurauit, nec non famosum cenobium pro sororibus
ordinis sancte Clare in honore saluatoris mundi, quod gloriosis
reliquiis sanctorum, uasis ac ornamentis preciosis ad cultum
25 diuinum pertinentibus, utpote diligens decorem domus dei
mirabiliter decorauit. Venientes autem quinque sorores ordinis sancte Clare de Terdento,[2] que ad peticionem ipsius de
fauore sedis apostolice sibi fuerant destinate, cum magna
spiritus exultacione ab ipsa recepte, memoratum cenobium
30 honorifice introducte sunt. Et in proxima festiuitate sancti
[Fol. 171 r.] Martini septem[3] uirgines de reg|no Bohemie generis ualde
clari, sponso uirginum castitatis nexibus uinciri cupientes,
habitu & conuictu adiuncte sunt sororibus antedictis.

---

[1] M., W. and B2. leave out "& stella." but add "vnd sezt dar zu diner vnd
kneht". See note VIII., p. 171.

[2] M., W. and B2. add "in welschen landen". See note IX., p. 171.

[3] M. and W. "vi."; B2. "sechs".

Claren orden möcht kumen, des sy von gantzem hertzen begert ;
der dannocht gar new waz, den die gottes mynnerin vnd
vsserwelte junkfraw sant Clar angefangen hat vnd mit den
engelschen vnd himelschen lylien irs ordens die end der welt
erfült hat mit heiligkeit vnd mit loblichem bild. Da sagten ir 5
die brüder die regel sant Claren, da stund, wer zu den orden
sant Claren | will komen, der sol nach dem rat des heiligen [Fol. 188 r.]
Ewangely verkoffen alles das er hat vnd sol es den armen
geben ; da sy daz hört, da ward sy erfült mit vnseglicher fröd
vnd durchgossen mit himelscher[1] trost vnd sprach "Diss ist, 10
daz ich lang von gantzem meinem hertzen begert han,"
vnd zu hand hiesz sy alles daz verkoffen, gold vnd silber
geschmeid vnd edelgestein vnd als ir kleinetter, ir kosperes
künigl[ich]es gewand vnd waz sy von farndem[2] gůtt het, des
on massen vil waz, vnd hiessz es alles den armen geben, vnd 15
hiesz da von irem erb ein gross herlich spital machen,[3] als ir
mům sant Elisabet det, do man all dürfftig solt in enpfahen
vnd machet daz selben spital in sant Francisen er vnd gab irs
eigens vnd irs erbes gar on massen | vnzelich fil zu dem selben [Fol. 188 v.]
spital, vnd sant zu hant geistlich lüt dar zu, die hiessent crütz- 20
herren vnd tragent rötte crütz vnd einen sternen,[4] die solten
des guttes pflegen vnd den dürfftigen von dem selben gůt mit
trüwen geben. Sy macht auch von irem eigen gut ein herlich
vnd loblich closter in sant Frantscisen er, do sein brüder in
solten wonen vnd vnsern herren deinen ; sy macht auch gar 25
ein richlich closter in der selben stat zu Brag die ir eigen waz,
den schwestren von sant Claren orden, die in dem selben
closter auch vnsren herren solten deinen, vnd namp das selb
closter in vnsren lieben herren eren des behalters aller der
welt ; vnd gab auch gar fil gulden vnd gar gross heiltum zu 30
dem closter vnd silberin fasz kelch vnd nepf vnd aller hant
gezeirt vnd illter gewand und was man zu gottes | deinst [Fol. 189 r.]
bedarff oder sol han, des gab sy on zal vnd an mass vil dar ;
vnd waz diz mit dem richlichesten vnd besten als man
erzügen möcht ; vnd bat den babst Gregorium, das er ir 35

---

[1] MS. "fröd" deleted. [2] MS. reads "faradem".
[3] MS. reads "machem". [4] See note VIII., p. 171.

Considerans tandem uirgo prudens quod in naufraga uita
presenti continue fluctibus nostre mortalitatis iactamur, nec
superna contemplari ualemus propter tumultum mundanarum
causarum, amore celestium ardencius inflammata, in Penthe-
5 coste proximo sequenti, presentibus septem epyscopis et
domino rege fratre suo ac regina cum multis principibus &
baronibus, nec non innumera utriusque sexus diuersarum nacionum multitudine, spreto regni fastigio et omni gloria
[Fol. 171 v.] mundana contempta, cum septem nobilissi|mis regni sui uir-
10 ginibus, ut columba innocua de diluuio nequam seculi ad
archam sacre religionis conuolauit. Cumque in monasterio,
crinibus tonsis, uestes regias deposuisset fletibus et luctui, ut
Hester altera, apta indumenta suscepit,—quatenus Clare matris sue pauperi se habitu conformaret & gestu. Sic[1] [se]
15 elongauit fugiens a periculosis mundi procellis, [et] salutis sue
anchoram supra petram que Cristus est[2] fiducialiter collocauit.
Ad hanc religionis solitudinem pennis affeccionis transmigrauit, ut in ea puritatis & pacis interne soliditatem seruando
suauitatem eterne dulcedinis palato mentis pregustaret. In
[Fol. 172 r.] hoc an|tro paupertatis[3] amore pauperis crucifixi et dulcissime
21 matris eius usque ad mortem se recludens, quasi mirra electa
suauem diffudit fragranciam sanctitatis. Nam ipsius exemplo
plures illustres persone Polonie partibus ceperunt monasteria[4]
construere, innumere nobiles uirgines & uidue ad religionem
25 confluere, et in carne preter carnem uiuentes celicam uitam
actitare.

---

[1] MS. repeats "sic".   [2] M., W. and B2. add "der war got".
[3] M., W. and B2.: "in der hol ganczer vnd rehter armut".
[4] M.: "grosse munster sant Clarn ordens in irn ern". W. omits "in irn
ern". B2. omits "sant Clarn ordens".

schwester sant von sant Claren orden, die den orden anfeng[1]
vnd lert.   Do sant ir der babst funf schwestern von santen
Claren orden ; die enpfeng sy mit grosser fröd vnd begirt irs
hertzen vnd würden mit aller er vnd andacht in daz closter
gefürt an sant Martins tag ; vnd des selben tags do füren auch 5
siben junckfrawen mit ir in das selb closter, der aller edelsten
höstgeboren[2] die in dem kunigrich waren mit grossen eren
und wunderlicher geziert.   Dar nach da das[3] geschach,
do ward die loblich magt vnd die gottes erwelte gemahel
Angnes noch hitziger vnd hertzlicher enzindet mit göttlicher 10
mynn vnd mit himelscher | begird vnd gedacht daz sy die welt [Fol. 189 v.]
vnd all weltlich er vnd wirdigkeit, fröd vnd gezeirt, gentzlichen
wolt lan vnd sich vnsrem herren wolt geistlich opfren vnd
geben vnd got dienen in volkumner armůt vnd demüttigkeit ;
vnd besamlet einen kuniglichen vnd herlichen hoff vnd lůd zu 15
den hoff siben bischoff, die höchsten vnd[4] achtberesten die in dem
künigrich waren vnd iren brüder den[5] kunig vnd sein frawen
die kunigin vnd ander ir frund ein mihel teil vnd ander fursten
vnd herrenfryen gar fil vnd ander edel lüt beiden frawen vnd
man on zal vnd on massen fil ; vnd cleidet sich selber mit 20
aller der zirt vnd richlicheit vnd bereitsaft, als die welt geleis-
ten mag vnd ire junckfrawen siben mit ir, die waren in all masz
gecleidet vnd gezieret als sy selbs.   Vnd an dem heiligen [Fol. 190 r.]
pfingst tag da leit disse edele furstin ir küniglich cleider vnd
alle ir gezeirt von ir vor dem kunig vnd der kunigin vnd 25
vor ander ir frunden vnd vor den siben bischoffen vnd den
andren fürsten vnd herren, die sy all zu den hoff geladen
het, vnd ward do vor allen die, die da gegenwirtig warent
gecleidet mit dem aller ermesten vnd verschmesten gewand
als die schwestren von sant Claren orden tragent, daz het sy 30
ir heissen bereitten ir vnd den siben junckfrawen, die sich mit
ir ergabent vnd koment in demselben armen verschmechten
gewand in daz closter das sy gemacht het sant Claren orden

---

[1] MS. "anfang".   [2] MS. "gerboren".
[3] MS. reads "dar nach dar nach," but a second hand has deleted the first
"nach" and added "da das" in margin.
[4] MS. "obersten" deleted.   [5] MS. "dem".

DE MAXIMA HUMILITATE IPSIUS & OBEDIENCIA.

Qvia uero spirituali fabrice humilitas est necessaria, tamquam ceterarum uirtutum stabile ac solidum fundamentum,
quam tocius perfeccionis exemplar dominus Jhesus Cristus
uerbo docuit & exemplo, ideo Agnes, ut uera Cristi disci-
[Fol. 172 v.] pula | in oculis suis humilis, de se semper humilia senciebat,
6 omnes superiores se arbitrans in uirtute.   Propterea toto tempore uite sue prelacionem sui ordinis declinauit,[1] parere malens
humiliter quam aliis imperare, et inter Cristi ancillas minima
& abiecta ministrare pocius quam ministrari summi exemplo
10 magistri.   Stupam calefacere & coquinam pro conuentu sororum parare uirgo egregia non horrebat, sed & specialia fercula
suis mundissimis manibus cum magna deuocione parata infirmis ac debilibus fratribus mittebat, cum Martha[2] ministra
Cristi sollicita, dominum in suis pauperibus reficere satagendo.
[Fol. 173 r.] Scutellas & cetera coquine uten|silia cum magna cordis hylari-
16 tate lauabat, habitacula[3] quoque sororum & diuersas in-

---

[1] See note X., p. 171.

[2] M.: "wann sy in der arch irs gots vnd irs herrn ein fleiszige dinern wolt
sein".   W.: "in der archa ires gotes".   B2.: "in der archen irs gotes".   The
translations suggest that in Y "Martha" was corrupted into "in archa".
This would happen very readily as "m" would be read as "in" and the letters
"t" and "c" are often almost indistinguishable in MSS.

[3] MS. "habitabula".

zu Brag in der stat.   Da ward weinen vnd clagen überal von
reuw vnd andacht vnd von grosser besserung vmb[1] so vnge-
hörttes vnd vngewonliches bilds, daz ein so höhe fürstin so
grosse er vnd wirdigkeit der wölt het verschmecht | vnd so ein [Fol. 190 v.]
verschmecht vnd arms leben an sich het genumen.   In dem 5
closter da beschlosz sy sich innen, als ob sy lebendig begraben
wer; da enpfloch[2] sy allen wittenden wettren disser welt, als
auch ir heiligen mûter sant Clar det, der sy sich gelichet an
dem gewand vnd an dem leben vnd an dem bild, der edlen
nachvolgerin vnd tochter sy waz worden.   Vnd nach irem 10
bild da warent vil höher vnd edler frawen, die auch closter
machten sant Claren orden vnd da innen vnsren lieben herren
deinten in himelschlichen vnd[3] engelschen leben bysz an iren
tod.

DAS VIERD CAPITEL VON IRER GROSSEN DIEMIETIKAIT VND
GEHORSAMKAIT.

Wann[4] nun daz geistlich gebeuw aller tugent vnd volkumnes 15
lebens nit bestan mag, es en hab denn einen starcken vnd edlen
grund die heiligen demût, die ein behutterin vnd ein behalterin
ist aller tugent vnd göttlicher lieb vnd gnad vnd gab an | den [Fol. 191 r.]
menschen, die got selbert het der ein [*exemplar*][5] vnd form was
aller volkumenheit vnd heiligkeit [*vnd*] wolt[*e sy*][6] [*l*]eren vff 20
ertrich mit wortten vnd mit bild ; . . . des ware jungerin vnd
nachvolgerin disse edle kunigin Angnes was; die sich selber
so gar ser verwarf, daz sy die nyderst vnd die verschmecht
wolt sein vnder den andren schwestren an allen dingen vnd
achtet sich selb nit andres denn als ob sy wer ein hinwurf 25
aller lüt.   Sy wolt nie kein ampt in dem orden han vnd hielt
sich nit anders an allen dingen, als ob sy der andren aller[7]

---

[1] MS. "un ".   [2] MS. "enpfalch ".
[3] MS. repeats "und ".
[4] The construction is distinctly faulty at this point.   Some words must be
supplied before "des waren ".
[5] MS. first reads "explan" deleted, and then "expēlar".
[6] MS. "welt eren vff ertrich mit wortten und mit bild des waren jungerin
vnd nachvolgerin dissen edlen künigin Agnes was ".
[7] MS. reads ". deinst vnd " deleted.

mundicias furtim purgabat, omnium facta peripsima [1] propter
Cristum. [2] Sed & stupende humilitatis excessu deliciositatem
obliuiscens ingenitam, infirmarum sororum ac leprosorum hominum fetentes pannos & sordidos pia sibi cautela procurans
5 afferri teneris manibus abluebat, adeo ut ex frequenti talium
locione propter mordacitatem lexiue et smigmatis manus
haberet sepius sauciatas. Vestes insuper eorundem laniatas
sub noctis silencio consuebat, nolens eorum que gerebat alium
quam deum inspectorem habere, a quo solo mercedem piorum
[Fol. 173 v.] expectabat | laborum. Igitur, ut gemmula carbunculi in orna-
11 mento auri, sic et generositas huius preclare uirginis humilitatis
decore preradians, ipsam deo amabilem et ceteris imitabilem
reddidit, et ad amplorum diuinorum carismatum ubertatem
illius uirtute qui ponit humiles in sublimi prouexit. Cum
15 autem sanctitas mirabilis ad aures sanctissime Clare uirginis
peruenisset, illa tam nobili prole diuina gracia fecundata
gaudens, magnificauit altissimum, eamque [3] crebrius suis graciosis litteris materne reuerenter ac affectuosissime consolans,
studiose in sancto proposito confortauit, regulamque suam
20 per bone memorie Innocencium quartum confirmatam ueluti
[Fol. 174 r.] pignus here|ditarie successionis eidem transmisit. Quam agna
Cristi deuote suscipiens denuo per felicis recordacionis dominum Alexandrum quartum pro se & sororibus sui monasterii
perpetuis temporibus obtinuit confirmari. Cuius sacre regule
25 professioni se uinciens districcione obediencie que prepollet
uictimis, quasi uite hostia pacificorum mactabat assidue pro-
priam uoluntatem. Toto nempe conamine mentis regularis
obseruancie intendebat, non iota statutorum uel apicem pre-
termittens, ut sine offendiculo uiam mandatorum dei percurreret
30 superiorumque iussionibus quoad uixit cum humilitate &
[Fol. 174 v.] reuerencia magna parebat, iugum sancte obedien cie ac onus

---

[1] An allusion to 1 Corinthians iv. 13.

[2] M., W. and B2. add : " daz die swester ir zell vnd wonung rein vnd sauber
funden vnd daz sy in reinikeit wurd vor dem anplik gotes vnsers herrn gefunden
vnd in rehter dymutikeit ".

[3] M., W. and B2. : " die lieben junkfrawen sant angnesen ".

deinerin wer.   Es was kein werck in dem closter so vnrein
noch so verschmecht, sy nem sich es an, es wer in der kuchin
oder anderswa.   Die schusselin vnd die heffen vnd waz in die
kuchen gehort, daz[1] wüsch sy alles mit grosser fröd vnd
begirt irs hertzen ; der schwestren hüsslin vnd andren iren 5
vnsubren ding flisz sy sich inen zu sybren ; den siechen vnd
den krancken brüdren vor dem closter vnd auch andren
siechen, den wolt sy nun selbert kuchen vnd mit als grosser
begird vnd andacht als ob sy es got selb solt dûn, des gelider
sy warent.   Vnd so sy denn die spisz wol bereit het, so sant sy 10
es für daz closter den siechen, den sy es bereit het.   Sy sant
auch zu den vssetzigen vnd wassersichtigen lütten, | daz sy [Fol. 191 v.]
allen ir vnreinen vnd schmackenden tücher santen vnd wusch
inen vnd sant sy inen rein vnd schön wider.   Sy wusch auch
den schwestren allen ir vnreinen dücher, die sy hetten in dem 15
closter, daz ir zart hend dick schrunden vnd zerbrachen von
den scharpfen lögen.   Den maltzensichtigen[2] vnd andren armen,
vnd dürfftigen, den nat sy vnd macht in ir alt zerbrochen
gewand wider vnd sas dick nachtes dar ÿber, daz es nemet gewar
wurd oder sech, denn got allein, durch des mynn sy auch alle 20
ding det.   Vnd als die edel gemmen[3] carfunckelstein schinet
in der geziert des goldes, also macht sy ir grosse deimiettig-
keit loblichen vnd mynnigklich schinent vor got vnd den lütten,
wann ir heiligkeit ward bekant[4] ver vnd nach.   Vnd[5] ward
auch sant Claren, der heiligen mûtter, ir heiliges leben kunt 25
geton ; do ward sy vnmessigklich frö vnd lobt den almechtigen
got, der ir so ein edle vnd so ein gar heilige tochter[6] het
geben ; vnd schrib ir gar mynnigklichen | vnd lieblichen bryff [Fol. 192 r.]
an dem[7] sy sy mit mûtterlichen truwen gryst vnd trost sy
vnd störckt sy in got, vnd an seinem deinst vnd an seiner 30
mynn ; vnd sant ir die regel die ir der babst Innoccencius der

---

[1] MS. reads " swûsch ".
[2] MS. reads " wassersichtigen," of which " wasser " is deleted ; " maltzen "
is added in the margin.
[3] MS. reads " gennen ".   [4] MS. " bedanck " altered to " bekant ".
[5] MS. adds " nach " deleted.   [6] MS. reads " ir " which is deleted.
[7] MS. " demen ".

virdt het geben.　Wann da sant Clar den orden anfeng, da bat
religionis artissime propter amorem domini suaue reputans et
leue.

DE SANCTA & UERA PAUPERTATE IPSIUS.

Paupertas altissima,[1] qua humiles spiritu mercantur regnum
celorum, tanto federe menti ipsius inheserat, quod in rebus
5 transitoriis atque caducis nil proprium uellet habere, nichilque
cuperet possidere in terra moriencium, ut porcio eius & here-

---

[1] M., W. and B2. all mistake nominative for vocative, " O du hohe armut ".

HOW SAINT AGNES BY VIRTUE OF SAINT CLARE'S PRAYERS IS
SAVED FROM BEING CARRIED AWAY FROM HER CONVENT.
(From MS. M.281 Royal Library, Dresden.)

sey den selben babst, daz er ir die regel rechter armůt wolt
bestetigen vnd beiden vns zu trost vnd vnsren orden zu eren
vnd zu bestetigung. Da schrib ir der babst mit seiner selb
hand die erst form vnd mas der regel; die sant die heilig
můter sant Clar der heiligen sant Angnes, die enpfing sy gar 5
fröchlichen vnd begirlichen vnd bat den babst Alexander, daz
er auch auch ir vnd irm closter die selb regel bestetet in ewiger
armut, daz weder sy noch daz closter eigen noch erb nymer
gewinen solt. Des gewerd sy der heilig vater der babst nach
allem irm willen. Disse regel gelobte sy zu halten vntz an 10
iren tod, vnd hielt sy auch als gar strenglichen alles | daz sy [Fol. 192 v.]
von ir regel oder von ir setz oder von des ordens gewonheit
halten solt, daz heilt sy alles mit grossen flisz vnd andacht bisz
vfi den jungsten punctum, wann sy wist wol den geistlichen
menschen nit nützers noch loblichster vnd got ge*n*emer[1] ist 15
von einem jeglichen menschen, daz geistlich ist, den[n] rechten
waren volkumen gehorsam; wann da mit werden sy den mar-
tarrer gelichet, vnd verdienent auch der martarer lon vnd grösser
lon denn die martarer, wann die martarer opferent sich mit einem
tod vnsrem lieben herren, doch schier nempt es ein end, aber 20
geistlich lüt die lyden als mengen tod als sy iren eigen willen
brechent, wann als dick vergiessent sy irs hertzen blůd. Als
auch der prophet spricht von geistlichen lütten "*propter te
mortificamur tota die*". Daz spricht in tuschem also " Herr,
wir werden all tag[2] gemartret vnd getödtet durch deinen 25
willen" mit dem schwert stetiger gehorsam. Vnd da von
was ir auch die strengen vnd des schwert der heiligen | gehorsam [Fol. 193 r.]
sonst licht vnd susz durch die mynn vnszers lieben herren
Jhesu Cristi.

DAS FÜNFT CAPITEL VON IRER WAREN VND WILLIGEN
ARMŮT.

Die waren vnd willigen armůt, mit der die demuttigen 30
gottes rich kuffent vnd an sich ziechent als zu einem eigen
erb—als auch vnser lieber her sprichet in dem ewangelio

---

[1] MS. " gememer ".   [2] MS. repeats " ge ".

ditas esset dominus in terra uiuencium. Vnde cum uenerabilis dominus Johannes Gayetanus [1] sedis apostolice cardinalis,
tempore concilii Lugdunensis sub decimo Gregorio celebrati,
per litteras sibi suasisset ut propter maliciam dierum & in-
[Fol. 175 r.] stancia tempora periculosa possessiones | aliquas pro se & suis
6 sororibus compararet, forti restitit animo, magis se uelle
astruens omni penuria & egestate deficere quam a Cristi
pauperie, qui propter nos egenus factus est, ullatenus declinare.
Cumque a germano suo domino rege Venzezlao & aliis principi-
10 bus large sibi elemosine mitterentur, uolens sibi facere de
mammona iniquitatis amicos, unam partem ad decorem reli-
quiarum uasorum ac ornamentorum ecclesie, cum omnia
magna diligencia acquisisset, conuertebat, alteram uero pro
necessitatibus suarum sororum, terciam uiduis orphanis leprosis
15 aliisque pauperibus occulte procurabat erogari, ut sic pondere
[Fol. 176 r.] terrenorum tamquam | gippo cameli deposito per angustam
portam paupertatis in eterna tabernacula & amplissimas celi
diuicias foret ydonea introire.

Denique annorum plurium labente curriculo post mortem
20 incliti domini regis Premisserii cognomento Ottakari, qui eam
non ut amitam sed ut matrem diligens honorabat et omnia
necessaria largiter ministrabat, deo permittente qui electos suos
in hoc mundo quandoque sinit egere, ut felici commercio pro
terrenis celestia & pro perituris recipiant se[m]piterna, tantam

---

[1] See note XI., p. 171.

"selig sind die armen, wann daz himelrich ist irer"—daz hat
die heilig junckfraw vnd disse furstin mit gar grosser begird
vnd mynn an sich genumen, daz sy nichtz zergenliches guttes
wolt haben noch begert zu haben hie vff erttrich durch die
mynn vnsers lieben herren, Jhesu Cristi, der auch in der 5
höchsten vnd strengesten armût leben wolt durch vnsren
willen all sein tag die er vff erttrich lebt.   Vnd es sant ir ein
erber man, der hiesz Johannes Gaytanus,¹ ein cardinal der sant
Claren ordens vnd der mynder bruder ordens pfleger was,²
wann er | waz dem orden gesetzt von dem heiligen vatter dem [Fol. 193 v.]
babst, der sant ir sein briff vnd bat sy gar flissiglichen vnd 11
reit ir mit vetterlicher truw, das sy vnd ir closter eigen vnd erb
solten haben durch meinger hand freiss vnd kumer vnd not
des lands, von mysswaschen vnd menger hand ander sach vnd
freiss.³   Do wider stund sy mit festem hertzen vnd gemût vnd 15
sprach, sy wolt ee von gepresten vnd von armût ee sterben e
dann sy sich wolt von der heiligen armut scheiden, von der
nachvolgung vnsren lieben herren Jhesu Cristi, der durch
vnsren willen wolt arm sein hie vff erttrich vnd wolt leben in
der strengen armut ; dem wolt sy nachvolgen vntz an iren tod. 20
Ir bruder der künig vnd ander fürsten santen ir dick gar
richlich vnd nützber almusen.   Daz heisz sy denn teillen in
try teil vnd hiesz sy geben, [*eyn teil*] zu dem gotz deinst vnd
altter gezieirt vnd zu andren gottes deinst ;⁴ daz ander teil
gab sy den schwestren zu ir notturft ; daz tryt teil hiesz sy 25
heimlichen geben weissen vnd wittwen vnd vssetzigen vnd
andren durftigen, mit dem sy den ewigen [*schatz*]⁵ in gottes rich
wolt gewinnen ; als auch der heilig sant Laurencius⁶ von dem
schatz der im | geben ward, den gab er durch gottes willen vnd [Fol. 194 r.]
gabs den dürfftigen vnd den armen.   30
    Nun geschach es darnach nit lang, daz ir bruder der
kunig starb vnd ward sein sunn kunig zu Beham nach im ;
der het sy lieb vnd ert sy nit als sein bassen, sunder er het sy

¹ See note XI., p. 171.   ² MS. reads " vnd schrib " deleted.
³ MS. reads " vnd kumer vnd not" deleted.
⁴ MS. adds "in hart " deleted.   ⁵ MS. " sachtz ".
⁶ See note XII., p. 172.

incurrit inopiam [1] ut uix alimenta & quibus tegeretur haberet, quod tamen cum maxima paciencia tolerauit. Quadam namque

[Fol. 176 r.] sexta feria cum | ad missam sedisset, sorores magnam debilitatem eius cernentes eam de pisciculis reficere cupiebant; sed
5 unde id facerent non habebant, grandi mesticia uexabantur. Quod cernens uirgo deo dilecta, palmas protendens in celum, dulcissime risit & pro tanta penuria dominum omnipotentem benedicens, sororibus dixit: "Laudate, filie, dominum quia pauperem uitam gerimus, & si paupertatem seruauerimus ut
10 debemus, non deseret nos dominus in tempore malo".[2] Et ecce deus tocius consolacionis desiderium pauperum exaudiuit et tante necessitati prodigio dignatiuo succurrit. Nam soror

[Fol. 176 v.] portaria pro quisbusdam negociis uadens ad rotam, per | quam res necessarie sororibus immittuntur, inuenit stantes in dicta
15 fenestra pisces fundulos nuncupatos, quibus ancilla Cristi libenter uescebatur, omnino secundum eius placitum preparatos. Quibus repertis pulsans rotaria, interrogans quis nam eos adtulisset, cui ne assignare deberet, nullum inuenit responsorem. Tandem cum magno gaudio eos Cristi famule
20 afferens, modum quo ipsos inuenerat enarrauit. At illa plus de miseracione diuina ex qua sorores in paupertatis proposito firmarentur quam de refeccione sui corporis agens gracias bonorum omnium largitori, in Cristo salutari suo domino exultauit.

---

[1] M., W. and B2. : "vnd der selb kunk Octagarus in solche armut fiel". The common German source Y1. evidently misunderstood this whole passage, representing the king as being the subject of it, instead of Bl. Agnes. Thus later: "Do die swester wolten zu tisch sizen vnd gedohten dez kungs grosse armut" !

[2] M., W. and B2. add: " er gibt vns hie genod vnd dort daz ewig leben ".

lieb als sein eigen mutter vnd gab ir alles daz, das sy vnd ir
closter bedorfft, die wil er lebt; aber darnach do er gestarb,
do verhengt got uber sy durch merung irs lons vnd vm ir
ewigen seligkeit vnd durch bewerung ir tugend vnd ir volkumenheit, daz sy in so grossen gepresten kam vnd armut, daz 5
sy fil kum ir bar notturfft mocht han an spisz vnd an gewand,
daz sy ir lebens natur da mit kom mocht hin bringen vnd kam
dick zu grosser kranckheit vnd armut, daz ir von armut ge-
prösten wolt sein, das sy nit zeleben het.   Vnd zu einem mal
da sy zu disch sasz, da ward sy gar kranck; da hetten ir die 10
schwestren geren kleine fiszlin geben oder etwas anders, da
mit sy sy möchten wider bringen; da enhetten sy ir nichtz
nit zu geben noch nichtz da mit sy ir wider möchten geholfen
han, vnd waren dar vmm ser betribt.   Da sy daz sach, die
gelybte gottes gema|hel vnd die edel furstin, da lachet sy gar [Fol. 194 v.]
frolichen vnd hůb ir hend vff gegen den himel vnd lobt got 16
von hertzen, da sy sellichen gepresten sach vnd armut,
vnd daz sy sellichen gepresten vnd armut solt durch gottes
willen lyden, vnd sprach denn zu den schwestren " Fil lieben
schwestren, loben i den ewigen got, der vns dar zu erwolt hat, 20
daz wir sellichen armut vnd gepresten sollent lyden vm vnszers
herren wyllen, der ouch vmm vnszern willen arm wolt sein vff
erttrich; vnd sind des sicher, beliben wir stet an der heiligen
armut, als wir sollent vnd als wir got gelopt hand, got
lat vns nymer".   Da det der milt got nach seiner gewon- 25
lichen gütte vnd erbermt, vnd trost die armen schwestren in so
strenger nott mit einem wunderlichen zeichen.   Da die weind
meisterin an die winden wolt gan, da man vss vnd in gibt
vnd verzichtet was man bedarf, da sach sy angefert in ein
fenster, da stunden cleine grindelin, wan die as sy geren, vnd 30
warent gar wol bereit nach allem iren willen.   Die porttnerin
wundret gar ser wer vyschlin [1] dar bracht het, oder wie sy dar
kumen werint vnd klopfet an der | winden vnd fraget.   Ir [Fol. 195 r.]
kund nemet dar von sagen, wer die vischlin [2] dar bracht
het oder wie sy dar werend kumen; da ward sy gar fraw vnd 35

---

[1] MS. " fislin " deleted.   [2] Ibid.

[Fol. 177 r.]   Alio tempore, cum fames ualida | regnum Bohemie premeret
uehementer, die quadam in monasterio sororum diuinis officiis
consumatis instabat hora prandendi, et nec unus panis habeba-
tur, unde famis periculo subueniri potuisset. Quo a dispen-
5 satrice comperto, fiduciam habens in domino ad oracionem
confugit, obsecrans ut misericors dominus qui aperiendo
manum suam implet omne animal benediccione, ancillis eciam
suis daret escam in tempore opportuno.[1]   Interea[2] soror hostiaria
pergit ad rotam, fratrem aliquem petitura ut pro sororibus per
10 auxilium panis acquiratur, de quo unaqueque saltem modicum
[Fol. 177 v.] quid accipiat ad malum inopie temperandum. Et apro|pinquans
rote inuenit eam candidissimis panibus plenam.   Quis autem
eos attulerit & ibi reposuerit, solus ille nouit qui nichil ignorat.
Credendum est sane illius uirtute panes predictos pro inclusis
15 Cristi uirginibus illuc fuisse repositos, cuius miranda potencia
Danieli intra lacum leonum incluso prandium ab Abacuc[3] est
allatum, cuiusque ineffabili prouidencia iumentis & uolucribus
indeficiens exuberat alimentum.[4]

DE GRAUI MACERACIONE CARNIS.

Qvanta rigiditate discipline felix hec uirgo castigauerit cor-
20 pus suum existens in habitu seculari, ex superioribus satis
claret.   Cum autem gradum regularis perfeccionis conscen-
[Fol. 178 r.] disset, | ut palmam spiritualis certaminis apprehenderet, primo
domesticum hostem gule uidelicet appetitum graui domabat
inedia, ut carnalia desideria que militant aduersus animam po-
25 testatiue reprimeret et carnem resipiscentem legi spiritus subiu-
garet.   Nam per plures annos in religione nullis leguminibus
usa est sed tantum cepe crudo, et aliquos fructus sumebat in
cibum, cupiens non uentrem cibo uoluptuoso sed mentem
pocius pabulo diuine gracie saginare.   Sanitatis quoque tem-

---

[1] MS. "opertuno".

[2] M., W. and B2. add: "als die heillig junkfraw sant angnes pet ".

[3] See note XIII., p. 172.

[4] M., W. and B2. add: "vnd auch gibt vnd keinerley arbet nit haben denn
allein der hymlisch vater der speist sy ".

bracht sy ir über den disch vnd seit ir, wie sy ir worden
werend. Do lobt sy vnsren lieben herren von hertzen dar
vmb vnd waz fil fröwer dar vmm, daz got die schwestren
gesterckt het mit dem zeichen der heiligen armut denn si
durch ir selbs willen von den vischen wurd gespist oder 5
getrost.[1]

Zu einer andren zit da waz grosses hungerjar über alles
kunigrich zu Behem, vnd da sy zu disch solten gan, da
en hetten sy in allem dem closter nit als fil als ein einiges
brot; da geng die schwester, der da daz bevolen waz zu ir 10
vnd bat sy daz sy vnseren herren bett, der die vogel spiset
in den lüfften vnd die tier in dem wald, daz der auch vns
arme kind well besorgen vnd für sehen. Vnder des, da die
schwester mit ir redt, da geng die portnerin an die winden,
daz sy einen bruder wolt vsz senden, der in brot precht, daz 15
doch eiglicher schwester etwas brottes wurd, do mit sy den
tag hin kumen mocht. Da die portnerin zu der winden kam,
da fand sy die winden vol des aller wissesten | vnd besten brotz [Fol. 195 v.]
daz iye gesechen ward. Wer daz brot dar bracht oder wie es
dar kem, daz weist der allein, der die seinen in notten nit lat. 20

DAS SECHST CAPITEL VON IRER STRENGEN KESTIGUNG IRES LEIBS.

Wie gar schwerlichen vnd strenglichen disse heiligen vnd
loblichen magt vnd junckfrawen sich selber kestiget, da sy noch
in weltlichem gewand waz, daz mag man dar an mercken,
wan da sy nun acht jar alt was, da vnder zoch sy ir selbs
alles daz das ir lustlichen möcht sein oder tröstlichen, es wer 25
an spisz oder an andren dingen vnd[2] den advend vnd die
gemeinen vasten der cristenheit übervastet sy all vss, daz sy
nit anders asz denn win vnd brot; vnd da sy dennocht vil
jung waz, da trůg sy ein hert herrin hemet an irem zarten
jungen lyb vnder kuniglichem gewand vnd gezeirt,[3] aber 30

---

[1] MS. adds " mit fiszen " deleted.
[2] MS. reads " vnd fastet in dē advend," etc., with " fastet " deleted and " in "
added in later hand.
[3] In MS. " ziert " written above.

pore in quadragesima communi [1] & quadragesima sancti Martini [2] quarta & sexta feria & ultimos dies ante quatuor festa
[Fol. 178 v.] uirginis gloriose | ac omnium sanctorum per anni circulum
in pane & aqua ieiunauit, ut ipsis suffragantibus ad gloriosam
5 ipsorum societatem pertingere mereretur. Sed nec defecto
ieiuniis corpusculo indulgebat, quin penas ipsius augeret et
graues apponeret cruciatus. Portabat cilicium de pilis equo-
rum nodose confertum quod eciam corda de consimili pilo
facta stringebat ad carnem. Teneros quoque artus ac
10 inbecillos flagello nodoso de corrigia facto dure frequencius
uerberabat. Non iam uestitu deaurato, ut regina, preful-
sit : non amiciebatur mollibus ut olim existens in domo
regia, que eciam tunc proposse uitabat ; sed ut pauper-
[Fol. 179 r.] rima Cristi serua utebatur contempto in|dumento, non ad
15 ornatum corporis sed ad nuditatis tegumentum, ut omnis
gloria filie regis esset ab intus in puritate consciencie &
decora uarietate uirtutum. Igitur propter magnam austerita-
tem diu patratam decor uultus eius deperiit, corporis uigor
emarcuit, oculi caligauerunt pre lacrimis et consumptis carnibus
20 ossa pelli coherebant. Sic dominice passionis sectabatur uesti-
gia, sic penalitates multimodas perferebat, cupiens pro tem-
poralis affliccionis amaritudine ad eterne consolacionis brauium
peruenire.

DE STUDIO ORACIONIS & MIRA DEUOCIONE IPSIUS ERGA
SACRAMENTUM ALTARIS.

[Fol. 179 v.]   Ignis deleccionis diuine, qui in ara cordis uirginei semper | ar-
25 debat, sic ipsam per iugem deuocionem sursum agebat ut inter

---

[1] M. and W. have nothing corresponding to "in quadragesima communi";
B2. "in der gemeinen vasten".

[2] See note XIV., p. 172.

darnach da sy zu geistlichem leben kam, do erdott sy gentzlichen an ir selb all lyplich gelust vnd begirt, die all zit
stritten sind vnd fechten wider den geist, vnd durch daz daz
sy ir selbs lib dar zu brecht, daz er dem geist vndertenig wer
vnd gehorsam. | Da waz sy vil jar in dem orden, daz sy [Fol. 196 r.]
gekochter spisz weder von schmaltz noch ander gekochet [6]
spisz wolt essen, sunder all zit ass sy nun rochen zibel vnd
knoploch vnd etlich ander rochen [1] frucht, daz sy da mit die
natur hin brecht mer dann daz sy von der spisz keinen lust
mocht haben.   Da sy gesund waz, so vastet sy all zit in der [10]
vasten vnd in sant Martins vasten [2] an der mitwochen vnd an
dem fritag zu wasser vnd brot vnd vor jeglichem hochzit
vnser lieben frawen auch zwen tag [3] vnd aller der heiligen die
durch daz jar sind, der abe[n]t vastet sy auch all zu wasser
vnd brot.   Sy trůg auch ein hert herrin hemet zu nechst an [15]
irem lib, daz waz gemachet vnd zusamen gestrickt mit grossen
hertten knoden vnd ross har, vnd daz selb hemmet gürt sy
vmm sich mit einem starcken seil auch von ross har gemacht,
daz man ir die knoden in irem lib sach.   Sy nam auch starck
vnd vngefug disciplin mit einer handgeisel, da warend gross [20]
knefp [4] an gemachet.   Die marter vnd daz liden | vnsers lieben [Fol. 196 v.]
herren lag an irem hertzen vnd in irer sel als ein mirren
büsselin; da von waz ir licht die liplich kestigung vnd pin,
die sy ir durch mynn irs gemyntten gemahels, Jhesu Cristi,
antůn mocht oder liden durch got.   Sy het sich selb dar zu [25]
bracht mit strenger abstinentz vnd pin, die sy von iren kind-
lichen tagen ir selb an getan het, daz ir kuniglich antzlitz vnd
farb verblichen vergangen waz, vnd das ir alles ires libes
kraft gentzlich engangen was, das sy kum der blossen hut hett
ob dem bein vnd warend ir ougen vnd ir gesicht von überigen [30]
weinen dunckel worden.

Das sibend capitel von irem gebet vnd von irer
andacht.

Das fur göttlicher mynn bran stettiglichen vff dem altar irs
megentlichen hertzen, daz sy auch krefftlichen vff zoch in got,

---

[1] MS. "spisz" deleted.   [2] See note XIV., p. 172.   [3] MS. "vor" deleted.
[4] So MS.; an unusual form for "knepf".

capedinem suum dilectum quereret, a quo pariete mortalitatis
seiuncta eidem vniri spiritu gestiebat. Secretum namque oratorium nacta, clauso ipsius hostiolo quasi continue solitaria
manebat, illis horis exceptis quibus eam communitati sororum
5 oportebat adesse. Ibi diuinis desideriis inardescens pennis
contemplacionis supra se leuabatur. Ibi lacrimarum fluentis
consciencie stratum rigabat, ibi oracioni perseueranter insistens
dulce ac familiare colloquium cum dilecto serebat. Contigit
enim aliquociens quod sorores, reditum eius ab oracione propter

[Fol. 180 r.] necessitatem aliquam circa oratorium | ipsius prestolantes, ipsam
11 ad dominum loquentem audirent, & quasi uirilem uocem
ualde suauem eidem perciperent respondentem. Quando uero
egrediebatur de oratorio, facies eius multociens sic lucebat
quod uix eam aliquis intueri ualeret, quia nimirum eterne
15 lucis radius, qui contemplantis mentem interius celesti claritate perfuderat, mirabili redundancia carnem exterius splen-
descere faciebat.[1]

Quadam denique sexta feria quodam nobili uiro ex parte
regis ad eam directo, una de sororibus nomine Benigna[2] que
20 sibi seruiebat ad oratorium ipsius cicius properauit ut eam ad
prefatum nuncium euocaret. Vt autem predictum oratorium

[Fol. 180 v.] latenter | intrauit, uidit eam totam mirabili claritate quasi nube
lucida circumdatam, propter quam faciem eius nullatenus
uideri potuit, sed effigiem tantum humani corporis in ipsa luce
utrumque conspexit. Qua uisione nimirum stupefacta silenter

---

[1] M., W. and B2. add : " als ein liehten stern ".
[2] M., W. and B2. : " Benignosa ".

wann all ir synn vnd irs hertzen begirt warend vff gericht zu
iren gemyntten, den sy all zit begeren was mit grosser begirt,
wann sy enscheit jetzunt nit anders von got denn die dynn
wand irs libs vnd das töttlich leben.   Sy hett ein heimlich vnd
ein sunder betthûsz, da was sy all zit inn, wann sy by der 5
gemeint nit solt sein oder von gehorsam nit anders | hett zu [Fol. 197 r.]
tûn, wann die gehorsam noch die gemein versumpt sy an
keinen dingen.   So sy denn in irem betthûsz was, so ergab sy
sich denn dem gebet[1] vnd der andacht also gar inerlichen, daz
sy mit begir vnd mit mynn enphlamet ward vnd in ir selb 10
erhaben ward über sich selb mit lütterer contenplacion vnd
vff gezogen.

Da wûsch sy vnd reinet ir concientz mit iren trehern, so
hett sy denn ein heimlich kossen mit irem gemynnten
gemahel.   Es ges[ch]ach[2] dick, so man ir bedorft vmm 15
etlich sachen, daz denn die schwestren vsswendig vor der tür
stonden vnd wartteten, wan sy selb her[ûsz][3] kam.   So
hortten sy, daz sy gar lieblichen vnd mynnklich redt mit
vnsrem herren vnd hortten auch denn gar ein lieblichen susse
stim, als ob ir vnser lieber her wider entwurt aller ir red ; 20
vnd wenn sy denn herûsz kam vnder die sch[w]estren, so
schin vnd licht ir antlitz mit als grossem liecht vnd wunderlicher clarheit, daz man sy kum mocht an sehen, wann daz
liecht der himelschlichen clarheit het ir hertz vnd sel innwen-
dig als krefftiglichen durchgangen vnd erlicht, daz es an iren 25
antlitz vss prach vnd schin mit wunderlicher clarheit.

Zu einem mal sant ir bruder der kunig einen | herren zu ir, [Fol. 197 v.]
der ir etlich bottschaft von seinen wegen solt sagen.   Da der
her dar kam, do geing ein schwester nach ir, die hiesz Benigna
vnd wolt heimlichen zu ir gan.   Da sy hin in kam, da sach 30
sy das sy ein himelsch liecht het vmmvangen oder vmbgeben,
vnd waz daz so gar starck vnd clar, daz sy ir nit anders mocht
gesehen denn als eins menschen bild enmitten in dem liecht.
Da die swester daz gesach, da erschrack sy vnmeslichen ser
vnd geng still schwigent wider vss vnd sprach zu dem herren, 35

---

[1] MS. " gebott ".   [2] MS. " gesach dich," " dich " being deleted.
[3] MS. " her hûsz ".

egreditur, dicens nuncio memorato quod eam in oracione
positam non presumeret impedire.

Alio tempore in die ascensionis domini cum duabus sororibus Benigna & Petrusca[1] in orto ultra chorum sororum horas
5 dicendo, in medio earum disparuit. Quibus pre stupore loqui
mutuo non audentibus, quasi post unius hore spacium in
eodem loco in quo prius steterat iterum repente apparuit. In-
[Fol. 181 r.] terrogata uero a sororibus predictis ubi fuisset, | dulciter quidem
risit, sed ad interrogatum non respondit. Credendum sane
10 est quod ascensiones uirtualium graduum in corde suo dis-
posuerat, & post Cristum ascendentem corde conscenderat ;
ideo eam diuina uirtus eciam corporaliter uehebat. Quadragesimali eciam tempore misteria redempcionis humane
ad memoriam crebrius reuocando, tanto suspendebatur deuo-
15 cionis excessu ut quasi continue celestibus inhians, magis
angelicam quam humanam inter homines ageret uitam. Dum
oracione consumata ueniebat aliquando ad sorores, quod tamen
erat satis rarum, non ociosum seu uanum aliquid ex eius ore
processit, sed flammea & mellica uerba de celestibus pro audien-
[Fol. 181 v.] cium edifica|cione promebat, uix ualens reprimere lacrimas &
21 singultus, cum de domino deo aliquid inter sorores diceret,
legeret uel audiret. Cuius moleste ferens hostis antiquus
sanctitatem, cum uice quadam ab oracione de loco in quo
circa unam fenestrulam quandoque legebat & orabat per
25 gradus descendere uellet, ipsam per dictos gradus precipitauit
sic grauiter, quod cubitus ipsius a iunctura debita separatus
magnum ei dolorem pluribus diebus inflixit. Quem diuini
amoris medicamine leniens, a sororibus quantum potuit occul-
tauit. Referam unum de multis quod uirtute oracionis eius
30 dominus operari dignatus est. Accidit quodam tempore ut
[Fol. 182 r.] filia fratris | sui domini regis infantula moreretur et ad monas-
terium in quo Cristi uirgo degebat causa sepulture deferretur.
Cumque uidisset dominam reginam matrem defuncte ploran-
tem, nimia compassione permota procidit in faciem suam

[1] M., W. and B2. : "die ein hiesz benignosa, die ander peters ". W. omits
names.

sy möcht im nit werden, sy wer an irm gebet vnd sy getürst
sy nit dar an geirren.   Zu einem andren mal an einem heiligen vffartag, do stond
sy by zwein swestren; eine hiesz swester Benigna vnd [*die
ander*] swester Petrosilia vnd sprachen ir zit mit ein ander;5
vnd da sy by ein stunden, da ward sy in genumen, daz sy nit
wustent wa sy hin kumen waz.   Da erschracken sy als ser,
daz keine zu der andren reden möcht von schrecken.   Dar
nach über lang ward sy wider[1] bracht an die selben stat
dannen sy genumen waz; da frageten sy sy, wa sy gewessen 10
wer; da lachet sy gar güttlichen, | sy wolt es aber in nit sagen [Fol. 193 r]
vnd hetten dar für, das sy mit andacht vnd mit begirt mit
vnszerm herren geistlich was uff[2] gefaren, das sy auch mit got
liplich vff gezogen ward.   Sy het sich dem gebet vnd der
andacht als gentzlichen vnd als inerlichen ergeben, daz sy 15
gewonlichen getrostet ward von got mit himelschlichen trost
vnd het me ein engelsch leben vff erttrich denn ein men-
schliches leben.   Vnd wenn sy denn von irem gebet kam
vnder die swestren, daz doch selten ges[*ch*]ach,[3] so warent ire
wort also hitzig vnd füren vnd so gar süss vnd honigflissig, 20
daz alle die getrost vnd gebessert wurden, die sy hortten.   Vnd
wann sy von got redt, so mocht sy sich von weinen vnd
süffetzen nit enthalten.   Des mocht der tüffel nit geliden so
grosser andacht, vnd da sy zu einer zit stund an einem hohen
fenster, da sy gewonlich bettet, vnd her ab wolt gan, do hub 25
sy der tüffel vff vnd warf sy von dem obersten grat herab, das
ir ein grin verenckt ward vnd ir des armes geleich[4] vss der
stat kam, vnd daz sy lang zit grosse pin vnd arbeit leid, vnd
verhellignet doch daz, so sy ymer meist mocht, vnd en wolt | [Fol. 198 v.]
kein artzney noch hilf dar zu dün, sunder sy wolt es lyden 30
durch got als lang er wolt.   Vnser her tett grosse vnd wunder-
liche ding, der ich nun eins hie will schriben.   Es geschach

---

[1] MS. " sy zu ir selb kumen " deleted.
[2] MS. originally read "mit begirt mit was uff gefaren". A second hand
has added in margin after " mit " "vnszerm herren geistlich" and also after
" uff " " vnsern herren ". The latter addition appears superfluous.
[3] MS. reads " gesach ".
[4] MS. reads " geliech " with " geleich " above it.

iuxta feretrum & orando sub silencio cepit dicere istud responsorium " Qui Lazarum resuscitasti & cetera ".[1] Et ecce exanime corpus & frigidum subito cepit calere et uene ut in uiuentibus mouebantur. Anima uero defuncte uirginem 5 Cristi orantem sic allocuta est " Cur me reuocas de gaudio in exilium & miseriam? Scito, si hoc feceris, nec parentibus meis nec ulli uiuenti fieri umquam potero in solamen."[2] Quod [Fol. 182 v.] audiens | uirgo dei orare pro ipsius resuscitacione destitit, et statim corpusculum, quod calore & motu uenarum uiuentem 10 premonstauerat, ad frigiditatem pristinam reuersum est. Et sic in uno eodemque facto uirtus oracionis humilis que nubes penetrauerat & condescensio dei benigna qua se ad suorum uota dignanter inclinat et orantis discrecio claresceret euidenter.

Circa sacramentum altaris hec uirgo preclara mira deuocione 15 flagrabat. Quando enim communicare uolebat, ab aliis sororibus sequestrata se oracionibus & meditacionibus deuotissime preparabat. Per unam fenestram sui cubiculi ad hoc paratam [Fol. 183 r.] corpus Cristi sumebat pluribus annis, | nolens palam facere diuine uisitacionis ac sue interne consolacionis secreta. Ibi 20 enim sciebat ut apicula mel dulcissime diuinitatis de petra & humanitatis oleum de saxo durissimo pregustare. Cum autem semel graui infirmitate detenta de uita corporali desperans, ad degustacionem inmaculati agni secundum morem solitum preparata deuotissime accessisset, auditu mirabili audiuit ad se 25 dicere illud quod sumebat dominicum corpus " Agnes, nequaquam putes te morituram, donec pene omnes caros tuos uideris ex hac uita migrasse ". Quam reuelacionem ut audiuerat prouinciali ministro[3] & aliquibus aliis personis sub specie [Fol. 183 v.] magni secreti | reserauit. Et ita factum esse rerum secutarum 30 probauit euentus.

---

[1] See note XV., p. 172.

[2] M., W. and B2. : " Wisz daz das du mich wider rufft vnd du es tust daz ich weder vater noch muter noch keinem menschen der lebendig ist nit anders denn betrubt vnd traurig wird vnd nymant mich da von mag erwegen vnd ich ewiklich nymer die weil ich leb in keinerley freud gesezt wird ".

[3] See note XVI., p. 172.

zu einem zyten daz irm bruder dem kunig ein kind starb,
ein töchterlin, daz ward ir tod bracht zu irem closter, daz
man es wolt begraben; vnd da sy sach das sich des kindes
muter als gar übel gehůb vnd so grossen jamer het, do
erbarmet es sy als ser, daz sy by der bar nider kuuwet vnd 5
bat stillschwigen für daz tod kind.   Zu hand ward daz kind
lebendig vnd die sel kam wider zu den lib vnd sprach daz
kind zu ir, "O we, was wilt du důn, daz du mich von als
grosser fröd scheidest vnd mich her wider bringest zu als
grosser jamerkeit.   Du solt wissen, tůst du daz, das ich lebidig 10
belib, daz all mein frund noch du noch kein mensch trost
noch lieb an mir nymer geleben noch gesehen mag."   Do
sy daz hort von dem kind, do liesz sy ab von irem gebet
vnd starb daz kind wider als vor.   Hie merckent wie gar
gross die krafft irs gebetz was, daz an einer stat daz tod kind 15
lebendig ward von irem gebet vnd da wider starb von irem
gebet; also merck auch die wunderliche gnad | vnd güttin [Fol. 199 r.]
gottes, der die seinen mit trüwen meinet vnd mynnet[1] vnd
inen so gar bereit vnd gehorsam ist.

All ir begird vnd gebett waz gen vnsers lieben herren 20
fronlichnam, wann sy den mit grosser andacht dick enpfeng
vnd mit grosser begird, vnd ward auch dick grösslich vnd
wunderlich von got getrost mit sunderlicher gnad vnd süs-
sigkeit die ir denn wider für, so sy vnsers lieben herren fronlichnam enpfeng.   Zu einem mal ward sy siech vntz vff den 25
tod, daz sy selb vnd all ir swestren vnd die lüt an ir verzwifflet hetten.   Do enpfeing sy vnsren lieben herren, wann sy
wand sy welt sterben, vnd do sy jetzunt vnsers herren fronlichnam enpfeng, do sprach vnser lieber her von dem sacrament zu ir "Angnes, du stirbest nit vntz daz du vil nach all 30
dein fründ überlebest" Das seit sy dem provincial[2] gar heimlichen vnd ettlichen andren iren schwestren vnd frunden, vnd
es geschach daz sy nach all ir frund überlebt.

---

[1] MS, "so gar bereit" crossed out.   [2] See note XVI., p. 172.

DE FERUIDO AMORE PASSIONIS & CRUCIS CRISTI.

Passionem et crucem domini Agnes fidelis eius ancilla
feruentissime diligebat & singulis sextis feriis circa cruci-
fixionem ipsius occupata, deuocionem suam usque in horam
nonam continuabat, stando pedibus affeccionis cum mestra
5 matre Jhesu iuxta crucem et dolorose mortis eius cernendo
supplicium, mentis obtutibus pre nimietate compassionis eius
oculus in amaritudinibus morabatur. Hanc preciosam crucem
baiulare propter Ihesum fidei sue brachiis & uirtutum, quoad uiueret non cessabat. Hec enim erat sue gloriacionis tytu-
[Fol. 184 r.] lus, hec | scala ascensionis in deum, hec lassitudinis eius suaue
11 reclinatorium. Hoc ligno salutifero[1] cunctos suos labores &
graues infirmitates aduersitatesque multimodas quas innocenter
pertulit, uelut aquas Marath dulcorabat. Hoc suco mirifico
languidis medelam prestabat et peruicacia demonum propel-
15 lebat, & ut de aliis taceam, pauca nunc succincte retexam.

Quedam nobilis domina, Sophya nomine, coniunx cuiusdam militis Prage qui Cunradus uocabatur, ante fores monasterii in quo famula dei morabatur residebat. Contigit autem

---

[1] The common German source Y1. must have misunderstood the Latin, making
this refer to Our Lord, instead of Bl. Agnes. Thus M., W. and B2.: "Mit dem
heilsamen heilligen holz des kreuzs hat der ewig got all sein arbet vnd auch swer
siechtagen . . . im selber susz gemacht," at which point M. and W. stop, having
nothing corresponding to "uelut aquas Marath". But B2. adds "als die wasser
Marath".

VEN DER MIN VND ANDACHT DIE SY ZÜ VNSZERS LIEBEN
HERREN MARTTER HET.   DAS [VIII] CAP.[1]

Die martter vnd den tod vnsers lieben herren hett disse
heilige vnd selige junckfraw gar innerlichen vnd krefftiglichen
zu hertzen geleit vnd übet | auch sich auch gewonlichen vnd [Fol. 199 v.]
flissiglichen darin vsswendig vnd inwendig mit meinigvaltiger
strenger pin vnd marter, die sy ir selb lyb an tet inwendig an 5
dem hertzen mit innerlicher mitlydung vnd mit emssiger
betrachtung seines lydens vnd seiner pin vnd aller meist sein
übermessige mynn, die in dar zu bracht, daz er so verschmecht lyden durch vns wolt han.   Vnd von über flyssiger
betrachtung ward sy dick innerlichen vnd süssigklichen von 10
got getrostet vnd geistlichen gespist.   Sy macht ir selber an
dem frytag einen karfrytag, daz sy denn die nacht über vnd
morgens allen den tag vntz gegen nun zit in stetten mitlyden
was mit vnsrem lieben herren in allen seinen lyden vnd in
ieglichen sunderlichen.   Sy half im sein crutz tragen mit den 15
armen ir begird vnd andacht.   Sy stund vnder dem crutz mit
seiner liebe[n] verweisten müter Maria ; sy half ir mit truwen
ires hertzen leid[2] klagen alles daz lyden ires kindes.   Sy
stund mit ir vnder dem crutz vnd het vil manig trurig angesicht
vff gegen vnsren lieben herren, der ir gegenwirttig hieng vor ir 20
an dem heiligen crutz.   Da sy zu geistlichen | leben kam, da waz [Fol. 200 r.]
ir die martter vnd daz lyden vnsers lieben herren ein anfang,
es waz ir ein vffgang an tugenden vnd an aller heiliger übung.
Sy was ein süsser trost vnd zuversicht vnd senfte rüw vnd
zuflucht allen deinen die in notten vnd arbeit hertzen vnd 25
lybs sind.   Sy vertreib mit dem zeichen des heiligen crütz die
tüffel vnd nert fil siechen, die zeichen, die ich doch alle vnder
wegen wil lossen vnd wil nun kürtzlich ettliche hie schriben.[3]

Es was ein ritter der het ein frawen die genas eines
kindes, vnd nach der geburt ward sy als kranck vnd als gar 30
übel mygent, daz all lütt an ir verzwiffelt hetten, vnd lag fil tag

[1] MS. "das IX. cap." which is wrong ; see note I., p. 169.
[2] MS. "tragen" deleted.
[3] VON ETTLICHEN ZEICHEN DIE SY BEY IREM LEBEN TET DAS X. CAP.   These
words form a heading in the MS., but B1. shows that no chapter heading is needed
here.

dominam memoratam quadam uice post puerperium in tantum
[Fol. 184 v.] debilitari, quod per plures dies nec cibum nec potum | gustans,
magis mortui hominis preferret effigiem quam uiuentis. Et
ecce quadam die quasi mentis excessum paciens cepit loqui
5 dicens "O si Agnes domina mea unum mihi pomum de manu
sua tribueret ad uescendum!" Fuerat temporibus multis
uirgini Cristi deuota. Conradus uero maritus eius, confidens
quod meritis alme uirginis coniunx eius adipisci possit sanitatem optatam, festinauit ad famulam dei, rogando flebiliter ut
10 pro sua coniuge intercedere ad dominum & ei pomum vnum
mittere dignaretur, asserens si ista fierent, consors eius cupitam
recuperaret sospitatem. At illa que super afflictos miserie
[Fol. 185 r.] uisceribus affluebat, militis merori compaciens | ad pomerium
monasterii celeriter transiuit; & nichil de pomis tam ipsa quam
15 sorores que eam secute fuerant in arbore ad quam declina-
uerant cernentes, signo autem mirifice crucis contra arborem
facto cum inuocacione beatissime trinitatis, tria poma vni
ramisculo coherencia conspexit, eaque festine carpens, memorate domine Sophye misit dicens, "Hec poma tibi a deo
20 miraculose donata secure commedas, quia ex eis prestante
domino non tantum corporis sed & anime percipies sanitatem". Reuertitur uir eius gaudens, ferens antidotum salutare,
et inuocato Cristi nomine ori coniugis fidenter apposuit. Que
[Fol. 185 v.] uirtutem dei pomis collatam senciens, continuo | attollens oculos
25 & poma predicta rapiens, tam auide cepit commedere ac si
nunquam infirmata fuisset. Sicque factum est ut uirtute sancte
crucis & meritis Agnetis pristine reformaretur sanitati; et
aliquibus temporibus interpositis, mortuo marito suo, sub
uiduitatis habitu domino seruiens in castitate, cunctorum pau-
30 perum per opera miserie mater effecta, uberiorem mentis, ut
uirgo dei predixerat,[1] obtinuit santitatem.

Alio tempore una de soribus monasterii eius, Elyzabeth
Azehmkonis[2] nuncupata, ob uehementem dolorem capitis de-
cumbebat, racione cuius nec caput mouere nec sursum respi-
[Fol. 186 r.] cere nec cibum nec potum | per triduum gustare ualebat.

---

[1] M., W. and B2. have nothing equivalent to "ut . . . predixerat".
[2] Name "Azehmkonis" omitted in M., W. and B2.

on essen vnd trincken vnd on reden vnd fur halb tod; vnd
eines tages da ward sy reden vnd sprach "O we, sante mir mein
fraw Angnes einen aphel, den sy in iren henden het gehebt,
ich genes aller ding!" Zehand[1] lief der rytter, der frawen
man, selb zu dem closter vnd bat die liebe junckfrawen sant 5
Angnes, daz sy seiner frawen einen aphel sant, den sy selber
in ir hand hett gehept.   Da geng sy selb in den bom gartten,
ob sy ir nenet keinen | aphel do mocht vinden, den sy der [Fol. 200 v.]
siechen frawen senden möcht.   Da fand weder sy noch alle ir
swestren in allem dem gartten keinen aphel.   Da kert sy sich 10
gegen einem[2] böm vnd macht ein crütz gegen dem bom vnd
riefft die heiligen trivaltigkeit an.   Zu hand do erschinen dry
ephel neben ein ander gegen ir, die prach sy ab vnd sant sy
der siechen frawen vnd enpot ir, daz sy die ephel ess, sy
werend ir wunderlich von got worden, von den selben[3] ephlen 15
solt sy genessen vnd gesund werden an sel vnd lyb von dem
gnaden vnsers herren.   Da für der ritter frölich wider heim
zu seiner frawen vnd leit ir die ephel in den mund; zu hand
det sy die ögen vff vnd tet als ein mensch der von einer andren
wölt komen wer, vnd ward essen vnd trincken vnd redt vnd 20
genas aller ding.   Dar nach über on lange jar starb ir der
man, vnd nach seinem tod blyb sy ein wittwe vnd dienet
vnsren lieben herren vntz an iren tod in keisheit vnd ward ein
demüttige vnd ein milte müter aller armen lütten mit den
wercken der barmhertzigkeit. | [Fol. 201 r.]
Es was ein[4] schwester in irem closter die hiesz Elysabet, 26
die het einen schweren siechtag vnd pinlich wee in irem hopt,
daz sy try tag was on essen vnd on trincken vnd mocht ir
hopt nit geregen noch erheben noch vff gesehen.   Do ward sy
zu sant Angnessen bracht; da sy ir grossen nott vnd arbeit 30
ersach, do erbarmet es sy gar ser, wann sy het ein süszes
vnd miltes hertz gegen allen denen die in lyden vnd arbeiten
hertz vnd libs warend, vnd macht ir ein crütz über ir hopt vnd
für ir stirnen vnd nam ir hopt düch von irem hopt vnd wand

---

[1] MS. repeats "zehand" deleted.   [2] MS. reads "gartten" deleted.
[3] MS. "tagen" deleted.   [4] MS. reads "es" for "ein".

Tandem per unam de sororibus ad uirginem Cristi difficulter adducta, cognita ipsius passione, deposito de capite suo albo uelo, infirme sororis caput iussit uelo predicto diligenter uelari & signum crucis saluificum tam capiti quam fronti pacientis 5 inpressit. Quibus gestis illico dolor omnis cessauit.

Vna uice ad oratorium suum properans uirgo Cristi per sororem Donikam Deszquotz[1] racione debilitatis sustentata est. Cumque ad ostium dicti oratorii peruenisset, uidit cum sorore prefata per fenestram eiusdem oratorii angelum tene-
10 brarum in humana specie horribili & distorta sub quadam
[Fol. 186 v.] arbore stantem, et | quasi eidem arbori se appodiantem. Ex- clamauit autem memorata soror pre timore, sed famula dei ne timeret eam confortans, signum sancte crucis contra demonem edidit in nomine deifice trinitatis. Qui uirtutem crucis non 15 ferens, protinus ualde celeriter discessit.

Alia uice innixa cognate sue domine sorori Elyzabeth im- peratrici[2] ad supradictum oratorium uadens, cum iam ultra limen calcare uellet, hostis malignus in specie bubonis ap- parens, antedicta sorore uidente, [initum][3] ipsius cauda sua 20 impedire uisus est. Que facto signo crucis dominice cruen- tam bestiam mox fugauit. Digne reuera sancte crucis uirtute
[Fol. 187 r.] mira faciebat, que innocentissimi | agni in ipsa pro nobis ymolati passionem iugiter in corde portabat.

De multa karitate ipsius erga sorores & alios quoscumque afflictos.

Karitatem qua uirgo Cristi proximos prosequebatur effec- 25 tus apercius declarauit. Deficientibus namque uiribus eius pre nimietate abstinencie, cum de uoluntate domini pape & precepto suorum superiorum oporteret eam licet inuitam necessaria uite plus solito percipere, de illis que sibi pro releua- amine debilitatis corpusculi mittebantur, debilibus & infirmis

---

[1] M. and W.: "die swester dronikam". B2., failing to recognise name, " die swester die sie an kom "!
[2] M. and W.: "frawen elspeten swester der kungin". B2.: "die swester elysabet die kungin". See note XVII., p. 172.
[3] MS. "inter".

es der schwester vmm ir hopt.   Da genas sy zu hand vnd stillt
alles ir we.

Zu einem mal fûrt sy ein schwester in ir kamer, wann sy
was gar kranck, vnd da sy in die kamer kam, da sach sy zu
einem fenster vss vnd sach den tüffel vnder einem böm stan 5
vnd hett sich an den bom geleinet, vnd waz ruch vnd gerump-
fen vnd als gar erschrockenlichen gestalt, daz die schwester
als ser erschrack, daz sy von schrecken schrien ward.   Da trost
sy die lieb schwester Angnes, daz sy sich nit solt förchten, er
wurd ir neitz dûn vnd | machet ein crutz gegen dem tüffel vnd [Fol. 201 v.]
zu hand verschwand er vnd kam von dem böm.   11

Zu einem [1] zitten da fûrt sy ir nechsten fründin, schwester
Elysabet, die keisserin [2] in ir kamer, wan sy kranck was, vnd do
sy über die schwellen wolt tretten, do waz der tüffel do in
eines hundes gelichnus vnd irt sy, daz sy nit mocht in gan. 15
Do tett sy ein crutz gegen im, zu hand mûst er dannen flüchen.
Sunst dett sy gar vil zeichen vnd wunder mit dem zeichen des
heiligen crütz, wann sy trûg den tod vnd die martter vnsers
lieben herren in irem hertzen, den er durch vnser willen lyden
wolt an dem crutz.   Da von waz nit wunder, daz sy auch 20
gewaltig grossz wunder vnd zeichen zu dûn mit dem zeichen
des heiligen crutz.

[DAS NEUNT CAPITEL]

VON DER LIEBIN DIE SY ZU DEN SCHWESTERN HET.

Sye het ein mynsam miltes vnd getrüwes hertz gegen den
schwestren vnd gegen allen lütten, vnd do sy von strenger
vnd hertter langer abstinentz vnd martter dar zu waz kumen, 25
daz ir der lib vnd ires lybes nattirlichen krafft gar vergangen
was vnd verdorben, da ward sy gezwungen von dem babst
vnd auch von irem prelaten daz sy ir da selbs genediglicher
mûst dûn dann ir gewonheit was an spis vnd an andren
dingen.   Daz doch wider alles ires hertzen willen waz ; dann 30
daz sy mit gehorsam dar zu gezwungen ward, so sant man ir
vnder | weillen gûtte wol bereitte spis, dar mit man ir wider [Fol. 202 r.]

[1] MS. " mal " deleted.   [2] See note XVII., p. 172.

sororibus prouideri faciebat. Ipsasque sepissime personaliter
uisitans, de omnibus eorum necessitatibus sollicitam curam
[Fol. 187 v.] gessit. Et quemadmodum gallina | pullos suos sub alis, sic
amplissimo miseracionis sinu materne eas & dulciter con-
5 fouebat. Circa uniuersos indigentes misericors & larga, sibi
uero nimium parca & rigida. Esuriens pascebat alios, et ore
pallente ieiuniis aliena fame torquebatur. Super omnes eciam
afflictos, tam in seculo quam in religione degens, compassiuam
mentem gerebat et cunctos ad se recurrentes aput deum &
10 homines piis remediis adiuuabat. Nam fugitiuos & incarceratos
pristine libertati reddebat, morte pro suis demeritis plectendos
uel quibuslibet suppliciis cruciandos liberabat, diffidentes con-
[Fol. 188 r.] cordabat, omnibusque ad uotum proposse | succurrens. Tanta
quippe pietate cor eius omnipotens deus repleuerat, ta[n]tam gra-
15 ciam in labiis diffuderat, ut non solum gauderet cum gaudenti-
bus & fleret cum flentibus, sed & si quempiam quacunque ex
causa dolor angebat, si urgebat calamitas, si aduersitas quem-
cunque frangebat, mulcedine dulcis eloquii omnium erat meren-
cium consolatrix. Si quando sororem aliquam corripiendam
20 censebat de aliquo, nequaquam silencio culpam supprimebat,
sed ut amatrix salutis proximorum, cum magna karitate ac
maturitate id agebat, illas seuerius arguens quas amplius diligere
uidebatur. Cum autem sororem correptam sanctis sermonibus
[Fol. 188 v.] ad bonum erudisset, | ad pedes eius humiliter se prosternens
25 dicebat. "Ignosce mihi, soror dilecta, si te in aliquo contris-
tam". Magno quippe cauebat studio, ne sororem aliquam &
maxime indebite perturbaret. Pro excessibus quoque ali-
quorum hominum de profundo cordis graues emittebat rugitus,
plus eorum lapsum spiritualem quam consanguineorum suorum
30 carorum mortem amaris lacrimis deplorando. Merito gaudio
dominus omnium eam dilexit, que tam sincere proximos
diligebat.[1]

---

[1] M.: "als leuterlich irn nehsten menschen in got als lieb het vnd durch
got". W. and B2. read similarly, but omitting "vnd durch got".

hült; der behůb sy vil lytzel vnd dick nütz über al vnd hiesz
sy andren siechen mit teilen, beiden in dem closter vnd andren
siechen. Sy kam dick selber zu den siechen vnd zu den
krancken vnd trost sy vnd stercket sy in iren arbeiten vnd
siechtagen mit süssen wortten vnd nützer ler vnd besorget 5
sy an irer notturft als fil sy mocht, als ein getruwe vnd milte
muter iren kinden důt. Sy waz milt vnd barmhertzig gegen
allen lütten aber, ir selbs waz sy gar streng vnd hert an
allen dingen. Alle die in notten [1] vnd arbeiten waren, es wer
an liblichen oder geistlichen vrsachen, der hilf an sy sucht, 10
den kam sy zu hilf gegen got vnd allen lutten, wann ir het
got gar ein süsz hertz geben, daz sy mitliden mit allen
menschen het, die in arbeitten hertzen oder libs warend, noch
do sy in wöltlichen leben was vnd auch in geistlichen. Got
het auch iren wortten so grosse gnad vnd kraft [2] geben vnd 15
warend ire wort vnd ir red so gar süss, daz alle die do besch-
wert vnd vngetrost zu ir komen, die schieden frolich vnd wol
getrost von ir, daz sy aun trost neimen liesz von ir scheiden.
Geschach es ettwen, daz ein schwester lichtfertig was, daz
strafber was, daz liesz sy niemer aun ιstraffung vnd besserung 20
hin gan. Sy straft es strenglichen vnd bessert es genug-
samigklichen mit muterlicher trüw vnd mynn vnd doch mit
grosser bescheidenheit nach der masz der schuld, vnd straft
die aller herttest, die man wand die ir die aller liebsten | [Fol. 202 v.]
werend; vnd so sy es denn getett, so fiel sy denn der selben 25
schwester zů füssen nider vff die erden vnd sprach "Fil liebe
schwester, vergib mir, han ich dich mit keinen dingen be-
schwert". Wann sy verschmecht niement der in sünd gefalen
waz oder sunst in sunden oder schweren gepresten waz, da von
hett sy als gross hertzleid vnd weinet vnd klaget des menschen 30
selen schaden, daz es was ir denn schwerrer, wenn werend·all
ir frund tod vor ir gelegen. Sy mynt gott von hertzen, wann
er mynt sy auch vnd alle die selen, die er mit sinem tod vnd
mit seinem myniglichen blut so gar tür gekofft [3] vnd ernar-
net hat.

35

---

[1] MS. "warent" deleted.   [2] MS. "krarft".   [3] MS. "hat" deleted.

DE REUELACIONIBUS DIUINIS SIBI FACTIS.

Nec hoc dignum uidetur silencio contegi, quod occulta &
absencia tamquam manifesta et presencia eo docente sciebat,
[Fol. 189 r.] qui revelat abscondita & profunda. | Cum enim filius fratris
sui dominus rex Premisserius,[1] dictus Ottakarus, ad bellum in
5 Austriam contra Rvdolfum,[2] regem Romanorum processisset,
sorores cum ligno sancte crucis & aliis reliquiis ambitum suum
processionaliter sepe girantes, psalmos penitenciales pro salute
dicti regis domino deuote promebant.   Quadam autem die in
processione cum aliis sororibus transeundo, uidit memoratum
10 regem grauiter uulneratum et duos uiros statura proceros eum
inter se ducentes.   Quam uisionem sororibus referens, ludifi-
cacionem demonum fore putabat, indignam se asserens ut talia
sibi diuinitus panderentur.   Eo autem tempore hec uisio erat
[Fol. 189 v.] suis | aspectibus presentata, quo prefatus rex ab inimicis uulner-
15 atus tentus & interfectus est.   Sic rerum series et ueritas &
narrancium postea declarauit.

Alio tempore ancille domini ex parte cuiusdam secularis
persone poma pulcra uisu per unam de sororibus transmissa
sunt.   At illa concupiscencia oculorum deuicta unum pomum
20 pro se seruauit & tandem, urgente consciencia, iterum reponens
omnia ut sibi missa fuerant presentauit.   Quam cum deo
dilecta uirgo fuisset intuita, pomum quod dicta soror concupie-
rat cum alio tollens porrexit ei dicens "Bene fecisti, filia,[3]
pomum reponendo: melius est enim tibi habere duo poma
[Fol. 190 r.] ab|sque scrupulo consciencie quam unum cum peccato".[4]
26 Vtique spiritus Helysei requieuerat in Agnete, que gesta
quibus corporaliter aberat, spiritu presens uidebat.

Alia soror, nomine Ermengardis[5] Parua, pro quodam ne-

---

[1] Name omitted by M., W. and B2.   See note XVIII., p. 173.
[2] M. and W.: "wider den romischen kunk," omitting both "in Austriam"
and "Rudolfum".   B2.: "wider den reinischen (!) chuning".
[3] M. and W. leave out translation of "filia"; B2. "tochter mein".
[4] M., W. and B2.: "denn vil mit beswerung der sund".   Probably Latin
original had "multa" instead of "unum" as B1.
[5] M. and B2.: "Ermgardis".   W. omits name.   "Parua": B2. takes this as
an adjective: "Ez was auch ain cleinen swester".   M. and W. "ein andere
swester".

[DAS ZEHENT CAPITEL]

VON DEN OFFENBARUNGEN DIE IR GOT THET.

Sy was so gar grosser heiligkeit vnd lütterkeit des hertzen
vnd mynt got so hertzenklichen von iren kintlichen tagen,
daz sy auch von got grosselichen gemynt ward, als er dick
schinberlichen erzeigt vnd ir zu erkennen gab.   Ir ward fil
heimlicher ding vnd verborgner ding von got kunt gethan; [5]
kunftige ding die sach sy vor, als weren sy geschehen.   Da
der künig von Beheim, der ires bruder sun was, zu stryt für [1]
wider den künig Rudloff den romschen kunig, da warnet [2] sy
in vor, daz er es nit tett, vnd tett er es, er wurd siglos.   Da
wolt er nit ablasen, vnd do sy zu stryt komen wider ein [10]
ander, da ward ir ein gesicht von got vnd sach das er wund
was worden vntz vff den tod vnd das in zwen schon herren
furtten [3] zwischen in.   Disse gesicht seit sy den schwestren
vnd erfand sich darnach, daz er da erschlagen vnd siglos was
worden. | [15]

Ain schwester bat zu einem zitten vnsren lieben herren [Fol. 203 r.]
vmm ein sach vnd tett gar fil gebetz vmm die selben sach, vnd
doch als gar heimlich, das neimen da von nit wust denn sy
vnd got; vnd zu einem mal kam sy zu ir vnd do sy sy gesach,
do sprach sy zu ir "Fil liebe schwester, lasz ab zu bytten [20]

---

[1] See note XVIII., p. 173.
[2] MS. "warend" with "warnet" written above.
[3] MS. "under" deleted.

gocio multas ad dominum occultissime preces fundebat.
Quam cum ancilla dei die quadam fuisset intuita, cum aliqua
seueritate dixit ei "Preces quas anxie pro tali negocio fundis
ad dominum multiplicare desiste, quia id pro quo postulas
5 deo non est acceptum!"

In obitu quoque sororum quibus conuixit pia miseracione
solebat semper adesse, & ibidem pro ipsis diuinam clemenciam
[Fol. 190 v.] suppliciter implorando, penas aliquarum & merita | frequenter
per spiritum intellexit. Vno enim tempore soror quedam,[1]
10 famula dei absente,[2] uerba contumelie protulerat & sine satis-
faccione condigna tempore aliquo interposito ex hac uita
migrauit. Cum autem uirgo dei sola in oracione die quadam
persisteret, audiuit iuxta oratorium suum animam sororis
uociferantem, recognoscendo humiliter culpam suam, et ob-
15 nixius flagitando ut sibi talem culpam propter deum ignos-
cere dignaretur, quasi a penis aliter liberari nequiret.[3]

Alia soror nomine Brigida,[4] que cum uirgine cristi religionem intrauerat, morum honestate pollebat et erat eidem
[Fol. 191 r.] ualde dilecta. Cumque post plures annos in ordine | laudabili-
20 ter transactos grauiter egrotaret & tandem ex hac uita migrasset, de infirmitate eius quidem multum doluit, sed pro morte
ipsius nullum mesticie signum ostendit. Viderat enim sanctos
angelos eidem assistentes, corpus eius thurificare et humanita-
tem sibi multam exhibere. A multis denique notatum est
25 quod quecunque uentura fore predixit, eciam post magni temporis decursum modo et ordine quo dixerat euenisse certitu-
dinaliter probata sunt, sicut de aliquibus infra patebit. Mens
quidem eternitatis repleta spiritu, cui nichil est preteritum,
nichil futurum, cuique omnia nuda sunt & aperta, non solum
[Fol. 191 v.] abdita sciebat cordium & actuum, uerum | eciam de futuris
31 quasi de presentibus uel de preteritis certissime disserebat.

---

[1] MS. adds "de".

[2] M., W. and B2. add: "vnd in gehaym an irm pet was".

[3] B1. has evidently lost the end of this story, which is supplied by M., W. and B2.: "Do sah sant angnes in dem geist daz der swester wart geben von got das ewig leben von dem sprechen der schuld".

[4] The name Brigida was either unfamiliar or corrupt in Y. For M. gives "pridavum," W. "prugda," B2. "bendit".

vmm die sach dar vmm du got gebetten hast, wann die sach
gefelt got nit, noch ist nit sein will ".

Wenn ein schwester sterben solt vnd an den tod lag, so
was sy allzit by in vnd bat denn gar begirlichen vnsren lieben
herren für die sterbente schwester, das ir got zu hilf köm in 5
iren nötten, vnd erkant auch denn dick wöliches lones vnd
wölicher wirdigkeit die schwester vor got was, die denn sterben
solt. Nun was ein schwester in dem closter, die was mit ir
in den orden komen vnd het fil gar in dem orden hertiglichen
vnd loblichen gelept vnd vnsren lieben herren mit grossen 10
flisz vnd ernst gedienet. Da die sterben solt, do was sy by ir
nach ir gewonheit, als sy all zit dett wenn ein schwester
sterben solt. Da sach sy die heiligen engel komen zu der
schwester end vnd trosten sy vnd dienetten ir mit flisz. Disz
ward man innen vnd mercknet man es an fil sachen, daz ir fil 15
heimlicher vnd verborgner ding von got geoffnet worden, als
man hernach vindet geschriben; vnd daz über fil jar vnd
über langen zit geschehen solt. Daz kunt sy vor vnd seit es
in alle die weisz, als es darnach geschach vnd ergeng.

De transitu eius & hiis que in eo facta sunt.

Apropinquante autem termino quo ancillam suam Agnetem ex hoc mundo Cristus uellet assumere & celestem thalamum introductam, propriis laboribus suis corona iusticie premiare, maioris quadragesime tempus instabat, quo non 5 solum a secularium personarum frequencia qui ipsam ob deuocionem uisitabant, sed eciam a sororibus secedere solita erat, exemplo Cristi qui quadraginta dies & noctes in deserto solitarius ieiunauit. Cum autem in dicta quadragesima soli [Fol. 192 r.] deo uacans in cinere & cilicio ieiunaret, et | orando cum lacrimis 10 misericordem deum precaretur ut siquid ei contagii ex allocucione hominum adhesisset, miseracionis sue lauacro expiaret, facta est una dierum manus domini super eam & tocius corporis uigor cepit diminui, languore uehemencius succrescente decubuit. Die uero dominica tercie quadragesimalis 15 ebdomadis adueniente, senciens instare suum felicem transitum ex hoc mundo, quem secrete reuelauit familiaribus suis ualde paucis,[1] iter suum salutari uiatico, corpore scilicet domini nostri Ihesu Cristi, ac sacri olei unccione, presentibus fratribus & sororibus, Cristianissima uirgo fideli deuocione communiuit.

[Fol. 192 v.] Et[2] dum hec agerentur, soror quedam | eiusdem monasterii 21 nomine Katherina Erhardi, que plusquam decem annis egritudine corporis et maxime dolore pedum grauata, lecto decumbens non sine magno sororum grauamine de loco ad locum portabatur, audiens famulam Cristi Agnetem, que ipsam 25 speciali affectu fuerat prosecuta, dominici corporis communione percepta oleo sacro perungi, altis clamoribus absencium pulsabat aures sororum. Quibus aduenientibus, instantissime postulabat ut ei preberetur auxilium ad Cristi uirginem ueniendi. Cumque ad eam perducta fuisset, plorabat inconsola-

---

[1] "Ualde paucis" not translated in M., W. and B2.

[2] M. and W. have nothing corresponding to the passage from "Et dum hec . . . usque ad horam sextam" [Fol. 194 v.]. B2. follows Latin text accurately down to "consolacionem a domino" [Fol. 193 r.], and then reads: "es was auch ein sichew swester mit andern swestern die begert fleissigleich das sie sich zeichet mit dem heiligen creutz; mit demutikeit enpfinge die heilig iungfrawe sand agnes dis red vnd berurd der swester smerzen". After that B2. follows the Latin text.

DAS[1] XI. CAPITEL VON IREM SÄLIGEN STERBEN VND
HINSCHAIDEN.

Do[2] die zit kam, das got ir lange arbeit vnd iren getruwen [Fol. 203 v.]
deinst, den sy got von iren kintlichen tagen het gethan[3] (wann
da sy dennocht in woltlichem leben waz vnd in geistlichen
leben was, do dienet sy got mit flisz): das wolt got der her ir
belonen mit himelschlicher fröd vnd ewige glori.   Da was es 5
auch in der fasten, das sy sich von allen lütten het gescheiden,
als sy allzit in der vasten gewonheit het zu důn, vnd vertrib
die vasten mit gepet vnd mit andacht, mit fasten vnd wachen,
als auch vnser lieber her die selben fiertzig tag in der wüstin
was vnd gescheiden von allen lütten vnd fastet.   In der 10
drytten wůchen der fasten da ward sy siech vnd meret sich
der siechtag als ser an ir, das sy nymen mocht vnd lag zu
bet.   Do erkant sy wol, daz sy solt sterben vnd von der welt
scheiden vnd seit das ettlichen iren gar sunderlichen vnd
heimlichen frunden der doch gar lützel was, und[4] sy hiesz ir 15
das heilig öl geben vnd enpfeng vnsers lieben herren fronlichnam mit grosser andacht vnd begird.

Do was ein schwester in dem closter, die heisz Kattarina,
die waz von schwerem siechtag darzu kumen das sy me denn
zehen jar stetlichen zu bet lag vnd nienet mocht kumen denn 20
also fer als ir die schwestren kum mit grosser arbeit gehulffen
von einer stat an die andren.   Do sy vernam daz man sant
Agnes[5] vnd bewart vnd bereittet het vff den tod, da schry die
schwester vnd rüfft den schwestern, wann die waren all by ir
vnd die siech schwester | was allein da beliben, wann sy mocht [Fol. 204 r.]
nenet kumen, man hulf ir dann.   Do sy die schwestren 26
hortten schryen vnd rüffen, do kumen sy zu ir.   Do det sy
so jemerlichen vnd bat die schwestren gar trülichen, daz sy

[1] MS. "zwelft ca" deleted.
[2] MS. "das" deleted.
[3] The construction of the sentence is broken by parenthesis, but the sense
is quite clear.
[4] MS. "vnd hiesz sich oleien" deleted.
[5] The words "sant Agnes" are written over an erasure. Note form
"Agnes," instead of the usual "Angnes".

biliter, uerbaque doloris ingeminans dicebat. "Heu me,
mater karissima, | vt quid filias tuas & me specialiter uis
derelinquere! Et quis me miseram consolabitur te, uirgo
dulcissima, moriente?" At uirgo Cristi miseria mota super
5 eam dixit, "Ne fleueris, Katherina, quia in breui recipies
consolacionem a domino!" Et cum infirma, una cum aliis
sororibus instantissime postularet, ut eam crucis signaculo
consignaret, illa propter humilitatem non assenciente, soror
paciens caute manum eius apprehendens loco doloroso appli-
10 cuit. Quod cum fecisset, tantus dolor ipsam inuasit, quod
omnes nerui eius pre doloris uehemencia quasi rumpi uide-
bantur. Post modicum autem sudorem resumptis uiribus
coram omnibus cepit ambulare, & deinceps usque ad mor|tem
suam optime ambulauit. Nulli dubium quin ad extollenda
15 ancille sue preclara merita dominus hoc operari dignatus est,
ut que uiuens fulserat sanctitate uite, eciam moriens redderetur
celebris miraculi claritate.

Licet autem iam fere nichil in ea corporearum uirium
remansisset, spiritu tamen fortis & feruida; nunc orabat
20 deuote, nunc sorores per suum decessum orphanandas ir-
remediabilibus lacrimis flentes benignis sermonibus demulce-
bat, nunc affectu materno ad apprehendum perfeccionis apicem
hortabatur dicens "Filiole mee karissime, karitatem ad deum
& proximum toto conamine obseruate, humilitatem & pau|per-
25 tatem quam tenuit Cristus & docuit imitari curate, semper
Romane ecclesie pedibus subiacentes, exemplo sanctissimi
patris nostri Francisci et alme uirginis Clare qui nobis hanc
uiuendi regulam tradiderunt, sciture pro certo quod sicut illos
misericors dominus numquam deseruit, sic nec nos eius dulcis

ir hilffen, das sy zu ir komen möcht vnd daz sy sy gesehen mocht vor irem tod, die schwestren tetten wie sy mochten, daz sy sy zu ir brechten. Da weinet sy hertzlichen ser vnd sprach "O we, O we, aller liebste fraw vnd mutter, wie wiltu dein verweist k[i]nd[1] hinder dir lassen vnd sunderlich mich 5 arme? Wer sol mich hinfür trosten in meinen liden vnd vngemach?" Do antwurt ir die gemynnt gottes gemahel vnd sprach "Katterina, lausz dein weinen sein, wenn du solt kürtzlich von got getrost werden" Da batt sy sy gar iniklichen vnd auch die andren schwestren mit ir, daz sy ein crutz 10 über sy macht, vnd sy getrüwet sy genessz von irem siechtag. Das verwidret sy zu dŭn, wann sy wer nit wirdig das ir oder iemant kein genad von ir solt geschehen. Da nam sy ir hand also kranck vnd bestrich die seichen schwester wa sy mocht vff ir hopt vnd an ir arm vnd wa sy mocht. Da bestunt sy zu 15 hand ein vnvertreglich vnd pinlich we in allen iren gelidern vnd andren vnd ducht sy das ir all ir synin vnd andren zerspringen vnd zerbrechen wolt. Dar nach bestund sy ein schweisz vnd genasz an der selben stat von allem irem siechtag | vnd von allerm ir pin vnd martter, die sy me denn [Fol. 204 v zehen jar gehept het vnd geng gesund selb dennen, die man 21 mit grossem arbeitten kum dar bracht, vnd geng darnach vntz an iren tod als wol[2] als sy je gedet. Mit dissem zeichen wolt sy got eren an iren tod, den sy vor all ir tag geerd het mit heiligem leben vnd volkumenheit aller tugent. 25

Sy was dar zu kumen, das sy lyplich noch leplich krefft nymen het, aber an dem geist was sy starck vnd hitzig, daz sy all zit bettet oder die schwestren trostet mit süssen wortten vnd mit heilsamer ler vnd sprach "O mein aller liebsten kind, habent got lieb vnd mynnent in vor allen dingen vnd behal- 30 tent sein gebot, dienent im mit flisz vnd mit truwen; vnd laut üch des nit verdriessen, wann das zit ist kürtz vnd die arbeit klein, aber der lon ist ewig vnd vnmassen grossz; vnd mynnent vnd behaltent die heilig arumŭt vnd demüttigkeit, als vns got selb das bild vor getragen hat. Die regel die vnser 35

---

[1] MS. "kund".   [2] MS. repeats "als wol" deleted.

clemencia ullatenus derelinquet, si eorum statuta & exempla
studiose fueritis imitate ".   Cum igitur hec & alia salutis monita
toto sero & nocte sequenti sororum cordibus inpresisset &
uice testamenti perpetui relinqueret inuiolabiliter obseruanda,
5 die altera, secunda uidelicet feria, quadam cepit hylaritate
[Fol. 194 v.] perfundi ac ridentis | speciem premonstare, totumque corpus
eius in candorem conuerti usque ad horam sextam.   Postquam
autem fratres dicta nona missam inciperent, circa horam qua
saluator humani generis pendens in cruce pro redempcione
10 nostra tradidit spiritum, hec deo gratissima famula in manus
patris celestis animam suam commendans, anno gracie millesimo ducentessimo octogesimo primo, sexto nonas Marcii [1]
in domino feliciter obdormiuit & angelicis fulta presidiis ad
eterna gaudia letanter intrauit.
15   O felix uirgo, que per quadraginta & sex annos in religione passionibus Cristi communicans, mortis eius horam
[Fol. 195 r.] seruauit, et depressa mortalita|tis caligine deum deorum in
sancta Syon irreue[r]beratis obtutibus limpide contemplatur !
O acceptissima deo anima, que carcere terreno soluta, libera
20 petens celum choris ymnidicis sociatur et inebriata torrente
deifico uoluptatis perpetue festiuitatis et graciarum accionis,
melliflua carmina pro euasione mundani studii ad laudem
regis glorie suaui personat armonia !

De sancti corporis eius sepultura.

Sorores igitur & filie tante matris solacio destitute, mon-
25 asterium replebant gemitibus & uirginales uultus uberrime
lacrimis irrigabant.   Accipientes autem sanctum corpus ad
[Fol. 195 v.] chorum deportauerunt, | ubi duabus septimanis stans inhu-
matum tam mirificum spirabat odorem, quod omnes ad ipsum
accedentes suauitate insolita replebantur.   Manus quoque
30 illius innoxie non rigide seu dure ut mortui, sed molles ac
ductiles ut uiuentis omni se prebebant palpanti.   Infra pre-

---

[1] M., W. and B2. all quote the Latin date " sexto nonas martii " without
translating it.

vater, sant Franciscus, vnd vnser hoch gelopte vnd aller
heiligste mutter, sant Clar, habent geben, daz die ir behaltent
demüttiglichen vnd volkumenlichen als ir auch got hand ver-
heiszen vnd ir sein schuldig sind zu halten; vnd sind des
sicher, haltent ir daz, das üch got nymer lat.   Er hab üch all 5
zit in seinem schirm vnd besorget üch all zit mit vetterlicher
trew aller ding der ir notturfftig sind zu sel vnd lyb."   Da sy
disse vnd ander | heilsame manung vnd nutzer ler allen den [Fol. 265 r.]
abent vnd die gantzen nacht fil mit in het gehapt vntz gegen
dem tag, da befalch sy in disse ler vnd disse manung[1] als zu 10
einem ewigen sel geret,[2] das sy sich darnach solten halden
vnd richten.   Vnd des morgens an dem mentag da lag sy als
sy mit newer fröd güttiglichen lachet vnd ward aller ir lyb
verwandlet mit einer wunderlicher wisz vnd schonheit; vnd
lag vntz sext zit, do sprachen die brüder non; vnd nach der 15
non fengen sy mesz an, wann es was in der vasten, vnd gen
non zit, als auch vnser lieber her verscheid an dem heiligen
crutz, da befalch disse heiligin vnd die gemynet gemahel
vnsrem lieben herren iren geist in die hend des himelschlichen
vatters vnd verscheid von disser wölt, da von gottes geburt 20
warend vergangen tussent vnd zwey hundert vnd ein vnd
achtzig jar, vnd ward ir heilige gebenedicte sel gefürt[3] von den
heiligen englen mit grosser fröd vnd glorie in gottes rich,
durch des mynn vnd ere sy verschmecht alle frod vnd rich
der wölt.   25

[*DAS ZWELFT CAPITEL, WIE SY BEGRABEN WARD.[4]*]

Do sy verscheid, da was leid vnd jamer vnd weinen vnd
clagen in allem dem closter über al.   Ire megtliche vnd reine
antzlitz wurden begossen mit trehern, das sy einer so heiligen
vnd seligen vnd trostlichen mûtter verweist warend, das sy ir

---

[1] MS. " in desser manung " altered to " disse manung ".
[2] MS. " begert " deleted : " geret " added in margin.
[3] MS. " ward " deleted.
[4] DYSZ CAPITEL SAGT VON DEN WUNDERZEICHEN, DIE GOT NACH IREM TODT
DURCH SY THET, ETC.   This is the heading of Chapter XIII. and should have
been inserted on p. 127.   The conjectural heading for Chapter XII. has been
supplied here.

dictos autem quatuordecim dies fratres minores [1] cottidie
claustrum sororum intrantes, missarum & uigiliarum celebra-
cionibus sacro funeri honorem debitum impendebant.　Sed et
tota pene ciuitas cum multitudine populorum adueniencium
5 omni die iuxta monasterium confluebat, instantissime postu-
lantes, ut felicem illum thesaurum larga dei pietate | donatum
saltem per cratem intueri ualerent.　Cum uero estuanti populo corpus frequencius monstraretur, multi anulis & cingulis
aliisque rebus ipsum cum magna deuocione contingebant,
10 sperantes se per gloriose uirginis merita ex rerum predictarum
contactu optata remedia percepturos, sicut factum esse postmodum diuina opitulante clemencia sepius expertum est.
Tandem sorores importunitatem hominum assidue inpulsan-
cium ferre ulterius non ualentes, corpus in archam nouam
15 ligneam cum reuerencia posuerunt & ostium eiusdem tena-
culis ferreis appendentes, clauo ferreo magno firmiter con-
cluserunt.

[Fol. 196 r.] (margin left of line 6)

Fol. 196 v.]　　Denique fama | de transitu preclare uirginis per regionem
ocius longe lateque procedens, ad dominam quandam nomine
20 Scolasticam de Sternberch,[2] moribus & genere nobilem, que
uirginem Cristi tenere dilexerat & deuote famulabatur eidem
ueredico relatu peruenit.　At illa cum omni qua poterat
festinacione ad ciuitatem Pragensem perueniens, rogabat cum
maximo fletu sorores, quatenus eam utpote licenciam ab
25 apostolica sede habentem,[3] monasterium sinerent introire &
corpus domine sue predilecte uidere.　Quibus asserentibus [4]

---

[1] M., W. and B2. read " die mynnern pruder dy parfuszen ".
[2] See note XIX., p. 173.　　　　[3] See note XX., p. 173.
[4] This whole sentence down to " annuerunt " is given by M. and W. ; B2. as
" dy swester erlaubten irs ".

nymer me ergetz solten werden, vnd trügen sy in den chor.
Da stunt sy XIIII tag | vnbegraben vnd geng so gar ein [Fol. 205 v.]
süsser vnd edel geschmack von ir, daz alle die die zu ir
mochten komen, die wurden erfült vnd gesterckt von dem
süssen geschmack. Ir hend vnd all ir gelyder warend als 5
lyplichen als eines lebendigen menschen, vnd die selben zwö
wüchen die wil sy vnbegraben stunt, da gengen die brüder all
tag in daz closter vnd sungen mess ob der heiligen lich vnd
butten ir schuldige ere vnd andacht mit messen vnd andren
gebet vnd ersamigkeit. Fil nach alle die stat vnd das folck 10
vss der stat gemeinlich ilten zu dem closter, vnd hetten daz
closter vss wendig vmblegt von andach, vnd batten alle
andechtiglichen vnd¹ flisz[ig]lichen durch die mynn vnd
erbermd gottes das² sye sy doch mochten durch einen gatter
sehen, vnd wurffen vingerlin vnd girtlen vnd ander ding vff 15
sy, daz sy von ir berurt mochten werden vnd daz in dann von
ir grosz heil vnd seligkeit solt widerfaren; als es auch
geschach³ vnd dick mercklichen befunden ward. Da was
den lütten so gar hitzig vnd begirlich zu ir vnd komend so
gar gemeinlich vnd gewonlichen dar, daz es die schwestren 20
nit geliden mochten vnd heissent einen hiltzenen sarch
machen vnd leitten die heiligen lich dar in vnd verschlugen
den baum vnd befessten in mit schlossen vnd starcken yssnen-
nen nagel.

Nun wassen die mer erschollen ver vnd nach über al als 25
wit in daz land, daz sy tod wer. | Da vernam es ein edele fraw [Fol. 206 r.]
in dem land vnd kam dar so sy aller schierest mocht, wann
sy mynnt sy gar ser; vnd do sy dar kam, da bat sy demüttiglichen vnd flisziglichen, daz man sy in daz closter liesz,
das sy ir lieben frawen die künigin mocht gesehen doch also 30
tod, wann sy das vrlab het von dem babst.⁴ Das widerretten
die schwestren gar fast vnd sprachent, es wer gar wider ir
gewonheit, das sy kein weltliche person in das closter liessent

---

¹ MS. repeats "vnd".   ² MS. "man" deleted.
³ MS. "gesach," of which "sach" deleted and "schach" written in
margin.
⁴ See note XX., p. 173.

contra morem dicti monasterii fore quod aliqua secularis persona, quamquam habens licenciam, quadragesimali tempore in-
[Fol. 197 r.] tromittatur, et adiungentes quod | eciam si intraret, corpus eius uidere nequeret, importunis precibus uicte peticioni ipsius
5 annuerunt. Qua monasterium intrante, et iuxta archam in qua prefatum corpus erat reconditum se cum amaris lacrimis prosternente, una de sororibus arche appropians cum murmure utrum aperiri deberet ingeminans, quia hoc ei laboriosum & difficile uidebatur, statim ad archam accessit, clauus[1] qui cum
10 uiolencia inpulsus fuerat, uidentibus qui aderant & stupentibus, per se exiliens super pauimentum strepitum fecit, aperta est archa, corpus patuit ad cernendum. Quod non nisi manu excelsi, qui habet clauem Dauid, ob merita eximie uirginis ad
[Fol. 197 v.] consolacionem amatricis | eius factum esse censendum est.

15 Interea nuncii a fratribus & sororibus ad honorabilem uirum, dominum Thobiam Pragensem epyscopum et postmodum ad uiciniores abbates destinantur, instancius postulantes ut aliquis ipsorum ueniens, corpus sanctum cum reuerencia congrua tumularet. Quibus propter occupaciones
20 diuersas, secretiori dei consilio aliud ordinante, uenire recusantibus—paulo enim ante mortem suam inclita uirgo predixerat quod nec epyscopus nec aliquis alterius religionis prelatus quam frater minor, et talis frater qui prius numquam uisus est in terra Bohemie, corpus eius sepelire deberet—adueniens uener-
25 abilis pater, frater Bonagracia,[2] generalis minister quartadecima
[Fol. 198 r.] die | a transitu eius, in sequenti die, uidelicet in dominica de passione,[3] preciosum illud pignus cum multis qui tunc aderant fratribus deuote ac honorifice in capella sacratissime uirginis Marie, in qua[4] tempore debilitatis audiebat missarum sol-

---

[1] M., W. and B2. have nothing corresponding to "qui cum . . . . stupentibus".

[2] See note XXI., p. 173.   [3] See note XXII., p. 174.

[4] M., W. and B2. have nothing corresponding to "in qua . . . petiuerat".

gan in der fasten, wie fil sy ymer vrlob dar über hetten; vnd
köm sy schon in daz closter, sy möcht ir doch nit gesehen, als
fast wer sy verschlagen vnd vermacht.   Do bat sy als gar
ernstlichen vnd hertzlichen, das die schwestren überwunden
wurden vnd liessent sy in daz closter.   Da kam sy zu dem 5
sarch, da sy inen lag vnd fiel nieder vff die erden neben den
sarch vnd weinet gar yniklichen von gantzem hertzen vnd
hett ir man ir den sarch geren vff gebrochen.   Da kund man
nicht erdencken wie das yemer geschehen mocht, also sterck-
lichen was er verschlagen; vnd do sy also redent wie man 10
daz mocht getůn, da sprang der gross vngefug nagel vss von
im selber, da mit auch der sarch aller krefftigest verschlagen [1]
was vnd für verrhin vff den esterrich mit grossem schall, wann
er was gar grossz vnd vngefüg, vnd tet sich selb vff vor ir
aller gegenwirttigkeit vnd angesicht, daz sy alle erschracken 15
vnd erbott sich die heilig lich selb zu sechen | iren getrüwen [Fol. 206 v.]
vnd lieben fründen, das nemen möcht geschehen sein denn
von wunderlicher gottes krafft.

Vnder dem da santen die brüder an den bisschoff, das er
kem mit den epten die in seinem bistum werend vnd sy mit 20
grosser err besteteten.   Do ward der geyrrt, als got wolt, daz
er‚ es nit getůn mocht, wann es was einem andren behalten [2]
von got, der sein wirdiger was.   Da nun brüder Bonagratia,
der brüder general,[3] dem disse genad von got behalten was,
kundt ward [4] daz sy tod wer, da kam er an dem dryzeenden 25
tag nach irem tod vnd der bestetet sy mit vil andren brüdren
des andren tags mit grosser er vnd andacht an dem sunentag [5]
so man singt *Judica me Deus;* [6] wann das het sy vnlang vor
irm tod geseit,[7] das sy kein bisschoff vnd ander prelat wurd
begraben, sunder ein mynder brüder vnd ein brüder der vor 30
zu Behem nie gesehen ward; also ward sy begraben in vnser
lieben frawen capell, als si begert vnd gebetten het.   Vnd

[1] MS. "ward" deleted.   [2] MS. "der es" deleted.
[3] See note XXI., p. 173.
[4] MS. adds "im kund" which is superfluous.
[5] MS. "der karwochen" deleted.   [6] See note XXII., p. 174.
[7] MS. adds "het," superfluous.

lempnia, sicut ipsa petiuerat, sepeliuit. Vbi[1] miri odoris fragrancia sorores causa oracionis intrantes diebus pluribus respergebat. Accidit autem die quadam ut una de sororibus predictam capellam ingrediens ad orandum, sompno grauata 5 uirginem Cristi uideret, cur tantus odor ex eius tumba manaret sollicite perquereret; que respondit hoc fieri propter sanctorum
[Fol. 198 v.] frequenciam angelorum, qui corpus ipsius˙ ui|sitabant. Erat re uera condignum ut corpus eius suauiter post mortem oleret, que, ut areola aromatum a celesti consita pigmentario, uirtutum 10 floribus dum uiueret delectabiliter fragrauit & nunc inter flores celicos transplantata, quasi flos rosarum in diebus eterne felicitatis gloria reflorescens, omnium aromatum suauitatem transcendit.

EPYLOGUS.[2]

Iam nempe a dilecto suo candido & rubicundo, pro cuius 15 amore sponsum spreuit mortalem, castis in celo amplexibus stringitur. Iam ab eo in ethereis mansionibus corona glorie pro cinere et oleo eterni gaudii pro luctu temporali humilis
[Fol. 199 r.] ancilla premiatur. Iam pro ex|trema pauperie thesauris felicitatis eterne ditata, in pascuis uberrimis ac iuxta fluenta 20 plenissima residet, deliciis diuine dulcedinis affluens pro parsimonia. Iam sacro concisso ueste iocunditatis induta, et tamquam sponsa monilibus dotum ornata, ueri cubiculum intrauit Asueri, nexibus precordialis amoris eidem prehenniter copulanda. Vbi cum filiabus syon exultans in rege suo faciem 25 eius uidet in iubilo, et saciatur infastidibiliter manifestacione glorie dei. Cuius glorie nos participes faciat per interuentum & merita huius inclite uirginis salvator piissimus Jhesus Cristus,
[Fol. 199 v.] cui cum patre & spiritu sancto sit omnis honor & gloria | per interminabilia secula seculorum. Amen.

---

[1] M., W. and B2.: " Do wart als gar ein suszer smak in der cappelle daz er alle menschen sterkt ".

[2] M., W. and B2. all give a much curtailed and inexact version of the original.

was darnach vil tag[1] also susser vnd edler geschmack da, daz
alle die zu den grab kament[2] vom dem geschmack[3] getrost
vnd gesterckt wurden, biede geistlich vnd lyblich.   Nun
geschach es daz ein schwester einest in die zell kam vnd wolt
da betten vnd die[4] entschlieff an dem gebet, | vnd indem da [Fol. 207 r.]
erschein ir disse heilige magt in er vnd wirdigkeit.   Da fragt[6]
sy die schwester wannen von der süssz[5] geschmack von irem
grab geng vnd so lang nach irem tod hett geweret.   Da
antwurt sy vnd sprach daz wer von der gegenwirttigkeit der
heiligen engel, die by irem grab weren vnd iren lyb vnd ir[10]
gebein da ereten ; von der gegenwirttigkeit kumt der edel gut
geschmack.   Vnd was daz wol zimlichen vnd billichen, die
lebendig was gewessen ein also lustlich wurtzgart aller edler
wyrtz vnd loblicher geziert mit allen edlen blumen aller
tugent, das auch von der toden lyb vnd von irem gebein also[15]
edeler geschmack solt gan.

[1] MS. "was" deleted.
[2] MS. "daz sy" twice inserted and deleted.   [3] *Ibid.*
[4] MS. "ensliff" deleted.   [5] MS. repeats "geng" deleted.

DE MIRACULIS DIUINA UIRTUTE PATRATIS PER EAM.

Omnipotens[1] deus, qui magno sue pietatis munere mirifi-
cat sanctos suos, Agnetem felicem uirginem in regno Bohemie
sanctissime Clare plantulam generosam, non solum precelse
uite meritis sed multis miraculorum prodigiis clarius illus-
5 trauit, ad inuocacionem nominis eius in necessitatibus &
periculis eius uirtute sue dextere misericorditer sucurrendo.
Vt gloriosus ipse deus in sanctis suis predicetur copiosius &
laudetur, ac fidelium deuocio ad ueneracionem huius illustrissime uirginis augeatur, aliqua de ipsis miraculis, pauca tamen,
10 sub breuitate censui perstringenda.

MIRACULUM.

[Fol. 200 r.]   Regina Bohemie, domina Guta coniunx[2] domini Venzezlai,
filiam suam Margaretam iam pene morientem, presumens de
meritis preclare uirginis Agnetis, ad monasterium in Praga
fecit deferri et super sepulchrum predicte uirginis poni, ca-
15 sulamque[3] preciosam ad honorem dei & uirginis memorate
super ipsius tumbam offerri. Que cum facta fuissent, ilico
puerulus super tumbam iacens ster[nu]tauit,[4] et lacte nutricis
refocillata delata est ad matrem omnino sana & pluribus
postmodum annis superuixit.[5]

20   Domina Elyzabet, regina Bohemie, consors illustris do-
[Fol. 200 v.] mini Iohannis regis regni prefati, | filium suum primogenitum
adhuc tenellum & unicum unice diligebat.[6] Cum autem uice
quadam ea in ciuitate regia que Praga dicitur existente, filius
eius prefatus in castro quod Cubitus nuncupatur a dicta
25 ciuitate plus quam duas dietas distante cum suis nutritoribus[7]
moraretur, vna nocte subita & grauissima infirmitate correptus
usque ad extrema perductus est, domina matre ipsius que
circa eum agerentur penitus ignorante. Et cum nocte

---

[1] This passage "omnipotens . . . perstringenda" is given by M. and W.
after the first miracle, instead of before it. B2. does not give it.

[2] M. and B2. give "wirtin"; W. "weib".

[3] M., W. and B2.: "messgewant".

[4] MS. "stermitauit".   [5] B2. breaks off at this point.

[6] M. and W.: "den liebt er gar ser.," referring by mistake to the king.

[7] M. and W. have nothing equivalent to "cum suis nutritoribus".

[DAS TRIZEHENT CAPITEL,]

VON DEN WUNDERZEICHEN DIE GOT NACH IREM TODT DURCH
SY THET,[1] ETC.

Der kunig von Behem, der ir bruder was, der het ein kind
das hiesz Margreta, daz lag an dem das es jetzunt me tod was
den lebendig. Do het des kindes muter die kunigin, die hiesz
Gutta also grosse zuverschicht zu der hochgelopte junckfraw
vnd heisz daz sterbent kind tragen hin zu irem closter, vnd 5
sant mit dem kind gar ein gut kosper casul, daz man das kind
solt vff ir grab legen vnd das casul auch vff ir grab solt
oppfren, ir zu lob vnd zu eren. Zu hand da daz kind mit
dem oppfer vff daz grab[2] ward geleit, da genasz das kind
aller ding vnd bracht man es gesund vnd frolich seiner mutter 10
der kunigin wider heim. |

[1] This chapter heading is supplied by transference from p. 119. Between the
end of this paragraph and the following one, the MS. has the heading "Von den
wunderzaichen".

[2] MS. "kam" deleted.

eadem memorata domina regina se sopori dedisset, audiuit
in sompnis uocem dicentem sibi "Numquid dormis?"
Qua in sompnis respondente "non," iterata uox ad eam
[Fol. 201 r.] sonuit dicens | "Cum petere soleas multos bonos homines
5 & deuotos, ut pro te ad dominum intercedant, cur non sup-
plicas auie tue sancte Agneti, ut eciam pro te dominum
interpellet, cum per ipsius merita omnium uotorum tuo-
rum cupitum consequi possis effectum?" Domina uero re-
querente ubi eam posset inuenire cum sit mortua, denuo
10 uox ad eam "Non est" inquid "mortua, sed manet in monasterio sancti Francisci et habet se ualde bene."[1] Ad que uerba
regina, ut sibi uidebatur, surgens de lecto ad prefatum monasterium celerius festinauit. Et appropians crati, hoc est
fenestre, ad quam sorores locuntur, dictam fenestram pulsibus
[Fol. 201 v.] cepit impetere & dicere "Est ne[2] hic aliqua de so|roribus?"
16 At una de intus respondente quid sit, interrogauit eam
"Numquid est hic in monasterio auia mea sancta Agnes?"
Denique sorore hoc affirmante, dicit ei domina memorata
"Vade" inquid "& dic ei quia ego sum Elyzabet, regina
20 Bohemie,[3] filia regis Venczlai et supplices ei ex parte mei ut
ad me uelit huc uenire". Qua tandem, ut ei uidebatur, ad
predictam fenestram accedente, uultum eius omnino in eadem
disposicione quam ante uiuens habuerat conspexit, excepto
quod decore mirabili & nimio candore uernabat. Quam cum
25 fuisset intuita, flexis genibus contra cratem dixit ei "Ora
[Fol. 202 r.] pro me, karissima auia, quia | uehementem cordis angustiam
pacior, licet causam caute ignorem, et scio quod quidquid a
domino pecieris impetrabis". Que auertens ab ea faciem
dixit ei "Cur pro te orabo?" At regina nimium contristata
30 corruit ante cratem dicens "Auia, ora pro me, quia de loco
isto non recedam, sed pocius hic iacebo & in cordis angustia
moriar, nisi pro me ad dominum intercedas!" Tunc uirgo
Cristi conuersa ait "Vade in pace, quia orabo pro te!" Die

---

[1] M. and W. have nothing corresponding to "et . . . bene".

[2] M. and W. curtail from "Estne . . . Agnes" thus: "Frogt ob iht sant
angnes ir pas dar innen wer".

[3] M. and W., "romische kungin".

9

uero sequenti nuncius de familia filii sui ueniens dixit ei
"Domina regina, date mihi mercedem pro nuncio, quia filius
uester de cuius salute desperauimus, deo auxiliante, conualuit".
[Fol. 202 v.] Que cum audis | set, de infirmitate quidem ipsius perterrita, sed
5 de conualencia nimium hylarata, sompnium quod uiderat
per rei euidenciam intellexit, statimque sororibus monasterii [1]
in quo uirgo Cristi sepulta est pulchrum cereum & pannum
preciosum ad ornatum sepulcri nec non elemosinam nota-
bilem destinauit, eas affectuose flagitans quatenus deo qui [2]
10 habet uite et mortis potestatem ac uirgini gloriose Agneti
graciarum debitas referant acciones, asserens unicum filium
suum per eius interuentum & merita a mortis faucibus
liberatum.

Alio tempore eadem domina Elyzabet, regina Bohemie,
[Fol. 203 r.] post partum secundi geniti nocte tercia | infirmitate grauis-
16 sima repente cepit urgeri, in tantum ut pre doloris uehemencia eos quos prius nouerat tunc minime agnoscebat. Et
cunctis qui aderant tam medicis quam aliis de eius uita diffi-
dentibus, ad alme uirginis patrocinium modo quo poterat se
20 conuertit, corde uouens & ore coram omnibus protestans, quod
si per merita eius gloriosa tam grauem languorem euaderet,
pro canonizacione ipsius totis uiribus & omnibus quibus
posset conatibus uellet fideliter laborare. Quod ut factum
est, diuina opitulante uirtute, incensi doloris ilico sensit iuua-
25 men, et optatam deinde recuperauit sospitatem. |

[Fol. 203 v.]   Puer quidam, Martinus nomine, filius domine Margarete de
ciuitate Pragensi, infirmitate graui correptus, in tantum defecit
quod nec uox nec sensus nec motus alicuius uene in ipso
perpendi ualeret. Quem auia sua nomine Kvnegundis [3] ac-
30 cipiens, utrum uiuum uel mortuum penitus ignoratur, intrauit
monasterium sororum, secundum graciam ab apostolica sede
sibi concessam, et posuit eum super sepulcrum sancte Agnetis
& facto uoto pro puero, cum omnes sorores alme uirginis

---

[1] M. and W. represent "monasterii . . . est" by "in daz selb kloster".
[2] M. and W. have nothing corresponding to "qui . . . potestatem".
[3] M., "sein mum kunn" apparently not recognising the name ; W. omits,
attributing the action to the mother.

Ain edle fraw het ein kind das hiesz Mar[t]inus, daz was [Fol. 207 v.]
von schwerem siechtag dar zu kumen, daz es weder stim noch
synn het, noch enkund neimen kein zeichen des leben an ym
gemercken noch kennen an seinem athem noch an seinem
schmack. Da nam es sein anfraw, die hiesz Kunigund vnd 5
trüg es in das closter, wann sy het vrlob von dem babst in
das closter zu gan, vnd leit daz kind vff ir grab vnd entheisz
ir da ein antheisz für das kind. Zu hand det das kind also
ob es wer von der hell her wider kumen vnd wart gesund
vnd starck.   10

auxilium implorarent, continuo puer quasi ab inferis suscitatus,
tantum a deo corporis recepit uigorem quod nutrici traditus |
[Fol. 204 r.] sic uiuide ubera mox sugebat, quasi nullam infirmitatem
pertulisset.

5 Soror[1] quedam, nomine Donika, filia domini Domazlai
Dezquotz, degens in monasterio uirginis Cristi Prage, quatuor
acutas habuit successiue. Cumque iam omnino deficere
putaretur, communione dominici corporis & sacri olei unccione procurata est. Deinde consobrina eius, soror Junka[2]
10 de Lisnik, pallio beate Agnetis eam mox ut credebatur morit-
uram[3] contexit. Que iacens sub pallio memorato, uidens
lucem magnam, ridere cepit, ita quod a sororibus astantibus
putabatur omnino racionem amisisse. Tantus autem odor de
[Fol. 204 v.] pallio predicto manabat, quod ipso confortata su|dare cepit &
15 Cristi uirtute conualuit.

Alia soror eiusdem monasterii, nomine Wratzka[4] de Ygezd,
passione quadam ualde grauata usque ad extrema perducta
est. Cumque, ut moris est, conductus eidem legeretur & ab
aliquibus mortua putaretur, iacens in agone opem Agnetis
20 sanctissime uirginis implorabat, ut ei pro signo sanitatis saltem
unam guttulam sudoris a domino impetraret, uotum faciens
de tribus missis ad honorem ipsius pocius quam ad suffragium
anime procurandis. Quo emisso, uirtute adiutricis sue curata,
uoti non inmemor missas legi procurauit; sed per incuriam
[Fol. 205 r.] sacerdotis non fuerunt consum[m]ate. Adueniente | autem an-
26 niuersario uirginis Cristi,[5] cum ceteris sororibus ad dicendas
uigilias circa tumulum eius properauit. Cumque ibi consis-
teret, a priori passione inuasa, cum magna difficultate peruenit
ad lectum. Intelligens tandem uotum suum non esse con-
30 pletum, ad ipsum denuo renouauit & perfici sollicite procurauit.
Tandemque per merita sancte Agnetis perfecte curacionis
munus accepit.

Alia[6] soror eiusdem monasterii, nomine Ludka de Tornow,

---

[1] M. and W.: "swester herrn domislaii tohter".
[2] M., "Juta"; W. omits name.
[3] MS. "Moraturam".
[4] M., "mit namen praczka"; W. omits name.
[5] See note XXIII., p. 174.   [6] W. omits this miracle.

Es waz ein schwester in dem closter die het fier[1] grosse
sucht nach ein ander vnd man het alle ding an ir verzwifflet
vnd ward bewart mit dem heiligen sacrament vnd bereit vff
den tod. Da nam ein schwester[2] der heiligen junckfrawen
mandel vnd leit in über die sterbente schwester. Da sy ein 5
weilen vnder dem mandel lag, da sach sy ein starck liecht ob
ir vnd ward lachen. Da wandent die schwestren, sy het die
synn verlaren vnd erschrackent. Da ward sy schwitzen vnd
ducht sy das so gar susser geschmack von dem mandel
geng, das si davon gesterckt ward vnd genas aller ding.   10
    Es was ein schwester in dem selben closter die kam von
schwerem siechtag vntz vff den tod, vnd do man daz gepet
sprach das man gewonlichen | sprichet ob den schwestren so sy [Fol. 208 r.]
wellen sterben, vnd ettlich wonden daz sy tod wer, da rufft
sy in ir selber die heiligen junckfraw an, daz sy genes, so wolt 15
sy schaffen, das ir dry messen gesprochen solten werden got
zu lob vnd ir zu eren. Zu hand da sy den antheisz gedet, da
genas sy zu hand an der stat von allem irem we vnd siechtag.
Da sy genas, da vergass sy irer gelypt vnd ires antheis nit;
sy befalch zu hand das ir dry messen gesprochen solten werden 20
zu lob vnd zu eren; aber der pryster versumet es, das sy nit
gesprochen wurden, vnd da ir tag kam[3] vnd disse schwester
mit den andren schwestren ob dem grab stunden, do kam all
ir siechtag vnd we herwider als von ersten, vnd gehalfen ir
kom mit grosser arbeit zu den[4] bett. Da erkant sy wol daz 25
man die messen nit gesprochen het, vnd erniiert da iren
antheisz, vnd schuff da zu hand daz sy gesprochen wurden.
Da genas sy zu hand vnd ward gesund als von erst.
    Es was in dem selben closter ein swester die hiesz Luca,

---

[1] MS. "sucht" deleted.
[2] MS. "die hulda die nam" deleted.   Name "hulda" scarcely legible and
uncertain.
[3] See note XXIII., p. 174.   [4] MS. "grab" deleted.

cardiaca passione uehementer afflicta, laborare uidebatur in
extremis.   Sorores uero accipientes uinum, in quo felicia ossa
sancte Agnetis lota fuerunt, ei dederunt ad bibendum.
[Fol. 205 v.] Cumque de ipso aliquan|tulum gustasset, uirtute dei conuales-
5 cere cepit.

Vir quidam, nomine Psribko, famulus[1] domini Cunssonis
de Hermanitz, Pragensis diocesis, in die secundo Pasce[2] cum
ceteris fidelibus ad ecclesiam properauit.   Cumque missa de
resurreccione domini cantaretur, stans in populo subito corruit,
10 coloreque faciei mutato protinus agonizare cepit.   Et ecce
uir nobilis nomine Nycolaus de Nazitz dixit astantibus "Cito
ad dominam coniungem meam properate, et capillos Sancte
Agnetis quos habet celerius apportate".[3]   Qui cum allati
fuissent & de aqua perfusi, aperientes os pacientis cum uio-
[Fol. 206 r.] lencia, predictam aquam ori ac gutturi eius inmiserunt.—Qua
16 gustata statim surrexit, & gracias agens deo ac inclite uirgini
Agneti, uidentibus cunctis et stupentibus, omnino sanus ab
ecclesia remeauit.[4]

Uirgo quedam, nomine Wanka Praga parua a multis apel-
20 lata, cum uice quadam Uulkanum fluuium transfretaret, habens
secum aliquantulum de capillis Agnetis, casu de naui lapsa in
fluuium, infra modici temporis tractum harenis in magna
quantitate cooperta est.   Sub quibus iacens pie uirginis
Agnetis subsidium inuocabat.   Et nautis tandem superueni-
25 entibus, de harenis quasi de loco sepulcri[5] incolumis est
extracta.

[Fol. 206 v.]   Alia uirgo, nomine Cristina, filia | Gotfridi procuratoris
fratrum minorum de Praga, uice quadam infirmitate grauata
totum corpus habebat ceruleo siue croceo colore perfusum, ita
30 quod omnes qui [e]am[6] intuebantur propter tam horrendam
inmutacionem coloris de uita ipsius desperabant.   Illa quoque,

---

[1] M. omits "famulus . . . hermanitz"; W. omits also name "psribko".
[2] M., "an dem heilligen ostertag".
[3] M. and W., "bringt mir des wassers (!) von sant agnessen".
[4] At this point W. departs from the order of the miracles in M. and B., and
here inserts the three miracles contained in passage beginning "sedes supra quam"
[Fol. 214 v.] to the end, "apponendi" [Fol. 216 r.].
[5] M. and W. have nothing corresponding to "quasi . . . sepulcri".
[6] MS. "tam".

die was von schwerem siechtag kumen vntz vff den tod. Da
nament die swestren des weines, da der junckfrawen gebein in
gewessen was vnd gabent der swester darab ze trincken, vnd
da sy des weines nur ein wenig getranck, da genas sy zu hand
von allem irem siechtag. | 5

Es was ein her in dem bystum zu Praug, der het einen [Fol. 208 v.]
knecht da, der an dem ostertag zu kirchen geng mit andren
lütten, vnd vnder der mess da stund er vnder dem volck. Do
fiel er nyder vor allem volck, vnd verwandled sein antlytz vnd
all sein farb vnd begund zu dem tod ziechen. Da was ein 10
edler her der heisz Nycholaus, der sant bald zu seiner husz
frawen, das sy im sant Angnessen hor sant, daz sy behalten
het. Do daz hor dar kam, da schyttnet man wasser dar über
vnd brach dem man den mund vff; vnd da im das wasser nun
inwendig inkam, da stund er zu hand vff vor in allen vnd was 15
aller ding gesund worden vnd geng gesund vnd frölich wider
heim vnd set genad vnd danck der edlen junckfrawen
Angnessen, die im geholffen vnd gesund gemacht het. Des
wundreten vnd frodten sich alle die da warend vmm daz
grossz zeichen daz sy gethan het.   20

Es was ein junckfraw in der stat zu Brag, die für zu einem
mal über ein wasser vnd hett ein wenig sant Angnessen har
by ir; die fiel von vngeschicht [1] vss dem schiff in daz wasser vnd
fiel zu hand zu grund vnd waz daz wasser so geschwind vnd so
starck, das es fil grys vff sy warff; vnd lag sy mit dem hor 25
daz sy by ir het vnder dem | grund als in einem [2] grab; vnd [Fol. 209 r.]
die will sy also lag, da rufft sy die myltten sant Angnessen an,
vnd da kament schifflütt dar vnd zugent sy vss dem grund
des gries herusz, als vss einem grab, vnd was gesund vnd on
allem schaden hervss genumen.   30

Ain ander junckfraw die hiesz Cristina vnd was her Got-
frydes dochter, der der mynder brüder schaffner was, die het
gar ein schweren vnd vngewonlichen siechtag, das aller ir lyp
von sellicher erschrockenlicher farb begriffen was, daz alle die
die sy sachen an ir verzwiffelt hetten, vnd daz sy kein zuver- 35

---

[1] MS. "sicht" deleted and "schicht" added in margin.
[2] MS. "grund" deleted.

de humana ope desperans, ad Agnetis suffragia se conuertit,
rogitando[1] cum lacrimis, ut eam suis sacris meritis ex hac
egritudine liberaret, firma sponsione se constringens, si uiueret,
in castitate transageret dies suos.   Mira res !   Virgo a uirgine
5 inuocata deuote celerem obtinet remedii salutaris effectum,

[Fol. 207 r.] eamque regine uirginum sectatricem.   Mox | enim ab infirmi-
tate sanata, religiosum habitum suscepit, & quod ore uouerat
opere solerter impleuit.[2]

Mulier quedam coniunx Martini ciuis Pragensis dicti de
10 Egra, diebus pluribus in puerperio laborando, fetum euadere
non ualebat.   Et mittens ad fratres minores, quibus erat amore
Cristi deuota, suppliciter flagitabat ut aliquam rem qua uenerabilis virgo Cristi usa fuit sibi a sororibus impetrarent, quam
apud se absque scrupulo consciencie infra tempus egritudinis
15 gestare ualeret.   Obtinent dicti fratres unum cingulum, de quo
corpus illius post mortem tactum fuit.   Quo cum paciens

[Fol. 207 v.] cincta | fuisset, inuocando uirginis piissime suffragium, eius
interuenientibus meritis ilico infantem peperit, salua prolis &
proprii corporis sospitate.

20   Una quedam, nomine Dobroslana,[3] de contrata Slauensi,
Pragensis dyocesis, magna matricis infirmitate grauata, & iam
pene deficiens pre dolore, diebus & noctibus lamentabiles dabat
uoces. Tandem de consilio fratrum minorum misit in Pragam
ad sorores, instanter petendo ut sibi de uino in quo propter
25 infirmos assidue rogantes tincte fuerant reliquie uirginis Agnetis, aliquantulum mitterent propter deum.   Quod allatum

[Fol. 208 r.] postquam gustasset, recepit omnimodam sanitatem. |

Nobilis quidam regni Bohemie, nomine Tatzo, habens intra
guttur quoddam apostema, petiuit humiliter fratres minores
30 in Praga, ut eum aliquibus reliquiis Sancte Agnetis con-
signarent.   Fratres uero capillos ipsius uirginis in uino in-
tingentes, collum pacientis uino predicto linierunt & residuum
bibere suaserunt, consulentes nichilominus quod uotum aliquod ad honorem dei sueque ancille Agnetis uoueret, &

---

[1] M. and W. have nothing corresponding to "rogitando . . . liberaret".
[2] M. adds " sy waz innig zu betrahten daz leben marie vnd sant Clarn ".
[3] M. and W., " broslana " omitting name of district.

sicht hetten zu menschlicher hilf. Da kert sy sich mit
gantzem hertzen zu der milten sant Angnessen vnd bat sy
weine[n]t, daz sy ir hilf daz sy genes, vnd gelopt ir, genes sy,
sy wölt vnsren herren in megtlicher reinigkeit denen vntz an
iren tod. Do sy disse gelupt getet, zu hand da genas sy von 5
allem siechtagen vnd we vnd ward gesund vnd starck. Da
vergass sy ir gelubt nit vnd ward geistlichen vnd denet
vnsren herren in geistlichem leben bisz an irem end.

Es was ein burger zu Brag in der stat, der hiesz Martinus,
der het ein huss frawen die geng fil tag eines kindes zu 10
arbeiten vnd mocht des kindes nit genessen. Da sant sy zu
den myndern brüder, wann denen was sy gar heimlichen vnd
ir sunder frundin, vnd bat sy daz sy ir hilffend, daz ir die
swestren ettwas santten | daz der loblichen junckfrawen sant [Fol. 209 v.]
Angnessen gewessen wer. Da ward ir ein gurttel gesant, die 15
ward vff sy geleit. Da sy mit der gurttel gegürttet ward, da
genas sy des kindes zu hand on allen schaden vnd freisz ir
selber vnd des kindes.

Es was ein ander fraw in dem bystum zu Brag, die het ein
gar schweren siechtagen vnd leid davon so grosse nott vnd 20
arbeit, daz sy kam fil nach vntz vff den tod vnd schry tag
vnd nacht jemerlichen vnd vngestymlichen vnd mocht ir
nemen gehelfen. Da riettent ir die brüder, das sy zu der
swester closter santte, daz sy ir schicketen des weines dar in
sy sant Angnessen heiltum ingedunncket hetten, durch aller 25
hand siechen die gewonlichen dar vmm batten vnd sy auch
dar von genasend von mainiger hand siechtag. Da sy des
weines ein wenig getranck, zu hand gestillet ir we vnd arbeit.

Es was ein edler her ze Behem, der gewann ein geschwer
in der kelen vnd mocht im daran nemen gehelffen. Da bat er 30
die brüder, daz sy ym ettwas von sant Angnessen heiltum
geben, das er genes. Da brachten sy im sant Angnessen har
vnd stiessent das in einen wein vnd bestrichent ym sein kelen
da mit, vnd den überigen gaben sy ym zu trincken vnd
rietten im, er solt ettlich antheisz dun, | almůsen den armen [Fol. 210 r.]
ze geben durch yr er. Das tett er vnd gelopt me denn sy ym 36
gerotten hetten. Da er den antheisz getan het, da genas er

pauperibus elemosinas largiretur. Qui cum non solum ea
que sibi suasa fuerunt deuote fecisset, sed eciam plura hiis
super[*erog*]asset,[1] perfecte curacionis munus adeptus est.[2]

[Fol. 208 v.] Alius multum nobilis dominus Linko de Duba[3] passione
5 squinancie frequenter uexabatur, tam grauiter quod propter
doloris uehemenciam linguam supra pectus turpiter exponebat·
Cumque nullo medicine remedio eidem posset subueniri, de
consilio sororum ordinis Sancte Clare in Praga consanguine-
arum suarum vinum in quo ossa beate Agnetis lota fuerunt
10 cum deuocione potauit, & nunquam deinceps memoratam pertulit passionem.

Iuuenis quidam, nomine Vencezlaus, notarius cuiusdam
militis nomine Protywerzonis[4] in Bohemia, grandem in gutture
paciebatur dolorem, racione cuius nec unum uerbum proferre
15 ualebat. Perductus tandem per dominum suum ad fratres
[Fol. 209 r.] minores in | Praga, nutibus cepit exposcere quod cum reliquiis
signaretur. Dominus autem ipsius nutus eius non intelligenti-
bus dixit " Ipse innuit & ego instanter peto, ut de reliquiis
beate Agnetis si quas habetis dolorem ipsius tangatis, quia
20 per hoc sperat se totaliter liberari". Properat subito unus
de fratribus et capillos uirginis quos ob deuocionem seruabat
attulit reuerenter, & intingens in aquam collum eius liniuit,
terque cruce signauit in honore deifice trinitatis, et quidquid
de aqua remanserat ebibere iussit. Qua difficulter potata,
25 aliquod enim diebus cibum non sumpserat neque potum,
[Fol. 209 v.] statim uocem emisit | ad modum ouis balantis. Quam cum
tercio emisisset, debilitari cepit & sudare, et post modicam
quietem in uerba exultacionis prorupit dicens " Benedictus sit
dominus noster Jhesus Cristus, qui me peccatorem per sanctam
30 Agnetem uirginem liberauit," Statimque equo ascenso cum
domino suo incolumis & letus abscessit.

Simili modo quidam uir Marzitus, nomine Hoholitz, Pragensis dyocesis, per octo dierum spacium propter grauissimam

---

[1] MS. "superegrotasset".   [2] M. and W. adds " vnd lobt got ".
[3] See note XXIV., p. 174.
[4] M. and W. omit name. Boll. I. and II. both give the name Vencezlaus
to the master instead of to the scribe.

zu hand von allem seinen siechtag vnd leist seinen antheisz
truwlichen vnd vollichen.

Es was ein ander edler her zu Behem, der het einen
siechtag vnd leid da von grosse not vnd arbeit, daz er dick
von bitterem we darzu kam, daz ym die zungen vss dem mund 5
dick heng vntz vff sein brust vnd en mocht im nemen gehelfen.
Da het der her ein nyffelin oder frund in dem closter zu Brag
die gab im des weines, da ir gebein ingewesen was. Zu hand
da er den wein getranck, da genass er gentzlichen von allem
seinen siechtagen.   10

Es was ein ritter zu Behem der het einen schriber, der
gewan einen schweren siechtagen in der kelen, vnd was ettwen
fil tag daz er weder reden noch essen mocht. Do furt in sein
her zu den brüdren, vnd bat sy ob sy nicht hetten von sant
Angnessen heiltum, daz sy ym sein kelen da mit bestrichen. 15
Da brachten sy ires hares, daz stiessent sy in ein wasser vnd
bestrichen im sein kelen, vnd gaben ym das zu trincken, das
da über was worden. Da er daz getranck, da liesz er ein
stym vss | zu dryen malen als ein schefflin daz da bleret, vnd [Fol. 210 v.]
ward gar kranck vnd ward schwitzen, vnd da er ein wil 20
gerüwet, da stund er frolichen vff vnd sprach "Ge'opt sy der
ewig got, der mich armen sunder generet hat durch der
heiligen sant Angnessen willen," vnd sass vff sein rosz vnd
fur frysch vnd gesund wider heym.

Es was ein ander man in dem bystum zu Brag, der was 25
acht tag daz er nie wort mocht gereden, also grosse martter
vnd arbeit leid er in der kelen, vnd mocht nit als fil als ein
wort gesprechen, vnd ruchlet jemerlichen vnd von byttrem we.

gutturis passionem nec unum uerbum proferre ualebat, sed
lamenta[*bi*]les rugitus doloris expressiuos. Cumque de capillis sancte Agnetis bibisset, nocte sequenti apparuit ei uirgo
[Fol. 210 r.] predicta in habitu sororum | ordinis sancte Clare, et dixit se
5 esse sanctam Agnetem, et duobus digitis in os eius usque ad
locum doloris inmissis, omnem dolorem tactu manus sue pro-
pulsauit.

Quodam tempore fluuio nomine Uulcana supra quem situm
est monasterium sororum in Praga nimium inundante, aqua
10 predictarum sororum monasterium ingrediens, eciam locum
sepulture uirginis Cristi repleuit. Cessante inundacione soror
Margareta, filia[1] Jacobi ciuis Pragensis, aquam de sepulcro
hauriens, multo tempore seruauit incorruptam, que multis extitit remedium salutare contra multimodas passiones. Quidam
[Fol. 210 v.] namque uir Albertus nomine & soror eius Ely|zabet in ciui-
16 tate Pragensi in morte decumbentes, haustu aque predicte totaliter a periculo mortis liberati sunt. Et multi alii a diuersis
egritudinibus liberati.[2] Propter tales autem inundaciones que
frequenter ibi contingunt timentes sorores omnes reliquias
20 uirginis incinerari debere, ossa ipsius de sepulcro leuantes
lota in uino per manus fratrum sacerdotum cum magna reuerencia in archa lignea condiderunt. Predictum autem uinum
per annum in cina conseruatum nec colorem nec saporem
mutauit, & multis egris bibentibus prestitit medelam salutis,
[Fol. 211 r.] sicut de aliquibus superius est expressum. |
26 Nobilis quidam de Bohemia, dictus Marquardus de Wlassym, habitis capillis Agnetis uirginis a quadam sorore ordinis
Sancte Clare de Praga, in ciuitate sua Wlassym multos febri-
citantes reperiens, aliquos quidem de predictis capillis bibere
30 fecit, alios autem tantummodo eisdem capillis benedixit et
quindecim ex illis meritis famule Cristi a vi febrium liberati
sunt.[3]

Soror Constancia que post mortem sancte Agnetis pluribus

---

[1] " Filia . . . pragensis " given by M. but not by W.

[2] Both M. and W. insert word " Nota " here.

[3] M. adds : " also eret got die der wertt zur hert in horn versmehent vnd lassen
absneyden vmb sein willen ". W. breaks off at " got ".

Da gab man im zu tryncken ab sant Angnessen har, vnd an
der nesten nacht dar nach, do erschein sy im in dem gewand
als die swestren sant Claren tragent, vnd seyt im daz sy es
wer vnd greiff im mit zweien vingern zu dem mund vnd
rürret in an die stat da ym we was. Da von was er genessen 5
von allem we vnd siechtagen.

Zu einem zytten ward ein wasser daz heiset Wiltana also
gross, das es übergeng vnd geng in der swester closter zu
Brag, vnd ward sant Angnessen grab vol wassers. Do scheffp-
fet man daz wasser von dem grab vnd gehielt das | wasser [Fol. 211 r.]
frysch vnd suber vnd beleib wol geschmack lang zit vnd 11
genasen fil siechen von dem selben wasser.

Ain man heisz Albrecht, der lag an dem tod vnd sein
swester heisz Elisabet, die lag auch an dem tod vnd man gab
ynen des selben wassers zu tryncken, vnd genasent alle beide 15
von dem tod vnd von allen siechtagen, vnd fil ander siechen
genassent do von aller hand siechtagen. Nun geng daz selb
wasser also dick in das closter, das die swestren vorchten das
sant Angnessen bein fillicht verlirt wurd, vnd besanten fil
priester vnd die brüder dar, die namen ir gebein alle uss dem 20
grab mit grosser erwirdigkeit vnd andacht vnd wuschen daz
gebein mit wein in einem zuber. Da stund der wein ein
gantz jar in dem zuber, daz er weder sein farb noch seinen
geschmack nie verwandlet. Von dem selben wein genassen
fil siechen die des weines trunckent vnd da mit bestrichen 25
wurden.

Es was ein man der heisz Martquart, der het ein wenig
von irem har, das hetten ym die swestren von sant Claren
gegeben, der ernert funfzechen siechen menschen da mit.
Etlichen gab er dar ab zu trincken, ettlichen bestrich er da 30
mit vnd genassen alle von ir hilf. | [Fol. 211 v.]
Es was ein swester in dem closter, die hiesz Constancia,
die het den rytten lang zit ; vnd in der nacht do sant Angnesz
starb, do tett er ir gar we ; vnd nach dem ymbysz, do die
swestren all in dem kor waren vnd daz *gracias*[1] mit andacht 35

[1] See note XXV., p. 174.

annis excursis monasterii ipsius extitit abbatissa, ante mortem
prefate uirginis gloriose pluribus accessionibus febrilibus
[Fol. 211 v.] grauata, in die tandem defunc|cionis ipsius plus solito cepit
uexari, ita quod quasi tenebrescebat ante oculos eius, et
5 totum corpus ipsius nimium erat ponderosum. Cumque sorores dixissent gracias in choro post prandium,[1] illa ueniens
procidit iuxta feretrum in quo corpus uirginis Cristi iacebat,
ipsius merita inuocando, ut cum aliis sororibus pro anima eius
nocte sequenti legere psalterium[2] posset. Surgens autem ab
10 oracione nullum dolorem sensit, nullumque grauamen, & quod
facere decreuerat, effectui mancipauit.

Alia soror, nomine Agnes de Sberzkowitz,[3] que eciam
post mortem alme uirginis sororum monasterii eius fuit ab-
[Fol. 212 r.] batissa pluribus | annis, ante quam gereret dictum officium,
15 grauissimam paralisim in cubito manus dextere perpessa est,
in tantum quod eadem manu nichil poterat operari, sed continue portabat alligatam in sinu cum corda. Die autem[4]
quadam inueniens archam ligneam in qua corpus uirginis
iacuerat, petiuit unam de sororibus ut eam iuuaret exponere
20 manum dolorosam de sinu, quia nunquam inponi poterat uel
exponi sine magno pacientis dolore pariter et clamore.
Cumque dictam manum prefate arche ut poterat applicuisset,
omni dolore semoto, restituta est usui & pristine sanitati.

[Fol. 212 v.] Qvedam nobilis domina, nomine Scolasti|ca, consors domini
25 Habhardi[5] de Zyrotin in Bohemia, dum adhuc Agnes felicis-
sima in carne degeret, massam quandam in latere sinistro diu
pertulit ex malorum coadunacione humorum. Quam per diuersa
medicorum remedia euadere non ualens, cum auia sua, domina
Scolastica de Sternberk[6] que licenciam habebat monasterium
30 sororum intrandi, claustrum in quo 'uirgo Cristi degebat ingrediens pia calliditate temptabat latus suum morbidum lateri
uirginali iungere, sperans se ipsius contactu cupitam recipere
sanitatem. Quod & factum est. Volens enim ab ancilla

---

[1] See note XXV., p. 174.
[2] M. and W., " pater noster," instead of " psalterium ".
[3] M. and W., " von kowiz ".   [4] M. and W. greatly curtail this miracle.
[5] M. " habrad " ; W. omits name.   [6] See note XXVI., p. 174.

sprachen, do kam auch die selb siech swester dar vnd strecket
sich mit arbeiten für die bar nyder vff die erden vnd bat sant
Angnessen, beide sy vnd all swestren mit ir, daz sy nun ir
hulf, daz ir nun so fil lichter wurd daz sy die nacht da by
sein mocht, so man den salter sprech als es gewonlich ist. 5
Do sy daz begirlichen bat vnd die swestren all mit ir, do
genas sy gentzlich von dem rytten vnd von allem we vnd ward
dar nach Eptissin in dem selben closter.

Es was ein ander swester in dem selben closter, die hiesz
Angnes, die het das parilis an einem arm also swerlichen 10
troffen, daz sy den gentzlichen verlor vnd must in all gepunden
tragen an einem seil; vnd zwei mal sach sy den sarch da sant
A[ng]nessen[1] lich zu dem ersten ingelegen was vnd bat ein
swester daz sy ir hulf daz ir der arm enpunden wurd, wann
der mocht ir nymer | enpunden werden on bytterlichem we [Fol. 212 r.]
vnd schmertzen.   Da ir der arm enpunden ward, do geng sy 16
zu dem sarch vnd leit iren siechen arm vnd hand in den sarch
als fil sy mocht.   Do genas sy zu hand gentzlichen von allem
siechtagen vnd von allem we, vnd ward dar nach Eptissin in
dem selben closter.   20
Es was ein edler her zu Behem, der het ein elichen frawen
die hiesz Scolastica; der wuschs gar ein vngefuger clotz an
der lincken sytten vnd en kont noch en mocht ir kein artzet
noch artzney[2] gehelffen.   Da geng sy ein mal mit der frawen
von Streubt, von der auch hie oben ist ges[ch]riben,[3] mit der 25
geng sy in daz closter do sant Angnes dennocht lept, wann des
het sy vrlab vom babst, vnd fugt sich mit einer keindigkeit zu
ir, so sy aller meist mocht, daz ir siechen sytten von ir berüret
wurd, so getruwet sy daz sy aller ding genes.   Vnd da sy von
ir scheiden wolt vnd ein ander gesegnetten, da vmmfeng sy 30
sy vnd det daz also, daz ir siechen sytten an sy kam, vnd ze
hand da sy von ir berüret ward, da genas sy des klotzen vnd

[1] MS. "Anessen".
[2] MS. "arney" with "artzney" written above.
[3] MS. "gespriben".

[Fol. 213 r.] Cristi licenciari recedendo, fuit eam amplexata, in quo | amplexu passionatum latus lateri eius ut potuit coniunxit, & quam nec herba nec malagina sanauerat, antequam de monasterio exisset sensit se omnino mirifica dei uirtute sanatam. Et ut 5 accepti beneficii gratitudinem demonstraret, egrediens de monasterio statim audientibus pluribus hominibus fide dignis uiue uocis oraculo fatebatur per merita eximie uirginis se a morbo grauissimo liberatam.

Alia domina clari generis, Ostyrhildis nomine, coniunx 10 domini Iobozlai de Sternberk, morbum qui fistula dicitur pluribus annis perpessa est. Audiens autem per merita beate Agnetis homines a diuersis egritudinibus liberari, totam se |

[Fol. 213 v.] contulit ad eius suffragia, ieiuniis & oracionibus et elemosinis imploranda deum ob reuerencia ancille Cristi uotum emittens, 15 ab omni dolore quem assidue passa fuerat sensit se immunem : sed aperturam fistule cernens omnino sanata[*m*], deo & gloriose uirgini Agneti gracias agens copiosas, uotum suum exsoluit.

Quedam alia domina, consors domini Inladote[1] de territorio Luchomericensi, annis pluribus fluxu sanguinis fatigata, in 20 exaltacione sancte crucis[2] ad monasterium in quo corpus sancte Agnetis requiescit peruenit ; et cum multe uirtutes et curaciones uariarum infirmitatum ad inuocacionem uirginis Cristi

[Fol. 214 r.] patrate, coram multitudine que tunc confluxerat | recitarentur, ad eius suffragia cuius audiebat magnalia se conuertit. Cum 25 ad honorem eius uotum in corde suo fecisset, continuo a profluuio sanguinis liberata, miraculum in se gestum ibidem protestans, multos audientes ad benedicendum & laudandum in sanctis suis dominum incitauit.

Soror Donika, ordinis sancte Clare de Praga, filia Do- 30 maslai Desquotz, quadam uice sororem que in coquina pro ceteris sororibus cibos parabat quantum poterat adiuuabat. Cumque uellet aquam fundere in cacabum qui super ignem pendebat, casu in ignem corruit secundum longum, et cadendo simulque in igne iacendo clamabat, " Sancta Agnes, adiuua |

[Fol. 214 v.] me ! " Surgens autem de uoracibus flammis, nullum adus-

---

[1] M. "nilado " ; W. "nicolao ".   [2] See note XXVII., p. 174.

alles iren anderen siechtagen vnd geng | gesund vnd frolichen [Fol. 212 v.]
wider vss vnd kundt allen lutten offenlichen die genad, die ir
von got vnd ir heiligkeit geschehen was.

Ain ander edle fraw die was des herren von Stainberg
elichen fraw, die het die fistel fil jar vnd mocht ir nemet 5
gehelffen. Da vernam sy von disser heiligen junckfrawen sant
Angnessen, daz sy ein gemeine nothelfferin wer aller der die
genad vnd hülf an si suchten, vnd daz sy also fil siechen
generet hett, vnd kert sich mit gantzer zuversicht vnd andacht
zu irer hilf, vnd mit gebet vnd mit fasten vnd mit almůsen 10
sucht sy ir hilf vnd ir genad demüttlichen, vnd enthiesz
antheisz, vnd genas gentzlichen von allem siechtagen, vnd seit
genad vnd danck dem almechtigen got vnd irer mylten vnd
getruwen notthelfferin vnd leist iren antheisz getrüwlichen.

Es was ein swester in dem selben closter, die was eines 15
edlen herren tochter, die solt zu einem zytten den swestren
helffen, die in der kuchen waren. Da sy wasser wolt schutten
in einen kessel, | da ful sy in daz für als lang sy was, vnd in [Fol. 213 r.]
dem fall vnd in dem für ligent, ruft sy sant Angnessen an vnd
sprach "Sant Angnes, hülf mir!", vnd do man sy vss dem 20
für zoch mit arbeiten, wenn die flamen des füres schlügen allent-
halbent ob ir vff, vnd was ir doch kein schad geschehen an dem
lyb, noch nie kein herlin ires gewandes besengt warden.

tionis uestigium in uestimentis suis habuit, nec in corpore
aliquam pertulit lesionem.[1]

Sedes supra quam uirgo Cristi sederat frequenter, ardente
quadam vice domo in qua tunc stabat sedes predicta, modicum
5 quidem in una sui parte adusta in medio magnarum flamarum
mansit inconbusta, que usque hodie in memoriam huius facti
conseruatur.

Quadam uice fluuius que circa monasterium sororum in
Praga in tantum inundauerat, quod magnam partem monasterii
10 & capellam in qua corpus sancte Agnetis fuerat tumulatum
[Fol. 215 r.] pro magna sui parte reple|uit. Cumque una de sororibus
nomine Elyzabet, filia domini Alberti de Lubressitz ad pre-
fatam capellam cicius peruenisset, uolens extrahere de sepulcro
casulam ligneam in qua erant ossa uirginis recondita, casu in
15 aquam lapsa, totaliter cooperta est aquis. Vna autem de
sororibus, nomine Sdinka Paulitonis, corda eidem porrecta ipsam
de aquis exire adiuuit. Cumque egressa fuisset nullum humid-
itatis uestigium apparuit in corpore eius uel in ueste, quod
utique meritis sancte[2] Agnetis factum esse credendum est.

20 Alia soror, nomine Iunka de Bessan, cum sancta Agnetis
adhuc staret insepultum, de pollice pedis ipsius, sororibus
[Fol. 215 v.] absentibus unguem pre|cidere uoluit et causa deuocionis ser-
uare. Quod cum facere cepisset, sanguis fortissime cepit
manare. Que nimium perterrita, sanguinem panno lineo abs-
25 tergebat, ita quod magnam partem ipsius dicto sanguine
rubricauit, qui postea meritis eximie uirginis multis infirmi-
tatibus extitit remedium salutare. Timens autem predicta
soror de prefato fluxu sanguinis nimium reprehendi & turbari,
procidit cum alia sorore iuxta feretrum, orans misericordem
30 dominum et uirginem piam ut predictum fluxum sistere dignaretur, quod et factum est.

Sunt quidem & alia multa signa que per huius gloriose |
[Fol. 216 r.] uirginis merita dominus operari dignatus est, non solum in
infirmantibus sed eciam in rebus perditis ut recuperentur adiu-

---

[1] M. adds " dez sprach sy allezit Deo gracias "; W. ditto, but mistaking
this for end breaks off at this point.
[2] MS. " sancta ".

Der stul da sy vff sass so bettet, der stund in einem husz, daz geng an vnd bran; vnd do daz husz verbran, do beleib der stul mytten in dem[1] für on allem schaden vnverbrent.

Ain gross wasser flosz vor dem closter hin, das zu einem zytten also gar gross daz es über geng vnd brach auch in daz 5 closter, daz ez ein sytten des closters erfüllet, vnd brach auch in die cappellen da sant Angnes in begraben was. Da lieff ein swester die hiesz Elisabet gar bald[2] in die cappelen da ir gebein in was, vnd wolt es her vss tragen vnd fiel von vngeschicht[3] in daz wasser, daz das wasser ob ir zu samen 10 schlug. Da komen die swestren zu geloffen vnd wurffend | ir [Fol. 213 v.] ein seil dar vnd zügen sy dar an hervss mit arbeiten; vnd do sy herusz kam, do en was ir weder am lyb noch an dem gewand nasz worden noch kein schad geschehen von sant Angnessen hilf.

Do sant Angnes gestarb vnd noch offen stund, do geng 15 ein swester über sy, die hiesz Gutta vnd warttet wenn die swestren alle hin vss kömen, so wolt sy denn sant Angnessen einen nagel ab der grossen zehen abschnyden vnd wolt in von andacht han behaltten. Do sy begund zu schnyden, do ward sy als ser blütten daz die swester vnmesslich ser erschrack, wann 20 sy vorcht daz man sy swerlichen dar vmm straffen wurd, vnd verhûb die zehen mit lynnen düchern, daz das blut verstan solt; aber es half nit, es blut als für sich. Do ward der swester als angst, daz sy nyder fiel nebent der bar vnd ein ander swester mit ir vnd battent den mylten got vnd die süssen 25 sant Angnessen daz das blut gestyllet; vnd also verstund daz blut vnd was des gar fil in die dücher kumen. Do von gar fil siechen genassen von[4] schweren vnd menger hand siechtag. |

Sy hett auch fil ander zeihen gethan vnd grosser loblicher [Fol. 214 r.] wunder, die got durch iren willen het gethan nit allein an den 30

---

[1] MS. " husz " deleted.   [2] MS. " vnd vnd wolt," deleted.
[3] MS. " sicht " corrected by scribe to " schicht ". Same mistake on fol. 208 v.
[4] MS. " swesren " deleted.

uando, et cunctis ad se clamantibus misericorditer sucurrendo. Predicta uero idcirco a me pauca sub compendio sunt transcursa, ut digniores & periciores [1] laudatores occasionem habeant plura si uoluerint ad laudem dei ac huius illustrissime uirginis
5 apponendi.

PRECACIO.

Eya, uirgo benigna, que [2] in littore celestis patrie secura in stacione letaris, intue minimum ac uilissimum seruorum dei, qui gesta tua gloriosa balbuciendo utrumque depromsi, oculis
[Fol. 216 v.] miseracionis intendas cum | ceteris tibi deuotis, ut qui adhuc
10 miseri in mari turbulento uersamur et procellosas eius uoragines corporis ratem trahentes ignoramus an ad soliditatem littoris peruenire possimus, tuis sanctissimis precibus de lacu miserie et de luto fecis educas, ne nos demergat tempestas aque multimoda scilicet tribulacio, neque dampnacionis eterne
15 absorbeat nos profundum.   Ora regem maiestatis, cuius nunc iocundissima frueris uisione, ut in fluctibus huius pelagi potenti sua dextera nos gubernare dignetur, quatenus inter Caribdim & Scillam [3] per medium sic tendamus, ut utroque periculo
[Fol. 217 r.] euitato salua naui & mercibus ad portum felicitatis perpetue
20 securi pertingere ualeamus.   Quod tuis sacris meritis & precibus ipse nobis prestare dignetur, qui est deus benedictus laudabilis & gloriosus in secula seculorum.   Amen.

Cristo deuota uirgo domina Agnes, soror Vencezlai quarti regis Bohemie, suscepit ordinem sancti Francisci : ad cuius
25 imitacionem, sicut pater sanctus Franciscus sub typo trium ordinum tres ecclesias erexit, ita ipsa tres sollempnes ecclesias construxit in Praga.   Primam uidelicet in honore saluatoris omnium, in qua se cum sororibus suis recollegit.   Secundam in honore sancte dei genitricis Marie et beati Francisci pro
30 fratribus minoribus iuxta se diuina sibi & sororibus ordinis
Fol. 217 v.] Sancte Clare ministrantibus. | Terciam in hospitali suo eciam in honore sancti Francisci pro ordine cruciferorum tunc de

---

[1] MS. "peririciores".   [2] M. omits from "que . . . profundum .
[3] M. "zwischen den vntern vnd den obern' ,

siechen die sy genert hett, sunder auch an den die in andren freiszen vnd notten warend, den sy myltlichen zu hilf kom, vnd auch an den dingen, die man verloren hett, den half sy daz es in wider ward, vnd alle die sy anrüfften vnd ir genad vnd hilf begerten, den kam sy barmhertzlichen zu hilf. 5

Die zeichen vnd wunder die got durch iren willen hat gethan, die lasz ich alle nun vnder wegen vnd han ir nun ein wenig geschriben vnd kurtzlichen überfaren durch daz, das die bessern meister, die des wirdiger sint denn ich, noch vil me von ir vindent zu schriben ob sy wollent zu lob vnd eren dem 10 obersten got vnd der aller heiligsten vnd loblichsten junckfrawen, sant Angnes von Brag. Amen.

Die arm swester, die es geschriben hat, begert das ir got für sy byttent mit einem AUE MARIA.

nouo per fratres minores de mandato ipsius domine Agnetis
creato, uidelicet cruciferis stelliferis quibus ipsum hospitale
copiosissime de propriis bonis regalibus dotatum conmisit, ut
ipsi debilibus & infirmis & omnibus miseris personis ibi re-
5 ceptis, tam in temporalibus quam in spiritualibus, fideliter
necessaria ministrarent.

SUBJECT UNCERTAIN : PROBABLY BLESSED AGNES OF
BOHEMIA AND TWO SISTERS.

(From MS. M.281 Royal Library, Dresden.)

HOW OUR LORD AND OUR LADY CROWNED SAINT CLARE
IN HEAVEN.

(From MS. M.281 Royal Library, Dresden.)

Dise brief sant die selig Sand Clar der edeln kvniginn der [Fol. 139 v.]
heiligen jvnkfrawen Agnesen, des aller edelsten kvnges tohter
von Pehaim, die da waz ze Brag in ainem closter Sand Claren
ordens do Sand Clar dennoch lebt auf ertreich, ze manen vnd
ze leren vnd ze sterken disev vorgesprochen jvnkfrawen Sand 5
Agnesen an dem dienst gotes, vnd an strenkait des ordens,
vnd auch zv ainem vrkvnde gaistleicher lieb die si zv ir het:
dar vmb sant ir Sand Clar dise brief die her nach geschriben sten.

Der ersamen vnd aller heiligsten jvnkfrawen Agnesen, der | [Fol. 139 r.]
tohter des aller wirdigsten vnd edelsten kvnges ze Pehaim, en- 11
bevt Clara, ain vnwirdige dienerin Jhesu Cristi[1] vnd ain
vnnvtzev dirn der beslozzen frawen des closters Sand
Damians von Assis, ir vndertan vnd dirn allenthalben, enpfil-
het sich selben ir in alle weise mit gaistleicher wirdikait 15
vnd wunschet ir daz si erwerbe vnd verdien die ere der
ewigen selikait.

[1] Ber. omits "ain vnwirdige . . . Cristi".

Ich hab gehöret den leimvnt ewres aller heiligsten wandels
vnd aller erwergsten[1] lebens der ist auch endleichen erhollen
niht mir alain, svnder nahen in allem vmbringe[2] der werlt,
vnd da von frewe ich mich vil in vnserm herren vnd pin vro.
[Fol. 140 r.] Von dem | ich mich niht alain mag frewen, halt alle die da tvn
6 und begern ze tvn[3] den dienst Jhesu Cristi. Wann da ir
genozzen möht haben vor anderr gezirde vnd ere der werlt
die wirdikait daz ir mit vbertrefender ere möht eleich gemehelt sein worden dem hohen kaiser, als ewerr vnd seiner wir-
10 dikait gezvmen het, disev dink habt ir ellev verwidert vnd habt
mit gantzem mvt vnd begirde ewres hertzen mer erwelt die aller
heiligsten armvt vnd gebresten des leibes vnd habt genvmen
ainen gemaheln ains edelern geslehtes, vnsern herren Jhesum
Cristum, der evren magtvm allezeit vngemeligt vnd vnbe-
[Fol. 140 v.] schedent[4] | wirt behüten. So ir den gemaheln nimmet, so
16 seit ir kevsche; so ir in an rvret, so wert ir dest rainer; so
ir in nemt, so seit ir ain jvnkfrawen; dez vermügenhait ist
sterker, des edel ist höher, des angesihte ist schöner, des
minne ist süzzer vnd alle sein gnad avzerwelter;[5] von des
20 vmbvahen seit ir iezvnt begriffen, der ewer hertze geziret
hat mit hohgültigen gestainen vnd evren oren gegeben hat
vnbetrehtenleich margariten vnd evech ellevsamt vmbgeben
hat mit blvenden vnd scheinenden gimmen, vnd evch ge-
krönet hat mit ainer gvldeinen kron, die offenbar ist mit
[Fol. 141 r.] dem zaich|en der heilikait. Da von, aller libstev swester vnd
26 auch vil ersamev frawe, wanne ir ain gemahel vnd ain mvter
vnd ain swester seit meins herren Jhesu Cristi vnd mit alle
wider gleistenleich seit gezaichent mit dem namen des
vnverwerten[6] magtvms vnd der aller heiligsten armvt, sc
30 schült ir stark sein an dem heiligen dienst des der arm an
dem crevtz gemartert ist, den ir habt angevangen inbrünstig

---

[1] MS. "erwersten" altered by addition of "g" in red. Ber., "erbersten".
B3. and W., "erwirdigsten".
[2] Ibid., "in aller der werlt".
[3] W. omits "und begern ze tvn".
[4] Ber., "vnvermaset vnd vngeschedigt".
[5] Ber. adds "für zytliche gemachel".
[6] Ber., "mit dem namen des unvermasten magtums".

an ewerr begirde, der für vns alle hat erliden die marter des creuces[1] vnd vns hat erlöset von dem gewalte des fürsten der vinsternvsse, von des gewalt wir gepvnden | gehabt waren mit [Fol. 141 v.] panden vmb die vngehorsam vnsers ersten vaters, vnd hat vns versvnet mit got dem vater.   5

O seligev armvt, den die si minnen vnd vmbvahen verleihet ewige wirtschaft! O heligev armvt, den die si haben vnd ir begern, den ist von got gehaizzen daz himelreich, vnd in wirt erpoten ewige ere vnd daz selig leben an allen zweifel! O miltev armvt, die vnser herre Jhesus Cristus der da verrihte 10 hat vnd noch verrihte[2] himel vnd erde, der mit dem worte geschufe die creatur, der hat si geruchet vmbvahen vor andern dingen,[3] wanne er sprach "Die fühse haben höler, vnd die vögel | des himels nest, aber des menschen kint, daz ist [Fol. 142 r.] Cristus, hat niht da er sein havbt genaige,"[4] svnder mit nider 15 genaigtem havbt gab er dem vater seinen gaist.[5] Da von seit als ain grozzer vnd ain sogetan herre kom in den megtleichen leip[6] vnd wolt erscheinen versmehter ellender vnd armer in diser werlt dar vmb daz die menschen die da waren aller ermest vnd dürftigen vnd die da liden grozze armvt an der himelischen 20 speise[7] reich würden in im vnd besezzen daz himelische reiche. Nv schvlt ir evch vil frewen vnd vro sein vnd wert erfvllet mit grozzer frevd vnd mit gaistleicher vrö|leichait.   Wanne [Fol. 142 v.] seit ev pas gevallen hat versmehde der werlt denne die[8] ere, vnd armvt pas denne zeitleicher reichtvm, vnd ir mere evren 25 schatz verbergen wölt in dem himel denn in dem ertreiche do in der rost niht verswendet vnd die milbe niht verderbet vnd die dieb niht avz graben noch stelen, so ist ewer lon gar vbernvhtig[9] in dem himel vnd habt ir verdienet daz ir pilleich genant werdet ain swester, ain gemahel vnd ain mvter des der 30

---

[1] Ber. adds "und den aller pittersten tod".
[2] Ber., "der da regirt himel," etc.
[3] Ber., "tugenden".   [4] W., "hynlege".
[5] Ber., "mit geneigtem hoft uff sein prust gab er uff sein geist".
[6] W., "leichnam".   [7] Ber. omits "an . . . speise".
[8] In B3. "di" is added in margin.   In W. it is omitted, which suggests that W. is copied from B3.
[9] Ber., "oberflusyg" instead of "vbernvhtig".

ain svn ist des obersten vaters vnd der ersamen junkfrawen vnser frawen.

Ich gelaube vestikleich ir habt erkant daz daz himelreich
[Fol. 143 r.] nieman von vnserm herren gelobt wirt vnd | auch gegeben
5 denne den armen, wanne swenn man zeitleiche dink liep hat, so verlevset man die fruht der minne;[1] vnd daz man got vnd irdischem gut niht[2] gedienen mvge, wanne aintweder ain herre wirt liep gehabt vnd der ander wirt gehazzet, oder man dienet ainem vnd versmeht den andern; vnd daz ain geklaiter mit
10 ainem nackenden niht geringen mvge, wanne der wirt schier an die erden geworfen, der da hat da mit er gehabt werd; vnd daz iemant ersam beleibe in diser werlt vnd daz himel-reich besitze mit vnserm herre; vnd daz ain ölpent[3] pas mvg
[Fol. 143 v.] gen durch ainer nadel öre denne der reiche mensche | avf gen
15 in daz himelreich.   Dar vmb habt ir hin geworfen die klaider, daz ist zeitleichen reichtvm, daz ir dem der mit ev ringet iht möht vndergeligen vnd daz ir durch den strengen wek vnd die engen porten möht gegen in daz himelisch reich.   Zwar ez ist ain grozzer vnd ain löbleicher wehselkavf verlazzen[4]
20 zeitleichev dink vmb ewigev vnd verdienen himelischev dink fvr irdischev vnd enpfahen hvndertvaltiges fvr ains[5] vnd ewicleich besitzen daz selig leben.

Dar vmb han ich geahtet ze flehen ewer wirdikait vnd heilikait als vil ich mag mit diemvtiger bet in den innedern[6]
[Fol. 144 r.] Cristi, daz | ir wölt gesterket werden[7] an seinem heligen dienst
26 vnd wahset von dem guten zv dem pezzern vnd von tugenden zv tugenden, daz der dem ir dienet mit gantzer begirde evrs gemvtes ev geruch ze geben den lon des ir da wünschet.

Nv pit ich evch auch als vil ich vermag in vnserm herren
30 daz ir mich ewer vnnvtzev dirn vnd die andern swester die bei mir wonent in dem closter, die da andehtig gen ev sint,[8] ev

---

[1] B3. and W. add "Ich gelaub ir habt auch der kant".

[2] Ber. adds "mit einander" in margin.   [3] Ber., "kemeltir"; W., "elefant".

[4] B3. and W., "daz man lezzet" instead of "verlazzen".

[5] W., "enphaen eyn zeitlichs von eyn ewiglichs" and omits "vnd . . . leben".

[6] Ber., "in der leib Cristi".   [7] B3. and W., "daz ir stark seit".

[8] Ibid., "die andacht haben zu ew".

lazzet enpfolhen sein in ewren andehtigen gebet, mit des
hilfe mvg wir erarnen die parmhertzikait Jhesu Cristi vnd
samt mit ev mezzen die götleichen anschawevnge. Nv seit
gesegent vnd wol mvgent in vn|serm herren vnd bitet fvr [Fol. 144 v.]
mich.   5

DAZ IST DER ANDER BRIEF.

Der tohter des kvnges aller kvnige, der dirn des herren
aller herren, der aller wirdigsten gemaheln Jhesu Cristi vnd
avch der edeln kvnigin frawen Agnesen, enbevt Clara, ain
vnnützev vnd ain vnwirdigev dirn der armen frawen iren grvz
vnd wünschet ir ze allen zeiten ze leben in der obersten armvt. 10
    Ich dank dem geber aller gnaden, von dem man gelavbet
avzfliezzen ain iegleich aller peste gabe,[1] daz er dich als vil
gezieret hat mit den zaichen der tugent vnd dich erlevhtet hat
mit dem gebrech[2] als grozzer | volkvmenhait, daz dv pist [Fol. 145 r.]
worden ain fleizzigev nachvolgerin des volkvmen vaters. Nv 15
mvzest dv verdienen daz dv volkvmen werdest, daz seinev
avgen ihtes iht vnvolkvmens an dir sehen. Ditz ist die volkvmenhait mit der dich der kvnk selber im zv gesellen wirt in
dem himelischen pravtbette,[3] daz dv versmehet hast die
höhe des irdischen reiches, vnd wenik geruchet hast dich ze 20
verpinden zv der kayserleichen e, vnd pist worden ain frevndin
der aller heiligsten armvt, vnd hast an gehaftet irn fvzsporn
in dem gaist der grozzen diemvtikait vnd der aller inbrvnstig-
sten minne, vnd hast erarnet zv gefvgt | werden irre gemahel [Fol. 145 v.]
schaft.   25
    Seit ich dich erkenne geeret sein[4] mit tugenden, so han
ich maz an langen worten vnd wil dich niht besweren mit
vberflitzzigen worten, swie dich doch nihtz vberflüzzig
dvnk von den dingen da dir etleich trost von kvmen
mag. Svnder wanne ains notvrftig ist, daz ain bezevg ich 30
vnd man dich durch die lieb des, dem dv dich geopfert

[1] B3. and W. add "vnd ein igleich volkvmen gab".
[2] *Ibid.*, "mit den zeichen der volkvmenhait".
[3] Ber., "gemahelpet".
[4] B3. and W., "daz du gereichet pist," instead of "geeret sein".

hast zv ainen heiligen vnd wolgevallenden opfer, daz dv
gedenkest deins fvrsatzes vnd, als die ander Rachel, alle zeit[1]
ansehest deinen anvank.   Daz dv da habst, daz hab ; daz dv da
[Fol. 146 r.] tvst, daz tv, noch | lazze sein ṅiht, svnder dv gange sicher
5 frewende vnd fröleich durch den wek als grozzer selikait mit
snellem lavffe, mit ringem gange, mit vnangestozzen füzzen,
daz dein genge iht ainen stavp enpfahen, daz dv nieman
volgest vnd nieman[2] gelaubest, der dich wolt wider ziehen
von disem fürsatz, der dir legt ain irrsal an den wek daz dv
10 dem aller obersten got iht wider gebest dein anthaizzen in
der volkvmenhait mit der dich der gaist vnsers herren geladen
hat.   Aber an dem daz dv den wek der gebot vnsers herren
dest sicherleicher durch gest, so volg nach dem rat vnsers
[Fol. 146 v.] ersamen vaters | bruder Helye des Generals[3]; den setz für an-
15 derr levte rete vnd aht in lieber denne alle gab.   Swer aber dir
ain anders sagt vnd dir ain anders rette, daz dein volkvmenhait
verirre vnd daz erscheine dein gotleichen rvffen oder laden[4]
wider sein, vnd ob dv in halt scholdest eren, so scholt dv doch
seinem rat niht volgen, svnder dv scholt den armen Cristum,
20 dv armev jvnkfrawe, vmbvahen.   Sihe, er ist versmeht fvr
dich worden, vnd volge nach seinev werk,[5] daz dv versmeht
seist durch in in diser werlt.   Sihe an deinen gemaheln, der
da schön waz vor aller menschenkinden, daz der vmb dein
[Fol. 147 r.] hail | ist worden der versmehst aller manne, versmeht, [_ze_]-
25 slagen[6] vnd an allem seinem leibe manikveltikleichen gegaiselt
vnd gestorben vnter der selben[7] angst des crevces.

Dv vil edelev kvnigin, sihe an, merke vnd schawe, beger im
nach ze volgen ! Mitleidest dv dem, so wirdest dv daz himelreich mit im besitzen ; klagest dv mit im, so wirdest dv dich
30 mit im frewen.   Stirbest dv mit im an dem creutze der be-
trvbsal, so wirdest dv in dem glantze der heiligen besitzen die
himelischen wonvnge, vnd wirt dein nam geschriben an daz bvch
[Fol. 147 v.] dez lebens vnd wirt noch kvnftig ersam vnter den | levten. Dar

---

[1] B3. has "allezeit" added in margin ; W. omits it, thus supporting the
possibility that W. is copied from B3.
[2] B3. and W. omit "nieman".
[3] See note XXVIII., p. 174.
[4] B3. and W. omit "oder laden".   [5] B., "also volg ym nach".
[6] MS. "der slagen".   [7] Ber., "grossen" instead of "selben".

vmb so wirdest dv immer ewicleich enpfahen die ere des
himelischen reiches fvr die irdischen vnd zergenkleichen dink,
vnd die ewigen gvten dink fvr die verdorbenleichen, vnd wirst
immer ewikleichen leben.

Nv pis gesegent vnd wol mvgent, aller libstev swester vnd 5
frawe, dvrch vnsern herren deinen gemaheln vnd pis fleizzich
daz dv mich vnd alle mein swester vnserm herren enpfelhest
mit deinem andehtigen gebet, wanne wir vns frewen von den
guten dingen vnsers herren die er mit seiner gnad an dir
würket.   Enpfilh vns avch vil[1] deinen swestern.   10

Daz ist der dritte brief.

Irre aller erwirdigsten frawen in vnserm herren Cristo vnd [Fol. 148 r.]
avch[2] der liben vor allen totleichen menschen[3] Agnesen des
edeln kvnges swester ze Pehaim aber iezvnd ain swester vnd
ain gemahel des kvnges von himelreich, enbevt die aller
diemvtigst Clara vnd ain vnwirdigev dirn vnsers herren, ain 15
dienerin der armen frawen, die frevd des grvzzes in dem merer
des[4] hailes vnd[5] daz peste des man begern mag.   Von deiner
gesvnthait vnd von deinem seligen wesen vnd[6] von deinem
gehvksamen nachvolgen da mit ich verstan dich eingen in
dem angevangen lavffe ze behaben den himelischen lon, da | 20
von wird ich als vil mer mit grozzer frevde erfvllet vnd kreftig [Fol. 148 v.]
mit frevden in vnserm herren, als vil ich erkenne vnd wene,
daz dv erfüllest den gebresten als wol an mir als an andern
vnsern swestern der wunderleichen nachvolgvnge der fvzsporn
des armen vnd des diemvtigen Jhesu Cristi.   Werleich ich 25
mag mich wol frewen noch nieman mag mich fremd gemachen
von als grozzer frevde, so ich daz han des ich vnder dem

---

[1] B3. and W., " fleizig " instead of " vil ".

[2] Ber. omits " irre aller . . . avch ".   [3] B3. and W. insert " swester ".

[4] *Ibid.* add " ewigen ".   [5] *Ibid.,* " wvnschet ir ".

[6] B3. read originally : " vnd von deinem gehvkke da mit ich verstan dich
gen in dem," etc.   This is altered by marginal additions to " vnd von deinem
gehvkkesamen nachvolgen da mit ich verstan dich eingen in dem," etc.   W.
appears to have copied from the uncorrected text of B3., for it reads : " vnd von
deinem globde (!) da mit ich vorstan dich dich gen yn dez," etc.   Both B3. and
W. omit " vnd von deinem seligen wesen ".

himel begert han, vnd so ich sihe dich vnderstevret sein mit
ainer wunderleichen fvrtreffenden wirdikait der weishait, die
da get von dem mvnde gotes selber vnd dich sihe vnersch-
[Fol. 149 r.] röckenleich vnd vnverwenleich [1] vertreten | die kvndikait des
5 listigen veindes, vnd die hohvart die da ist ain verderberin
menschleicher nature vnd die eitelkait die da törot machet
menschleichev hertzen, vnd dv avch den vngeleichen [2] schatz,
der verporgen ist in dem acker [3] der werlt vnd der mensch-
leichen hertzen mit dem daz gekavfet wirt von dem ellev dink
10 worden sint von nihtev, hast vmbvangen mit den armen
der diemvtikait vnd mit der tugent des gelauben vnd hast
avch vmbvangen die heiligen armvt. Ich mag avch aigenleichen [4] sprechen daz wort des zwelfpoten, "ich sihe daz dv
pist ain helferin gotes vnd ain avfheberin der nidervallenden
[Fol. 149 v.] gelider seines vnsegleichen [5] leibes". Wer sprech halt daz ich
16 mich niht schölt frewen von als wunderleichen frevden. Dv
aller liebstev, nv frewe dich avch ze allen zeiten in vnserm
herren vnd laz dich pitterkait vnd vinsternvsse niht verwalken.
O dv aller svzstev frawe in vnserm herren Cristo, ain frevde
20 der engel, ain kron der swester, leg deinen mvt [6] in den
spiegel der ewikait, leg dein sel in den schein der eren, leg
dein hertze in daz pilde des gotleichen wesens vnd pilde dich
selber gar mit ainem [7] anschawen in daz pilde der gothait
selbe, daz dv avch enpfindest des da enpfinden sein frevnd,
[Fol. 150 r.] daz dv versvchest die verporgen | svzzikait die got selber von
26 angeng hat avfgeslozzen [8] den seinen [9] die in lip haben, vnd
laz gentzleich vnterwegen ellev dev dink die in diser trvgleichen werlt ir blinten minner bestricken mit betrvbleichen

---

[1] B3. and W., "getvrstikleich" instead of "vnerschröckenleich vnd vnver-
wenleich".
[2] B. and W., "zv dem nihtes zv geleichen ist" instead of "vngeleichen".
[3] W., "kerker". [4] Ber., "wol" instead of "aigenleichen".
[5] Ber. omits "vnsegleichen".
[6] B3. and W., "sin" instead of "mvt".
[7] *Ibid.* add "contemplirenden". [8] *Ibid.*, "behalten".
[9] Ber., "denen" instead of "den seinen"; B3. and W., "den" instead of
"den seinen".

panden. Vnd[1] hab den alain gentzleichen[2] liep der sich gar
gegeben hat vmb dein minne, von des schöne wundert sich
svnne vnd mone, des lon vnd reichtvm kain ende ist, ich
sprich den svn des aller obersten[3] den ain jvnkfrawe geborn
hat vnd nach der gebvrd magt beliben ist. Der aller 5
svzsten mvter des selben svns scholt dv anhaften, die
ainen sogetanen svn geborn hat, den | die himel niht [Fol. 150 v.]
mohten gevahen,[4] den hat si braht in dem klainen slozze
irs heiligen leibes vnd hat in getragen in irr jvnkfravnleichen
schozze. Wer schölt niht schevhen die lag des menschen 10
veindes, der mit der selde diser kvrzen zeit vnd mit trvghait
der eren daz twinget ze niht werden daz grözzer ist den der
himel?[5] Nim war iezvnt ist scheinber daz die sel des gelev-
bigen menschen von der gnade gotes ist die wirdigest[6] aller
creatur vnd grözzer denne der himel. Den schepfer den die 15
himel mit den creaturen niht gevahen mvgen, des wonvnge
wirt alain ain gelavbige sel, vnd daz geschiht alain dvrch | die [Fol. 151 r.]
minne der die pösen darben, als die warhait, daz ist Cristus
selber, sprichet " Wer mich liep hat, der wirt liep gehabt von
meinem vater, vnd ich wird in liep haben, vnd wir werden[7] zv 20
im kvmen, vnd werden[8] ain wanvnge pei im machen ". Reht
als die jvnkfrawe aller jvnkfrawen in hat leiplich getragen, also
scholt dv nachvolgen die fvzspor[9] irr diemvtikait vnd avch
irre armvt: so maht dv in mit kevschem vnd megtleichem[10]
hertzen an zweifel ze allen zeiten[11] tragen vnd behaben den 25
von dem dv vnd ellev dink gehabt werden, daz dv besitzest
daz[12] daz dv mit gewalte sterkleichen besitzen wirst, | so anderr [Fol. 151 v.]

---

[1] B3. and W., " minne allein den der," etc.
[2] Ber. omits " gentzleichen ".
[3] B3. and W., " allerhöhsten,".   [4] W., " begreiffin ".
[5] B3. and W., " wer schölt halt niht schevhen die lage des veindes mensch-
liches geslehtes der da in diser kleinen zeit mit der trvgleichen ere dev werlt ze
niht pringet die edeln sel die grözzer ist denne der himel ".
[6] Ber., " wirdiger denn all creatur ".   [7] B3. and W., " wöllen ".
[8] *Ibid.*   [9] B3. and W. omit " die fvzspor ".
[10] Ber., " reinem " instead of " megtleichem ".
[11] B3. and W., " den tragen vnd behalten von dem du vnd ellev dink auf
gehalten werden ".
[12] Ber., B3. and W. omit " daz dv besitzest daz ".

reichtvm diser werlt hinget, an dem vil werltleicher kvnig vnd
kvniginne betrogen werden, swie daz ir hohvart avf gegangen
sei pis an den himel vnd irev havbt die wolken angervret
haben, die werden an dem ende verderbet als ain mist havfe.

5 Vber[1] dev dink die dv mir enpoten hast, die ich dir
offenne schol, wer die hohzeit sein vnd leiht als ich wen daz
dv mainest an der manikveltikait der speise, wie vns geleret
het svnderleich ze begen vnser aller ersamster vater sand
Franciscus, des antwurte ich deiner minne. Dein weishait schol
[Fol. 152 r.] bekennen[2] daz an die kranken vnd die siechen den hat er |
11 vns gemant vnd geboten ze tvn alle die minne die wir
vermvgen mit allerlai speise, vnd vnser kain die gesvnt vnd
stark ist newer alain vasten speise schölt ezzen als wol die
tegleichen tag als die höhzeitleichen, vnd alle tage vasten
15 avzgenumen die svntage vnd den Cristage ; an den scholt
wir zwir ezzen vnd avch an den pfintztagen[3] ze gewönleichen
zeiten ; nach iegleicher willen als ob si niht wolt vasten si wer
sein niht gebvnden.[4] Aber wir gesvnden vasten tegleichen
an die svntag vnd den Cristage. Wir sein avch, als Sand
20 Franciscen schrift spricht, niht gebvnden ze vasten in allen
ostern[5] vnd an den hohzeiten vnser frawen Marien[6] vnd der
zwelfpoten, ez kvmen denne dise sölhe hohzeit an den freitage.
Als vorgesprochen ist,[7] wir die gesvnt vnd stark sint, ezzen

---

[1] B3. differs considerably in this paragraph :—

" Als du mir enpoten hast daz ich dir offenn schol wer vnser hohzeit sein vnd
leiht als ich wen du mainest an der misleikeit vnserr speis, wie vns geleret het
vnser aller ersamster vater sand Franciscus svnderleichen zu begen daz ich
deiner minne dar vber antwurten schülle, so scholt du wizzen daz die kranken vnd
die sichen sein auzgenumen, den hat er vns gepoten ze tvn alle die minne die wir
vermvgen mit allerley speise. Aber vnser keinew die gesvnt vnd stark ist
schüllen niht denn alein vastenspeis ezzen peidev tegleich vnd hohtzeitleich
tagen."

W. is practically identical.

[2] Ber., " wyssen " instead of " bekennen ".

[3] Ber., " donstagen " instead of " pfintztagen ".

[4] Ber., " ob eine nit wil fasten, so ist sy sein nit schuldig " ; B3., " si were sein
niht schuldig noch gepunden an dem pfintztage ".

[5] Ber., " in der osterlichen zit ".

[6] Ber., " unser liebe frawen gotes müter Maria ".

[7] Ber. omits " als vorgesprochen ist ".

allezeit vasten speise. Zwar wanne vnser leip niht ein erein leip ist, vnd vnser sterk niht der stain sterke ist, vnd wir halt blöde sein vnd mit leipleicher krankhait nider genaigt sein so pit ich dich, aller liebstev, daz dv dich weisleich vnd beschaidenleich enziehest von etleicher vnbeschaiden vnd[1] vn mügleicher herbikait der abstinenci die dv hast angegangen, als ich wol erkenne. Vnd ich pit dich in vnserm herren daz dv lebende lobest vnsern herren[2] | vnd vnserm herren erbietest [Fol. 153 r.] deinen beschaiden dienst ; vnd dein opfer sei allezeit gekochet mit dem saltz der beschaidenhait. Nv[3] mvg wol ze allen zeiten[4] in vnserm herren, als ich mir selber wvnsche wol ze mvgen, vnd enpfilhe mich vnd alle mein swester deinen heiligen swestren.

DAZ IST DER VIRDE BRIEF.

Irre halben sel vnd der svnderleichen almarein der hertzenleichen lieb, der edeln kvnigin, der gemaheln des lambes[5] des ewigen kvnges,[6] frawen Agnesen, irr aller liebsten mvter vnd svnderleicher tohter vnter den andern, enbevt Clara ain vnwirdige dienerin Cristi vnd ain vnnvtzev dirn seiner dirn die da wonen | in dem closter sand Damians von Assis irn grvz, [Fol. 153 v.] vnd wvnschet ir ze singen ain newes[7] gesank mit den andern[8] aller heiligsten jvnkfrawen[9] vor dem tron gotes vnd des lammes[10] vnd dem lemlein nach volgen, swar ez ge.[11] O mvter vnd tohter, ain gemahel des kvnges aller der werlt, hab ich dir als emzzikleich niht geschriben als dein sel vnd auch samt die mein[12] begert vnd wünschet, da von scholt dv dich etwie

---

[1] Ber. omits " vnbeschaiden vnd ".
[2] B3. and W. omit " daz dv lebende lobest vnsern herren ".
[3] *Ibid.* " ich beger daz du wol mvgest alle zeit ".
[4] Ber. omits " ze allen zeiten ".
[5] B3. and W., " des himelischen lempleins ".
[6] Ber., " der gemahel des kings der ewigen eren ".
[7] Ber. omits " newes ".   [8] B3. and W. omit " andern ".
[9] *Ibid.* " meiden " for " jvnkfrawen ".
[10] *Ibid.* " des himelischen lempleins ".
[11] Ber., " wa es hin gat ".
[12] B3. and W., " als dein vnd mein sel ".

vil niht wundern, noch scholt kainigweise niht gelavben daz
daz fewer der lieb gegen dir iht dez minner svzleich brinne in
den | innedern deiner mvter.   Daz ist ez daz mich da irret hat,
[Fol. 154 r.] der | gebreste der boten vnd die offenbarn fraiṣe vnterwegen.
5 Nv schreib ich deiner minne vnd mitfrewe mich mit dir vnd
frewe mich in frevden, dv gemahel vnsers herren, wanne dv
pist reht als die ander aller heiligst jvnkfrawe, Sand Agnes,
wunderleich gemehelt dem vngemailigtem ¹ lemblein, daz da
tregt die svnde der werlt vnd hast versmeht die eitelkait diser
10 werlt.   Sicherleich er ist selik, dem daz gegeben wirt daz er
niezzen schol dise heilige gemahelschaft vnd anhaften dem
von gantzem   hertzen,² von des schön sich an vnderlaz ³
wundernt alle die selig ⁴ samnvnge des himelreiches, des
[Fol. 154 v.] begird begirige | machet, des contempliren wider bringet, des
15 gütikait erfüllet, des süzzikait machet vol, des gehvgnvsse ⁵
levhtet svzleichen, von des gutem smacke werden die toten
wider lebendig, des ersame angesihte machet selig alle die
bvrger der obersten Iherusalem, wanne er ist ain schein der
eren, ain glantz des ewigen lihtes vnd ain spiegel an mal.
20   Dv kvnigin, ain gemahel Jhesu Cristi, sihe an tegleiches
disen spiegel vnd erlvge ⁶ dein antlütze emzzikleich dar inne,
daz dv dich ellevsamt also inwendig zirest vnd geklaidet seist
vnd vmbgeben ⁷ mit der mankveltikait alle tvgent vnd daz
[Fol. 155 r.] dv alsu ⁸ in seiner | angesihte gezieret seist mit den blvmen vnd
25 mit den klaidern aller tugent,⁹ als wol gezimt der tohter vnd
gemaheln des obersten kvnges.   In dem spiegel wider scheinet
die selig armvt, die heilig ¹⁰ diemvtikait vnd die vnsegleich
minne, als dv wol durch vnd durch den gantzen spigel
schaven maht.
30   O wunderleichev diemvtikait, O erschröckenleichev armvt,
der kvnik der engel vnd der herre himelreiches vnd ertreiches
wart gelegt in ain krippen !   An der mittel des spiegels merke

---

¹ Ber., " vnvermaltigen ".   ² Ber. omits " von gantzem hertzen ".
³ Ber. omits " an vnderlaz ".   ⁴ Ber. omits " die selig ".   ⁵ Ber., "gedechnus".
⁶ Ber., " ersich " instead of " erlvge " : " emzzikleich " instead of " teglich ".
⁷ Ber. omits " vnd vmbgeben ".   ⁸ Ber. omits " vnd daz dv also ".
⁹ Ber. omits " gezieret . . . tugent ".   ¹⁰ MS. " armvt " deleted.

sein diemvtikait vnd sein selige armvt vnd vnzelleich vil arbait
vnd peinleichait die er geliden hat vmb die erlösvnge mensch-
leiches ge|slehtes.[1] Aber an dem ende des spigels schawe die [Fol. 155 v.]
vnsegleichen minne, mit der er wolt leiden an dem stammen [2]
des crevces vnd dar an wolt sterben mit dem aller lester- 5
leichsten tode vnter allen töden. Dar vmb do der selbe spigel
gesetzet waz an daz heilig crevtz, da manet er die da fvr
gingen ze merken disev dink vnd sprach "O we,[3] ir alle die
da gent durch den wek,[4] merket vnd seht ob kain smertz
sei als mein smertze". So schvlle wir im der da schreiet vnd 10
rvfet antwürten mit ainer stimme vnd mit ainem gaiste : [5]
"Ich wil [dein] [6] gedenken mit meiner gehvgnvsse vnd mein
sel wirt swelken in mir". Mit der inbrvnstikait diser minne |
scholt dv emzzikleich krefticleich [7] enzvndet werden, O kvni- [Fol. 156 r.]
gin des himelischen kvnges ! Dar vber so schawe sein 15
vnsprechenleich wirtschefte vnd reichtvm vnd ewig ere, vnd
rvfe vnd sevfzig [8] von grozzer begirde vnd minne [9] "Zevhe
mich nach dir, himelischer gemahel, in dem guten smacke
deiner salben. Ich wil lavffen, noch wil niht abnemen [10] pis
daz dv mich eingefürest in dein weincelle, vntz daz dein 20
linkev hant sei vnter meinem haubt vnd dein rechtev hant
mich selikleich vmbvahe vnd dv mich küssest mit dem aller
selisten kvsse deines mvndes." Swenne dv gesetzet seist in
ditz contempliren, so gedenke [11] deiner | armen mvter, vnd [Fol. 156 v.]
wizze daz ich dein selige gehvgnvsse vnverschaidenleich gesch- 25
riben han an die taveln meines hertzen vnd han dich lieber
vor allen menschen ! Waz schol ich vil sagen ? In deiner lieb
schol sweigen die zvnge des leibes vnd schol reden die zvnge
des gaistes.[12] O dv gesegentev tohter, wann die lieb die ich
zv dir han, die mag die zvnge des leibes [13] kainigweise niht 30

---

[1] Ber., " vmm vnser erlösung ".   [2] Ber. omits " stammen des ".
[3] Ber. omits " we ".   [4] Ber. omits " durch den wek ".
[5] B3. and W. add " vnd schullen sprechen ".
[6] Supplied from Ber., B3. and W.   [7] Ber. omits " krefticleich ".
[8] Ber. omits " sevfzig ".   [9] B3. and W. add " vnd sprich ".
[10] Ber., " ruen ".   [11] B3. and W. add " mein ".
[12] W., " die zunge der engel ".
[13] B3., " kein leipleichev zvnge " ; W., " deyn leipl ch zwng ".

avzgelegen. Ich sprich, ich han dir ditz kavm halbes geschriben, ich pit dich daz dv ez gütleich vnd andehtikleich
enpfahest vnd zv dem minsten dar inne merkest die mvter-
leichen[1] begirde da mit ich alle tage bekvmert pin mit in-
[Fol. 157 r.] hitzi|kait der minne vmb dich vnd vmb dein töhter, den
6 enpfilhe mich vnd mein töhter fleizzik in vnserm herren
Cristo. Die selben, mein töhter vnd ze aller vorderst
die aller weisest jvnkfrawe Agnes, mein swester, enpfelhent sich dir vnd deinen töhtern als vil si mvgen in
10 vnserm herren. Nv pis gesegent vnd mvg wol, aller libstev
tohter, mit deinen töhtern pis zv dem tron der eren des
grozzen gotes, vnd pit fvr vns. Vnser aller liebst brvder,
bruder Amatum,[2] der got vnd den leüten liep ist, vnd bruder
Bonamgraciam,[3] die dir bringent dise gegenwartig schrift, die
15 enpfilhe ich deiner minne als vil ich mag an disen gegen-
[Fol. 157 v.] wertigen | briefen.

[DAZ IST DER LETST SEGEN]

In dem namen des vaters vnd des svns vnd des heiligen
gaistes. Amen. Vnser herre gesegen dich vnd behüt dich
vnd zaig dir sein antlütze vnd erbarm sich vber dich. Er
20 kere sein antlutze zv dir vnd geb dir[4] vride, mein[5] swester
vnd mein tohter, Agnes.[6]

Ich Clara, ain dirn vnsers herren Cristi,[7] ain pflantz
vnsers aller selisten vaters Sand Franciscen, dein swester vnd
dein mvter vnd der andern armen[8] swester, doch ain vnwir-
25 digev, ich pit vnsern herren Jhesum Cristum durch sein parm-
herzikait vnd durch die pet seiner aller heiligsten mvter
Marien[9] vnd des heiligen fvrstengels sand Michels vnd aller
[Fol. 158 r.] gotes heiligen, vnsers | seligen vaters Sand Franciscen vnd

---

[1] Ber. adds " trw vnd ".   [2] See note XXIX., p. 174.
[3] Ber. reads " Bonagrum " which is deleted and then followed by " Bona-
graciam ".
[4] B3. and W. add " seinen ".   [5] Ibid. add " libev ".
[6] B3. adds in red " Daz ist der letst segen vnd der v briefe " ; W. adds in red
" Hiv hebet sich an der letzte segenn ".
[7] B3. omits " Cristi ".   [8] B3. adds " frawen vnd ".
[9] B3. reads first " Maria " altered to " Marien " ; W. reads " Maria ".

aller seiner heiligen vnd heiligine,[1] daz der himelische vater
dir gebe vnd bestetig disen seinen aller heiligsten segen in
dem himel vnd an der erden,[2] avf erden dich meren in gnaden
vnd in seinen tugenden vnter seinen knehten vnd seinen
dirnen[3] in der streitenden cristenhait, in dem himel dich 5
erhöhen vnd eren in der signvftenden cristenhait[4] oder samnvnge vnter seinen heiligen. Ich gesegen dich pei meinem
leben[5] vnd nach meinem tode als vil ich mag vnd mer denn
ich mag mit allen den segenne mit den der vater der parmhertzikait sein svn vnd sein tohter hat gesegent vnd noch 10
wirt gesegenne | in dem himel vnd auf ertreich vnd mit den ain [Fol. 158 v.
gaistleich vater vnd muter ir gaistleich svn vnd töhter gesegent hat vnd noch gesegenne wirt. Amen. Ich pin ze aller
zeit ain minnerin deiner sel vnd aller deiner swester. Ich pit
dich daz dv fleizzik seist ze behalten dev dink die dv vnserm 15
herren gelobt hast. Vnser herre sei mit dir ze allen zeiten,
vnd wölle got daz dv alle zeit seist in im.. Amen.

[1] B3. and W. omit " vnd . . . heiligine ".
[2] *Ibid.* " auf ertreich ".
[3] *Ibid.* "seinen dinern vnd dinerin ".
[4] *Ibid.* omit " signvftenden cristenhait oder ".
[5] *Ibid.* " lebendigen leib. " instead of " leben ".

APPENDIX I.

BIBLIOGRAPHY.

The following list does not profess to be a complete Bibliography, but merely to indicate the principal works bearing upon Blessed Agnes of Bohemia and the Order of Saint Clare.

Acta Sanctorum. Martii. Tom I., pp. 502-32. Paris. 1865.

Acta Sanctorum Ungariae. Tyrnaviae, I., 1743 ; II., 1744.

Arturus a Monasterio. Martyrologium Franciscanum. Paris. 1653.

Balfour, Mrs. Charlotte. Life and Legend of the Lady Saint Clare. London. 1910.

Baudrillant. Dictionnaire d'Histoire et de Geographie Ecclesiastiques, fasc. IV. 1911 [under Agnès de Bohême].

Chronica Nic. Glassberger. Analecta Franciscana, tom. II. Quaracchi. 1887.

Chronica XXIV. Generalium. Analecta Franciscana, tom. III. Quaracchi. 1897.

Cuthbert, Father, O.S.F.C. Life of Saint Francis of Assisi, chap. IV. London. 1912.

Dudik, Dr. B. J. P. Ceroni's Handschriften-Sammlung. Brünn. 1850.

Emler, Prof. J. Fontes Rerum Bohemicarum, vol. 5. (Ac. Prague Nadáni Palackeho.)

Gilliat-Smith, Ernest. Saint Clare of Assisi : Her Life and Legislation, part II., chaps. I.-III. London. 1914.

Glaubrecht, Dr. Julius. Die Selige Königstochter Agnes von Böhmen. Regensburg. 1874.

Greiderer, Vigilius. Germania Franciscana, I. Oeniponte. 1777.

Heimbucher, Max. Die Orden und Kongregationen der katholischen Kirche, vol. 2, pp. 475-89. Paderborn. 1902.

Hueber, Fort. Menologium . . . Sanctorum . . . ex triplice Ordine . . . S. Francisci. Munich. 1698.

Jentsch, Joh. Nep. Die selige Agnes von Böhmen (Kathol. Press-verein). Prag. 1872.

Jörgensen, Joh. Saint Francis of Assisi, chap. v. London. 1912.

Leitschuh, Friedrich. Katalog der HSS. der königlichen Bibliothek zu Bamberg, vol. i., part ii. Bamberg. 1897.

Lemmens, Fr. Die Anfänge des Klarissenordens. Römische Quar-talschrift, tom. xvi., p. 97 ff.

Lempp, E. Die Anfänge des Klarissenordens. Zeit. für Kirchen-geschichte, tom. xxiii., pp. 626-29.

Leon, Father. Lives of the Saints and Blessed of the Three Orders of Saint Francis, vol. i., pp. 339-48. Taunton. 1885.

Oliger, Père Livarius. De Origine Regularum Ordinis Sanctae Clarae. Archivum Franciscanum Historicum, tom. v., fasc. ii. and iii. Quaracchi. 1912.

Pontanus, Barth. Compendium vitae b. Agnetis de Bohemia. Contained in Acta Sanctorum, March i., p. 508.

Pontanus, Bartholdus a Braitenberg. Hymnorum sanctorum de . . . s. patronis regni Bohemiae. Prag. 1602.

Rejzek, Ant. Blahoslavená Anežka Česká. 1894.

Robinson, Fr. Paschal. The Rule of Saint Clare and its Observance in the Light of Early Documents. Philadelphia. 1912.

Robinson, Fr. Paschal. "The Writings of Saint Clare." Archivum Franciscanum Historicum, tom. iii., pp. 435-40.

Sbaralea, J. H. Bullarium Franciscanum. 1759.

Lebensgeschichte der seligen Agnes, Tochter Königs Přemisl Otto-cars I. *Schiffner*, Landespatronen ii., pp. 177-200.

Seraphicae Legislationis Textus Originales. Quaracchi. 1897.

Sláma, A. Rozbor legendy o blahoslavené Anežce. 1898-99.

Ussermann, Æmil. Episcopatus Bambergensis. 1802.

Wauer, E. Entstehung und Ausbreitung des Klarissenordens. Leipzig. 1906.

Zíbrt, Dr. Čeněk. Bibliografie České Historie, vol. 2. Prag. 1902. [This Bibliography contains, pp. 999, 1000, a list of the most important works relating to Blessed Agnes and to her convent in Prag.]

APPENDIX II.

NOTES.

I. The numbering and the headings of the chapters have gone wrong in the Introduction and also in the body of the text of Ber. It has been corrected as far as possible by comparison with B1. and B2. The source of the trouble is that the first scribe who wrote the whole of the text of Ber., including the Introduction, but not the chapter headings, has given in the Introduction a wrong description of chapter viii., has omitted chapter ix., has run chapters xi. and xii. into one, and has numbered the last chapter xii. instead of xiii. Possibly this is due to the marked Franciscan regard for the number xii. The second scribe had no difficulty in filling in the right headings in the spaces left in the text up to and including chapter vii. : she also inserted the heading for chapter xi.; at that point she ceased to insert the headings, probably confused by the Introduction. The third scribe then attempted to complete the headings and made several mistakes. She numbered as ix. the chapter which should be viii. ; she then inserted a chapter heading numbered x., where no space had been left for any heading. She put in an appropriate heading on page 107, but failed to number it ix., and an appropriate heading on page 111, but not numbered x. The right heading for chapter xii. has been omitted altogether, and instead the third scribe has inserted a heading which is really that of chapter xiii., and which has accordingly been transferred to its right position on page 127. The respective handiwork of the three scribes can be determined by a detailed comparison of the formation of some of the letters.

II. *Saint Hedwig.* Described in Boll. I. as "*religiosissima princeps Polonorum Hedwigis*". She was the wife of Henry VI., Duke of Silesia, sister-in-law of Andreas II., King of Hungary, and aunt of Saint Elizabeth. She died on 15th October, 1243, in the convent of Trebnitz in Silesia, a house of the Cistercian Order, and was canonised by Clement IV. in 1266 : 17th October was assigned for her cult by Innocent XI. B1. says

(169)

that Agnes was taught by the daughter of Saint Hedwig (*ex ore filie sancte Hegwidis*) : this would be Gertrude, who was abbess of the convent at Trebnitz. For full bibliography relating to Saint Hedwig, see Zíbrt, Bibliografie České Historie (Prag. 1902), vol. II.

III. *Doxan*, a convent of the Premonstratensian Order.   It will be seen that Ber. omits the name.

IV. Ber. here gives information which is materially different from that in B1. or any of the allied versions.   It states that shortly after she entered on her fourteenth year she was brought back to her home and that the prince to whom she was betrothed died.   B1. merely states that the marriage was deferred.   The son of the Emperor, to whom Agnes was betrothed, was apparently Henry.   According to Palacky, the Bohemian historian (Dějiny Narodu Českeho, vol. II., part I.   Prag. 1877), "at the beginning of the year 1213 the Emperor Frederick II. and Ottokar I. met in Frankfurt and there entered into an alliance, upon which occasion it appears that a betrothal of the children of the two kings took place, viz. of him who was afterwards Henry King of the Romans and the Bohemian Agnes ; which betrothal was broken off in 1225 ".   Agnes was committed to the charge of Leopold, Duke of Austria.   In 1225 Leopold sought a dispensation from Honorius III. to break off the betrothal between Henry and Agnes, and instead to marry his own daughter Margaret to Henry.   He succeeded, went to Naples to Frederick II., and in July, 1225, Frederick broke off the betrothal of his son to Agnes.   The marriage of Margaret and Henry took place in December, 1225.   This explanation of the postponement and ultimate abandonment of the betrothal is not inconsistent with the statement of B1. and the Bollandist lives : but it is inconsistent with the statement of Ber. that the prince died, to whom Agnes was betrothed.   If Palacky's story is correct, it goes far to explain Agnes' violent objection to the Emperor Frederick's suit.

V. "*Regis Anglorum.*"   This is Henry III. of England.

VI. "*Capellam domus regie [uel] ad ecclesiam kathedralem.*"   The Royal Castle here mentioned is on the Hradchin, overlooking the city.   The present castle is built on the site of an older building, which was destroyed by fire in 1303.   The Cathedral, dedicated to Saint Vitus, is on a site adjoining the Royal Castle ; the present building dates back to 1344, but it was preceded by an earlier building dating back to the tenth century. This would be the Cathedral referred to in the text.

VII. "*Uocavit fratres minores.*" Several of the Bohemian Chronicles, *e.g.* the Letopisy Českě, the Neplachova Chronicle, the Marignola Chronicle, etc., agree in stating that it was in 1232 that the Friars Minor were first brought to Prag, probably through the influence of Blessed Agnes.

VIII. "*Cruciferos cum rubea cruce & stella.*" The Crucigerous Knights are an Order of Hospitallers and were brought to Bohemia by Blessed Agnes. Their Church and Monastery are still to be seen in Prag in the position stated in the text, viz., at the foot of the bridge. The Order was confirmed by Gregory IX. in 1238, as stated in the following rubricated inscription in the Breviary still preserved in their Monastery and described on page 21 :—

> "*Anno incarnationis dominice Millesimo CCXXXVIII° per sanctissimum patrem Gregorium papam nonum confirmatus est ordo fratrum Cruciferorum cum stella de regula sancti Augustini quem fundavit adhuc in seculo existens Christianissima virgo Agnes regali genita ex progenie, etc.*"

IX. "*De Terdento.*" It will be noticed that Ber. is silent as to the place whence the first sisters were brought to Prag. Boll. II. says that they came "*ex Italia*". Some writers have stated that the first sisters were sent to Prag from the mother-house of San Damiano. The house referred to as "*De Terdento*" is probably the *Monasterium Sancti Michaelis*, which, according to Oliger, was in 1228 the only House of Clarisses outside Italy contained in the most ancient list of such houses given in the circular letters of Cardinal Raynaldo (18th August, 1228).

X. "*Prelacionem sui ordinis declinauit.*" This is scarcely accurate, for the Papal Bulls show that Agnes was Abbess of the Convent at Prag at any rate from 1234 till 1238.

XI. "*Johannes Gayetanus.*" A Cardinal Legate who became Pope in 1277 with the title of Nicholas III. It will be observed that he is described as being Protector not only of the Order of Friars Minor, but also of the Clarisses. According to Gonzaga he was the fourth Cardinal-Protector of the Order. His Protectorate, according to Nicholas Glassberger, lasted from 1263-77. The date of this incident is given by Bi. as "tempore concilii Lugdunensis sub decimo Gregorio celebrati". The

Council of Lyons, which was the Fourteenth General Council, met from 7th May to 17th July, 1274, under the Pontificate of Gregory X. Accordingly the incident here recorded may be assigned to the year 1274.

XII. *"Der heilig sant Laurencius."* His festival is on 10th August. The allusion here, which is confined to Ber., is somewhat obscure. In the Fourth Lesson for Matins on 10th August in the *"Sermo Sancti Leonis Papae"* we find ;—

"Postulat sibi ab immaculato Sacrarii Praesule opes ecclesiasticas, quibus avidissimus inhiabat, inferri, cui Levita castissimus, ubi eas repositas haberet, ostendens numerosissimos sanctorum pauperum obtulit greges".

XIII. *"Danieli . . . prandium ab Abacuc est allatum."* This reference to Habbakuk bringing food to Daniel in the den of lions is derived from the Apocryphal writing known as "Bel and the Dragon".

XIV. *"Quadragesima sancti Martini."* Saint Martin's Fast lasted from 11th November, Saint Martin's Day, to Christmas.

XV. *"Qui Lazarum resuscitasti."* This is the response following the second Lesson in the first Nocturn of the Office of the Dead.

XVI. *"Prouinciali ministro . . . reserauit."* Boll. II. gives the date of this incident as 1269, but omits any reference to the Provincial. The reference to the Provincial is interesting, as suggesting that the Clarisses were under the jurisdiction of the Provincials of the Friars Minor at that time.

XVII. *"Domine sorori Elyzabeth imperatrici."* Boll. I. and II. do not mention Elizabeth in their account of this miracle. It is not very clear which Elizabeth is meant. It is probably the same Elizabeth as the one concerning whom B1. records two miracles on pages 126-30, under the name *"Domina Elyzabeth, regina Bohemie, consors illustris domini Johannis regis,"* who instituted the petition for the canonisation of Blessed Agnes.

XVIII. *"Cum enim filius fratris sui,"* etc. The reference in this paragraph is to the defeat of Ottokar II., brother's son of Blessed Agnes, by Rudolph, Count of Hapsburg, King of the Romans, at Durnkrut on the Marchfeld in 1272, when Ottokar was slain. The passage illustrates the inferior historical value of the Bollandist lives. Boll. I. states that it was the father of Blessed Agnes, Ottokar I., who was slain. It will be noted

that Ber. states that Blessed Agnes warned Ottokar not to go
to war and that he refused, facts not mentioned by B1. or the
other German versions.

XIX. "*Scolastica de Sternberch.*" The name "Sternberch" or
"Sternberg" occurs ·frequently in Bohemian chronicles about
this time. Thus in the "*Anonymi Chronicon Bohemicum,*"
printed in Mencken's *Scriptores Rerum Germaniae,* vol. III.,
p. 1718, referring to an invasion of Prag by Tartars in 1254, we
read of "*quidam Nobilis de Sternberg, pro tunc capitaneus
civitatis eiusdem, de civitate progrediens impetum fecit in eos
viriliter*".

XX. "*Utpote licenciam ab apostolica sede habentem.*" Special licence
from the Pope was necessary to enable any person, not a
regular inmate of the convent, to be admitted to one of the
convents of Clarisses. Even the Friars Minor, who at first
were allowed to visit the convents, were by the Bull of "Quo
elongati" of 1230 forbidden to do so without a special licence
from the Pope. Thus the Bull of Gregory IX., "Cum omnis
vera Religio," says ;—

"*Nulla unquam Abbatissa, vel eius sorores aliquam Personam
religiosam seu secularem, ac cuiuslibet dignitatis in Monasterium
intrare permittant, nec omnino hoc alicui liceat, nisi cui atque de
quibus concessum a Summo Pontifice fuerit*" (Sbar. I., 265).

XXI. "*Frater Bonagracia, generalis minister.*" Tenth General of
the Order of Friars Minor, 1279-1283. The full account of
his career is in Chron. XXIV., Gen., in Anal. Franc., tom. III.,
pp. 367-82. From this it appears that Bonagracia was in
Germany in 1282, for he held a chapter at Strassburg in the
same year. At that chapter he directed Brother Philip, Minister
of Tuscany, to collect evidence as to the day and hour when
the stigmatisation of Saint Francis took place. Boll. I. omits
his name altogether : Boll. II. gives his name, but does not
identify him as the General.

XXII. "*Judica me Deus.*" This is Psalm xliii., which is said in the
Priest's Preparation before the Mass. It forms the Introit to
the High Mass on Passion Sunday and on Tuesday in Holy
Week, and is sung by the choir. It is somewhat curious that
Ber. should identify the Sunday in question in this way, while
B1. speaks of it as "*dominica de passione*".

XXIII. "*Adueniente autem anniuersario uirginis Cristi.*" Ber., "*da ir tag kam*". These references point to an early observance of the day of Blessed Agnes's death, which would naturally be the beginning of the cult leading up to the petition for her canonisation.

XXIV. "*Linko de Duba.*" B1. gives the name quite clearly as "*Linco.*," but Boll. I. and II. both give it as "*Hinco*". The name, "*Hynco de Duba,*" occurs under the date 14th August, 1300, as a witness in a contract of sale in Erben's *Regesta Bohemiae et Moraviae,* pars i., p. 801 (Prag. 1855). Hinko de Duba is given in a list of Burgraves of the Kingdom of Bohemia under date 1324 by Hammerschmid in his *Prodromus Gloriae Pragenae,* cap. xxiii., p. 713. Possibly "*Hynco de Duba*" is one of the witnesses from personal experience, from whom the anonymous writer claims to have derived his evidence.

XXV. "*Gracias . . . post prandium.*" The full form for grace after meals will be found in the *Benedictio Mensae* in the Breviary.

XXVI. An interesting confirmation of the historical character of the persons here mentioned, viz., Habhard de Zyrotin and Scolastica de Sternberk, is afforded by a Bull of Nicholas IV., registered by Potthast as No. 23362, under date 21st August, 1290, with the following description :—

"[*Iohannem*] *episcopum Pragensem dispensare iubet cum Hebardo de Sirotin et Scolastica nata quondam Sdezlai de Sternenberch, ut in matrimonio contracto, consanguinitate non obstante, remanere possint.*"

XXVII. "*In exaltacione sancte crucis,*" i.e. 14th September, the feast upon which Saint Francis received the Stigmata on Mount Alverna.

XXVIII. "*Bruder Helye des Generals.*" This is a reference to Brother Elias of Cortona, who was General of the Order until his deposition in 1239. It is noteworthy that the Latin version of the Letters describes Elias as "Minister-General of the whole Order" (*totius ordinis*), but none of the German versions add anything after "Generals".

XXIX. "*Bruder Amatum . . . vnd bruder Bonamgraciam.*" These brothers have not been identified. Bonagracia must not be identified with the Minister-General of that name, for of him it is said that he had never been in Bohemia before the time when he arrived for the funeral of Blessed Agnes.

APPENDIX III.

The following letter addressed by Wenceslas IV., King of Bohemia, to Pope Gregory IX., in 1237, is of special interest as it shows that he was writing in support of one of the two applications made in 1238 by Blessed Agnes to the Holy See. It is difficult to decide whether it relates to her application for the Convent at Prag to be allowed to renounce possessions, or to her application to be allowed to follow the modified form of the Rule of San Damiano :—

Wenceslaus IV. Boemorum rex Gregorio IX. papae gratias refert "pro eo quod vos carissimae filiae vestrae ac praedilectae sorori meae d. Agneti, de ordine pauperum dominarum, nunquam desinitis affectum benevolum impertiri. Nam ista hoc testatur, quod nullas preces vestrae sanctitati se unquam meminit porexisse, quarum mox optabilem effectum a paternitate vestra non fuerit consecuta. Proinde spondeo et promitto, quod exhoc vobis et sanctae Romanae ecclesiae semper promptior et paratior ex animo volo esse in omni necessitate seu opportunitate publica et privata : praesertim si [preces] praedictae specialis filiae vestrae ac dilectissimae sororis meae germanae, quas ipsa vobis porrigere impraesentiarum decrevit intra sacrarium exauditionis vestrae solita benignitate duxeritis admittendas, hoc certum et per omnia ratum habentes, quia per hoc, quod satisfacitis votis eius—me—cum omni virtute mea sub vestram omni respectu redigitis potestatem ; nec mirum, quoniam eam, ut verum fatear, sicut conjugem et liberos et universa bona diligo, cunctisque mortalibus praefero in affectu. Datum Pragae anno ab inc. dom. MCCXXXVII, regni nostro anno IX."

The letter is printed by Erben in the *Regesta Bohemiae et Moraviae*, pars i., Prag, 1855, p. 429.

APPENDIX IV.

While the argument contained in pages 23-30 and the quotations given prove that at all events M., W. and B2, form a group possessing characteristics of omission and addition which differentiate it from the group to which B1. and Ber. belong, yet it must be admitted that it is doubtful whether it is necessary to hypothecate for M., W. and B2. a Latin source Y different from the Latin original of B1. and Ber. It is not impossible that Y1., the common German source of M., W. and B2., may itself be merely a derivative from B1.; or alternatively a derivative from X. Such an explanation would account for all the 'phenomena' of the M., W. and B2. group. The diagrammatic representation of the MSS. containing the Legend would on that hypothesis be shown as below: the alternative derivation of M., W. and B2. from B1. is indicated by dotted lines.

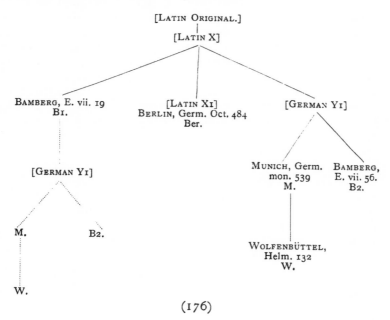